Planning and Developing the Company Organization Structure

*This report may not be reproduced in whole or in part
without the express permission of the Association.*

Fifth Printing, October 1957

RESEARCH REPORT NUMBER 20

PLANNING AND DEVELOPING THE COMPANY ORGANIZATION STRUCTURE

By ERNEST DALE

AMERICAN MANAGEMENT ASSOCIATION

1515 BROADWAY, TIMES SQUARE

NEW YORK 36, N. Y.

ADVISORY COMMITTEE

Appreciation is expressed to the following, who read the study in manuscript form and offered valuable criticisms and suggestions:

Preface

The application of systematic methods to the conduct of business is one of the most striking developments of the present day. The successful pursuit of business activities is increasingly based on carefully developed plans and well-ordered arrangements. The body of knowledge, called Organization, has become increasingly helpful in accomplishing the objectives of the enterprise.

This book is an analysis of the development and change of the organization structure of the individual company. It is an attempt to combine the systematic thinking on this subject with the "rule of thumb" of practical experience. It essays an integration of the formal structure of the enterprise with the human forces that mold and are molded by it. Thus it is designed to aid the practical man of affairs as well as the student of organization.

The study is confined largely to the organization of manufacturing companies, with some reference to retail and service activities. Limitations of space and time have made impossible a detailed discussion of such related and important topics as planning company activities, establishing policies, procedures, and controls. Each of these subjects merits a study of its own.

The main body of the report is divided into two parts: Part I deals with the dynamics of organization. This is an analysis of the major organizational problems as they arise at various stages of a company's growth. Part II deals with the mechanics of organization. It offers detailed guidance for analyzing the existing structure and modifying or changing it, in the light of the best established practices, to conform to the needs of the individual company.

Ernest Dale planned and executed the research and wrote the study over a period of two years. James O. Rice, Administrative Vice President and Secretary of AMA, provided help at all stages of the project. Clare Silva, of the AMA staff, aided on the survey, helped in checking the manuscript and reading the proof, and provided the index.

Grateful thanks are expressed to members of the AMA Advisory Committee, listed on a preceding page, who evaluated the study in draft form. The many companies and executives whose names appear on the following pages contributed generously from their rich experience to the factual material.

LAWRENCE A. APPLEY
President

Acknowledgments

In this study, the primary aim has been to provide a perspective on organization development which would combine basic truths with practical realities. The answers had to be drawn, in the first place, from the wisdom of the great authorities of the past. These were the pioneers in scientific management and their followers, and the economists who evolved the principles of profit maximization. They have discerned relationships not seen before which we cannot afford now to overlook. The wisdom of the past was then modified by the analysis of the experience of those who have applied these ideas. Without the test of experience, analysis and generalization remain sterile. However, willingness to share the results of its experience has long been one of the outstanding characteristics of American industry. All students of organization and management owe a great debt to the forward-looking business leaders who have made this possible.

It has been our good fortune to get help and counsel from some of the outstanding practitioners and thinkers in the field of organization. The study was undertaken at the initiation of Lawrence A. Appley, President of the American Management Association, and James O. Rice, its Administrative Vice President and Secretary. At many stages, this study has benefited materially from the guidance, through correspondence and personal discussion of Lt. Col. Lyndall Urwick, Chairman, Urwick, Orr & Partners, one of the foremost writers and practitioners in this field in England. It was he who suggested the study of organization problems as they may arise at various stages of the company growth. A number of issues on organization were discussed in correspondence and interview with General of the Army Dwight D. Eisenhower, who gave generously of his time, especially in regard to the concept of the "staff assistant."

The following companies and individuals gave valuable assistance through interviews and correspondence:

JOHN J. BASSILL, President, American Enka Corporation

CYRIL J. BATH, President, The Cyril Bath Company

C. E. BOSWORTH, Manager, Organization Department, Ford Motor Company

ALVIN BROWN, Vice President—Finance, Johns-Manville Corporation

ELLSWORTH BUNKER, United States Ambassador to Italy, formerly President, National Sugar Refining Company

L. BYRON CHERRY, Consultant, Management Consultation Services Division, General Electric Company

BERTRAM J. COHN, Vice President, Decatur Iron and Steel Company, Inc.

HAROLD V. COES, Retired Vice President, Ford, Bacon & Davis, Inc.

LOUNSBURY S. FISH, Organization Counsel, Standard Oil Company of California

O. ROGERS FLYNN, JR., Vice President, Seabrook Farms Company

HENRY FORD II, President, Ford Motor Company

SIR PATRICK HAMILTON, Chairman, Henry Simon (Holdings) Ltd.

JOHN M. HANCOCK, Partner, Lehman Brothers

SIR GEOFFREY HEYWORTH, Chairman, Unilever Limited

J. L. HEYWORTH, Director, Unilever Limited

C. F. HOOD, Executive Vice President—Operations, United States Steel Company

CHARLES R. HOOK, JR., Vice President—Personnel, The Chesapeake and Ohio Railway Company

The late HARRY A. HOPF

C. L. HUSTON, JR., President, Lukens Steel Company

IRA KATZ, Vice President, The Gruen Watch Company

DUDLEY M. MASON, Personnel Research Director, Armstrong Cork Company

FOWLER McCORMICK, Director, International Harvester Company

GERRY E. MORSE, Vice President, Minneapolis-Honeywell Regulator Company

KENDRICK R. PORTER, Vice President, Lester B. Knight & Associates

JOHN POST, Manager, Industrial Relations Department, Continental Oil Company

PORTER M. POWELL, Organization Planning, Continental Oil Company

SIR CHARLES RENOLD, Vice President, British Institute of Management; Chairman, Renold and Coventry Chain Co., Ltd.

L. L. PURKEY, Manager, Department on Organization, Standard Oil Company of California

DANIEL RHOADS, Assistant to the President, Armstrong Cork Company

HAROLD F. SMIDDY, Vice President, Management Consultation Services Division, General Electric Company

ALFRED P. SLOAN, JR., Chairman of the Board, General Motors Corporation

J. F. SOLES, JR., Assistant to the President and Manager, Central Plant, Line Material Company

SIR HAROLD WEST, Managing Director, Newton Chambers & Co., Ltd.

Parts of the manuscript were read and discussed by a group of organization specialists meeting from time to time in New York, including:

F. H. BRAGG, Assistant Director, Organization and Staffing, The Prudential Insurance Company of America

D. C. DOUGHERTY, Supervisor, Organization Planning, American Hard Rubber Company

H. A. FINLEY, General Supervisor, Coordination Division, Metropolitan Life Insurance Company

E. F. FITZMAURICE, Manager of Development Planning, Sales Division, General Foods Corporation

H. B. FREEMAN, Assistant for Organization, Johns-Manville Corporation

J. B. JOYNT, Assistant to the President, American Enka Corp.

J. E. McCABE, Secretary, Merck & Co., Inc.

J. G. NAGRO, Development Planning Specialist, Sales Division, General Foods Corporation

H. M. SISSON, Manager, Organization Planning Department, Merck & Co., Inc.

Contents

PART TWO: The Mechanics of Organization (*continued*)

Planning and Developing the Company Organization Structure

Introduction

ORGANIZATION is a subject which needs to be treated not only with respect, because it is fundamental to company planning, but with realism, because it is of value only insofar as it is practical. Perhaps the following story will make this point clear: Once the king of the cockroaches visited the king of the grasshoppers and complained bitterly about the unpopularity of his subjects. Frankly, he had come for advice — to find out how to make cockroaches better liked. The king of the grasshoppers promised to take the matter under advisement. Some weeks later the two kings met again. The king of the grasshoppers came forth with his solution in a pompous fashion. "All you cockroaches can easily become popular by becoming grasshoppers," he announced. The king of the cockroaches thought this very good advice, but he still had one problem: "How can we cockroaches become grasshoppers?" he asked. The king of the grasshoppers thereupon lost patience and replied: "What a silly question! Why, I make policy — I think up the ideas. It's up to my subordinates to put them into practice!"

The AMA Study

In most of the discussion we hear about organization, there is too much generalization based on personal opinions, off-the-cuff observations and hunches; there are too many unverified theories which defy systematic analysis. The rules of thumb are useful only if we know when and how to apply them. For example, "Keep your lines of communication short" and "Have a short span of control" are both wise precepts, but they are also contradictory. In short, too many executives speak about organizational problems in terms of what they believe they *ought* to do rather than in terms of what they *are* doing.

For this reason an attempt has been made to emphasize the realities of organization in AMA's two-year research study of company organization. In the course of this study, we visited some 40 companies believed to have harmonious organization structures. We participated in the work of changing company organizations. We examined and analyzed over several hundred organization manuals and organization charts. We talked to and corresponded with scores of outstanding thinkers and practitioners on organization, among them General Dwight D. Eisenhower; Lt. Colonel Lyndall Urwick of England; T. S. Petersen, Lewis L. Purkey, Lounsbury Fish and their associates at the Standard Oil Company of California; L. F. McCollum, President of the Continental Oil Company; Alfred P. Sloan, Jr., Chairman of the Board of General Motors Corporation; Alvin Brown of Johns-Manville; Luther Gulick, Chief of the New York City Management Survey; the late Harry Hopf; Henry Ford II, President, Ford Motor Company; J. L. Heyworth, Director, Unilever Ltd.; and many other persons too numerous to mention. We made an extensive survey of the existing literature on organization, both American and foreign. We then submitted our study to a distinguished group of organization specialists for review and discussion. Finally, an AMA committee of company presidents read and commented on the completed AMA guide to organization.

Definition of Organization Planning

Organization planning is the process of defining and grouping the activities of the enterprise so that they may be most logically assigned and effectively executed. It is concerned with the establishment of relationships among the units so as to further the objectives of the enterprise. The following basic characteristics of organization should be kept in mind in any discussion of organization planning:

1. Organization is a planning *process*. It is concerned with setting up, developing and maintaining a structure or pattern of working relationships of the people within an enterprise. It is carried on continuously as changes in events, personalities and environment require. Thus organization is dynamic. However, the resulting structure is static—i.e., it reflects the organization only as of a given moment of time.

2. Organization is the determination and assignment of duties to people so as to obtain the advantages of fixing responsibility and specialization through *subdivision* of work.

3. Organization is a plan for *integrating* or *coordinating* most effectively the activities of each part of the enterprise so that proper relationships are established and maintained among different work units and so that the total effort of all people in the enterprise will help accomplish its objectives.

4. Organization is a *means to an end*. Good organization should be one of the tools of accomplishing the company's objectives, but it should not become an objective in itself.

The Importance of Organization

Organization has been in existence ever since the first group of men banded together to hunt, to build and to fight. Constructing the wonders of the Ancients, such as the pyramids and the Hanging Gardens of Babylon, required the organization of large labor forces. As early as Biblical times, it was written: "Seest thou a man diligent in his Organization? He shall stand before Kings; he shall not stand before mean men." (*Proverbs* xxii, 29.) The great armies of antiquity such as Alexander's and Julius Caesar's and others were superbly organized. The churches, the military and the political states have offered much evidence of man's organizational ingenuity and folly.

As time went on, man's accumulated experience was written up to guide his fellows on organization. Consider, for example,

John Ford's *Serious Address to Men in Business, Concerning the Right Ordering Their Affairs; with advice in the case of those who have unhappily mismanaged* (London, 1733) which gave such rules as the following:

> Undertake no more than you can manage;
> Perform with delight and a kind of unweariness;
> Have your eyes upon your own business and trust not wholly to servants;
> Be watchful over strangers;
> Trust not your Memory, but immediately make Entrys of things in the proper books;
> At proper times inspect your affairs;
> He who observes the Rules laid down, will be likely to thrive and prosper in the World.

With the development of the study of economics, organization was treated more systematically. Some writers, like the great economist Alfred Marshall, classed organization with the three basic factors of production, land, labor and capital. Marshall regarded organization as the activity which brings the three other agents together into productive use.

The increasingly systematic planning of management organization was developed during the industrial revolution. It was assembled into a usable body of knowledge by the writers on scientific management, the great trio — F. W. Taylor, H. L. Gantt and F. Gilbreth — and their successors, and the work of numerous executives, so that today it has widespread application. For example, more than half of the companies participating in the 1950-52 AMA seminars on organization have a department or an individual in charge of organization planning. An AMA random survey of 150 large and medium-sized companies revealed that about four-fifths have one or a series of organization charts, and a substantial proportion have an organization manual.

The experience of the past and the thinking of many writers and practitioners have created a body of knowledge on organization which may enable its users to solve their own organizational problems with increasing success. The value of organizational knowledge in improving the accomplishment of the firm's economic and non-economic objectives goes a long way toward explaining its importance.

The factors which must be taken into account to ensure the survival and prosperity of the company have become increasingly complex. The relatively simple problems of the owner-manager in adjusting himself to the demands of the market have multiplied in difficulty. Modern management is largely divorced from ownership, yet it must take into account not only the owners' interest in its decisions, but a host of other influences. Its organization must be so geared as to adjust to the vagaries of the market, of competitors, labor unions and employees, governmental and community relationships, technology and inventions, and the impact of foreign relations. Only careful organization planning makes it possible to marshal and deal adequately with this multitude of factors.

This importance of organization planning may grow with the increasing size of companies — with the larger number of plants controlled by one firm and the growth in the size of plants themselves. As the company grows in size, the chief of the operational unit (plant or division) is further removed from headquarters and his control over policies that affect him becomes reduced. On the other hand, the number of over-riding uniformities and controls that must be adhered to is also likely to multiply. Those who lay down procedures and policies and receive reports at headquarters are increasingly removed from the "feel of the situation." Increasing size also introduces the staff specialist, possibly with long chains of command behind him, and the dilemma arises between his advisory position to the line and the need to get his ideas accepted and carried out. Finally, more systematic organizational structuring is required to make a success of increasing executive participation at all levels through delegation of decision-making. The growing complexity and specialization of business functions thus necessitates more systematic organization planning.

The need for organization planning varies not only in accordance with the importance of the factors already enumerated, but with the nature of the company's objectives and business (e.g., the single-product versus the multiple-product firm), the complexities of the production and selling problems, geographical location, the personalities involved, individual and group capacity for handling people and problems, and the history and traditions of organization in the particular industry.

Advantages of Organization Planning

There are distinct advantages to organization planning. It is of value in defining, discussing and evaluating the company's objectives. It indicates in clear and easily understood terms, where responsibilities lie. The resulting organization chart and manual are like a contour map of a geographical area — at a glance or with relatively little effort an executive can grasp the whole company structure and his relation to it. For this reason the chart and the manual may constitute excellent training devices.

As a consequence of organization planning, top executives may be enabled to drop overloads of responsibility and thus have more time to devote to long-run planning, reviewing, coordination, and innovation, or whatever happen to be the company's most important activities. Representatives of different departments may be able to work more closely together in the interest of over-all company objectives.

As another result, executives may have a greater opportunity to utilize their abilities, plan their own activities, develop and train themselves and others. Organization planning may provide the basis for estimating manpower resources and requirements and thus enable a company to improve its system of executive succession and replacement, and, in the process, offer better promotional opportunities to its younger men.

Organization planning may help to integrate personalities with the objectives of the enterprise and make for improved human relationships. As a famous sociologist put it: ". . . There is no reason why . . . the labour of supplying society with all the material goods needed for its general comfort should not become both agreeable and attractive. There is no necessity of waiting for the slow action of evolution in transforming human character. The result can easily be brought about by the transformation of human institutions."[1] Thus conditions may be consciously developed

[1] Lester F. Ward, *Applied Sociology*, Ginn & Company, Boston, 1906, p. 336.

to remove innumerable artificial obstacles to better cooperation.

Finally, organization planning can help to remedy some of the ills common to many business organizations: It may reduce or eliminate duplication of effort (resulting in executive manpower saving); do away with "red tape" (by shortening lines of communication and assigning definite responsibility and authority); improve coordination between different functions (such as manufacturing and marketing); eliminate unneccessary functions (checking the tendency of empire-building through a manpower budget or, better still, through financial audits); eliminate friction (through reduction of the number of levels of management and clearer, more logical and more definite allocation of responsibilities); tend to reduce mistakes by placing decision-making nearer to the problems; improve specialization, and properly balance the expansion of various management functions.

Organization planning provides for continuing adaptation in order to meet changes in people, resources and environment. It aids in keeping the units of the organization in balance, avoiding excessive or deficient strength among the company's departments. The classic example of over-preparedness is the armored dinosaur who was so well protected that he finally failed to earn a living (the analogy cited by Henry S. Dennison in his pathbreaking book, *Organization Engineering*).

We may summarize the advantages of organization planning in the words of the late Dr. H. A. Hopf, as follows: "That a business cannot permanently occupy levels of effectiveness higher than those clearly determined by the capacity of its executives is self-evident, but it is not generally understood that the influence of superior organization upon the accomplishments of mediocre executives can raise the enterprise to heights not otherwise attainable."[2]

[2] Copyright 1938 by Harry Arthur Hopf, New York. Quoted from an address delivered at a joint meeting of the Montreal Branch of the Engineering Institute of Canada, Montreal Personnel Association, Chartered Institute of Secretaries, Society of Chartered Accountants of the Province of Quebec, and the Canadian Society of Cost Accountants and Industrial Engineers, and published in the *Engineering Journal* (Canada), Volume XX, No. 12, December, 1937.

Part I

The Dynamics of Organization

A Study of Organization Problems at Various Stages of Company Growth

T HE major problems of organization can perhaps best be studied in dynamic terms, i.e., as they arise and change with the evolution of the company. In this dynamic setting the causes and nature of organization problems can be recognized most easily. Each major problem can be analyzed at the stage of the company's growth when it typically arises,[1] when there are few complications and the organizational problem is centered about just one factor or change in the company's mode of operation. Just as it is easier to study the workings of democracy as they arise in one of the small towns of New England rather than in the United States as a whole, so it appears to be desirable, in dealing with a subject of such scope as organization, to isolate and study the major problems individually.

Organization studies usually are devoted to the study of large scale enterprise because information about larger companies is generally more widely recorded and more readily available. Because of this, more emphasis needs to be placed on organization planning in the smaller firms. It was at the suggestion of Lt. Colonel Lyndall Urwick that AMA undertook this study of com-

[1] It is not suggested that these problems necessarily arise at the stage at which they are discussed in this study. This is merely a method of exposition to aid in treating organization problems in a systematic fashion. Obviously, the major organization problems discussed here may arise at almost any stage of a company's growth.

25

panies of different sizes, as a means of improving our knowledge of organization—a field in which he has made major contributions.

Many of the larger companies face small-scale problems in their subsidiaries and small units. However, those starting work in the large firm find it difficult to visualize the evolutionary process on which their company's present operation is based. Therefore, it may be of interest even for large companies to study the various stages of growth, up to and including, of course, their own present stage of development.

It is proposed in this book to study the various stages of growth in representative companies. At each stage a new factor of organization pertinent to that stage will be analyzed in isolation. It will then be related to previously noted factors in organization.

In this approach it would be ideal to confine the analysis to the development and growth of a single company which would be representative. Unfortunately, the existing histories of business enterprise give little or no attention to the problems of growth in relation to organization. Time limitations and absence of essential records made it extremely difficult to conduct first-hand studies of the problems of growth as related to one organization, though this certainly needs to be done to obtain real continuity and comparability. Therefore, for our present purposes, we must focus our study on different businesses at various stages of growth.

The detailed study of each company to be presented here will be suplemented at each stage by a summary of the experience of a number of companies and a general framework of analysis which will aid in solving the particular organization problem under discussion. In the development from the small one-man business to the large company, seven major organizational problems arise. Each of these problems is identified in the accompanying chart at the approximate stage of company growth at which it arises.

SEVEN MAJOR STAGES OF COMPANY GROWTH

Stage of Growth	Size[2] (No. of Employees)	Organizational Problem and its Possible Consequences
I	3-7 (Any size)	Formulation of Objectives: *Division of Work*
II	25 (10)	Delegation of Responsibility: *The Accommodation of Personalities*

Seven Major Stages of Company Growth *(continued)*

Stage of Growth	Size[2] (No. of Employees)	Organizational Problem and its Possible Consequences
III	125 (50-100)	Delegation of More Management Functions: *Span of Control*
IV	500 (50-300)	Reducing the Executive's Burden: *The Staff Assistant*
V	1,500 (100-400)	Establishing a New Function (Functionalization): *The Staff Specialist*
VI	5,000 (100-500)	Coordination of Management Functions: *Group Decision-Making*
VII	465,000 (over 500)	Determining the Degree of Delegation: *Decentralization*

2 The first figure indicates the actual size of the company studied. The second figure in brackets indicates very broadly the size of the company when the particular organization problem may arise for the first time. The rise of the organizational problem is, of course, not necessarily tied to the size indicated, but merely reflects very roughly the findings of our limited sample.

Stage I: Determining the Objectives and Dividing the Work Accordingly

ILLUSTRATIVE CASES

THE organization structure is a mechanism designed to help in the goals of the enterprise. However small an organization, it must start by determining its objectives. For the resources of any organization are limited and must be properly utilized if the company is to survive and to prosper. This requires a formulation of objectives and an assignment of responsibilities. Allocation of responsibilities is essential, even if the organization consists of only one man, for he must divide his time as effectively as possible. The allocation of responsibilities becomes even more important when there is more than one person in the organization. For responsibilities which are not assigned are likely to be neglected. If no one is specifically charged with the replacement of inventories, for example, many items of merchandise may not be available to customers. Specific assignment of responsibilities also assures that they will be placed with those who can exercise them best.

Even a small store owner must determine his objectives in order to build his organization. After deciding on location, types of customers and merchandise, he must determine sales potentials, prospective revenues, and costs. These factors influence the number and type of functions that must be exercised. Let us say that the proprietor of a store decides that he needs a salesman and delivery-man in order to meet the objectives set. His organization is as follows:

THE W. TONNE GROCERY STORE

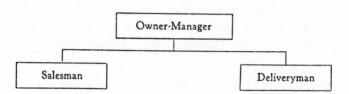

At this point, the specific functions should be allocated:

Owner-manager	*Salesman*	*Deliveryman*
(The husband)	(The wife)	(The children)
Order merchandise	Sell merchandise	Deliver orders
Set inventory minima and maxima	Answer phone	Open and close store
Control slow-moving inventory and stock shortages	Check on inventory	Keep store clean
Get prices and discounts	Arrange window displays	
Supervise selling and sell		
Arrange advertising		
Pay bills		
Control expenses		
Keep records		
Handle bank account		
Handle taxes		
Make contacts		
Handle complaints		

Similarly, in the small manufacturing organization, the basic activities must be determined as soon as the objectives are set. Usually these consist of two basic organization functions — production and selling and possibly finance. In the beginning the two functions may be exercised by the owner, with his wife perhaps acting as secretary, and with a few workers added gradually:

THE F. SILVA PRINT SHOP

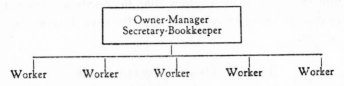

As a company grows its objectives can be broken down in greater detail, as was recently done, for example, in the A. C. Gilbert Company,[1] New Haven, Conn. (a medium firm):

Over-all objectives—
    a. Preservation of the American Way of Life (opposing monopoly in any form, whether in industry or labor unions).
    b. Being a good citizen in communities of operation; assuming a share of community responsibilities.
    c. Research, development of know-how and an ever-advancing technology.
    d. Making the company a better place to work; getting enjoyment out of work; good wages; fair play; recognizing the dignity of the individual, maintaining a progressive personnel program.

Organizational consequences—
    a. A limit to the expansion of the organization; absence of tie-in agreements and other organizational devices which might aid monopoly.
    b. Establishment of a "Department of Relationships."
    c. Establishment of a separate research department.
    d. Establishment of a personnel department.

Financial objectives—
The company should make enough profit to:
    a. Continually improve plant facilities and working conditions so that production may become more efficient and work more pleasant.
    b. Provide a reasonable return to common stockholders.
    c. Aim toward maintaining the soundest financial structure possible, with particular emphasis on maintaining a good liquid position.

[1] See also the excellent statement of the General Objectives of Management and the Requisite Conditions for Meeting Them in *The Management Guide* of the Standard Oil Company of California, 1948, p. 28.

    d. Consider banks as friends and as absentee members of the company; their interests to be recognized in the financial policies.

Organizational methods of accomplishing these objectives include—
    a. Capital budget procedures and follow-ups.
    b. A centralized department for the establishment of accounting, cost and budget controls with additional decentralized advisory departments and control agencies.
    c. A centralized fund and bank loan procedure.

Sales objectives—
    a. Highest quality products.
    b. Sales exclusively through company organization.
    c. Maintenance and improvement of the firm's market position (percentage share of sales in major product markets).

Organizational consequences—
    These objectives led to the organizational establishment of (a) a quality control department; (b) an extensive sales organization, with branches in different parts of the country; (c) centralized market research, marketing budgets, and closely centralized control of results.

Public relations objectives—
    Managerial co-workers shall do their share of worthwhile civic activities and strive to further the good name of the Company in all walks of life. In the conduct of their personal lives they shall do nothing to bring censure or discredit to the Company.

Organizational impact—
    This led to the establishment of a separate public relations function.

Production objectives—
    a. Emphasis on diversification: Through diversity in products, seasonal peaks and valleys can be minimized and unfavorable changes in public acceptance of any one product hedged against.
    b. In order to provide full employment, existing plant facilities shall be utilized fully and sub-contracting done systematically only when found advisable for reasons of capacity, economy, or lack of specialized machinery and know-how.

Organizational consequences—
>   Division of production work into different product depart-
>   ments; establishment of production and engineering control
>   departments; coordination of production and sales through a
>   committee of the executives concerned.

Even this broad statement of company objectives shows how
closely they can be linked to and influence the organization pattern. The organization specialist can neglect them only at his
own peril.

GENERAL ANALYSIS

The Division of Basic Company Activities

The alternative methods for dividing the work of a company
toward the accomplishment of its objectives are numerous. They
include, traditionally, function, product, location, customers,
process, equipment, and time. It should be noted that in many
companies these various bases of division are combined, and co-
ordinated by checks and balances. But there is usually one predominant type of subdivision of the major company activities,
made by the chief executive officer himself, called "basic subdivision," "basic delegation," or "departmentation."

The first step in the division of work is the determination of
the primary responsibilities of the enterprise — that is, the purpose of the enterprise, and the major functions necessary to accomplish it. Thus, in a manufacturing enterprise, production is
one basic responsibility; in merchandising, it may be advertising;
in public utilities, the maintenance of equipment; in the liquor
business, the determination of credit risk; in flour milling, the
purchase of flour.

The principal or primary subdivision of the activities of an
enterprise may then be divided on the following bases:

1. *Function.* Major subdivision by function, subject-matter or
principal activities is found in many enterprises where actual
control throughout all hierarchies and over all locations is exercised by the heads of managerial functions — such as finance;
production (including plant design, construction and maintenance, purchasing); manufacture; engineering (product design
or research, possibly quality control); law (claims, tax laws, cor-

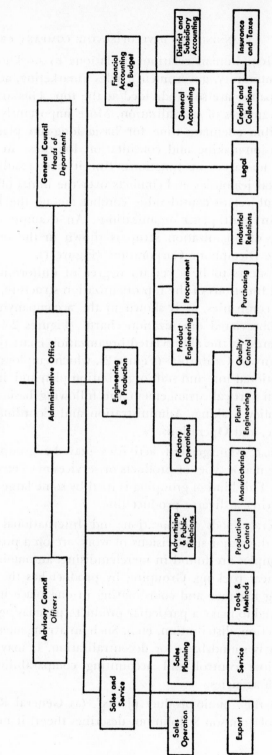

FIG. 1. A FUNCTIONAL ORGANIZATION (THE DICTAPHONE CORPORATION)

porate affairs); human relations (relations to stockholders, employees, community, government); sales (marketing, advertising). Many compaines are so subdivided at the top. This arrangement has the advantages of specialization. More importantly, it should make possible adequate time for basic long-run planning and major decision-making and consultation for those in charge of the major management functions. But it may result in interdepartmental jealousies and conflicts over the limits of authority. It is also subject to considerable conflict among the local plant managers in multi-plant organizations. An example of a functional type of organization setup is shown in the organization chart of the Dictaphone Corporation (Figure 1).

There appears to be a certain degree of uniformity in basic managerial functions of the top organization structure, at least in very large companies, as is shown in the accompanying illustrations of abbreviated organization charts (Figures 2-4). Of particular interest is the abbreviated organization chart of Standard Oil Company of California (Figure 2), which employs the use of the conventional line and staff organization plan and, in addition, identifies in vertical arrangement the following basic functional groups: Policy Making, Administration and Coordination, Staff and Service, and Operations.

2. *Product*. Management activities may be grouped on the basis of the major types of products or services marketed, and sold separately. This kind of grouping is used by some large companies manufacturing a diverse product line.

At General Foods Corporation and International Harvester Company, the major subdivisions of work are on a product basis. Other examples are found in merchandising, automobile, chemicals and meat packing. Grouping by product has the advantage of bringing together and coordinating in one place major activities required to make a particular product (purchasing, engineering, production, distribution, etc.). Such an arrangement provides a particularly sound basis for decentralization. It may also make possible close control and accounting comparability through central staff agencies.

Even in the "mono-product plants" (as General R. Johnson, President of Johnson & Johnson, describes them) it may be wise to make "little ones out of big ones." For example, at the General Electric Company the refrigerator cabinet is made separately from refrigerator compressor units. Or in the production of locomotives, the cabs and running gear are made in separate sections, erected and assembled in another section; the rotating units are made in another shop; and control gadgets in still another. In making control gadgets of infinite variety, the necessity for a multi-product plant really arises.

Figure 5 shows the product organization at The Kendall Company, a medium-sized company which is famous for its work in scientific management.

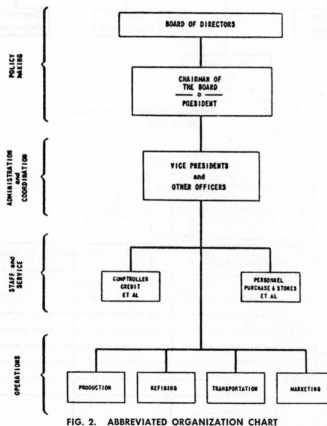

FIG. 2.   ABBREVIATED ORGANIZATION CHART
(STANDARD OIL COMPANY OF CALIFORNIA)

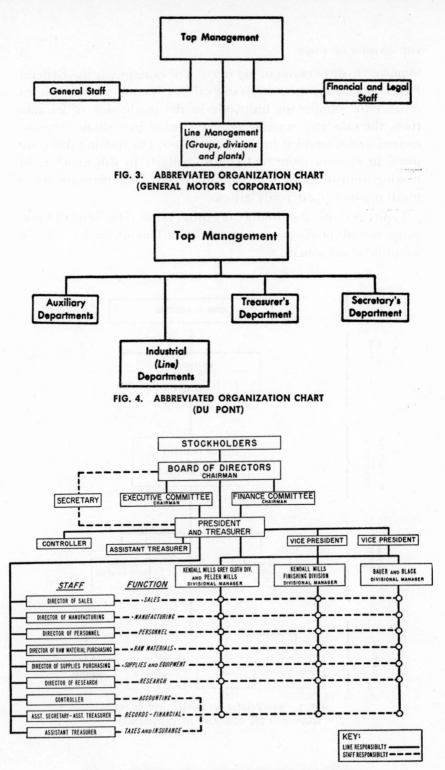

FIG. 3. ABBREVIATED ORGANIZATION CHART
(GENERAL MOTORS CORPORATION)

FIG. 4. ABBREVIATED ORGANIZATION CHART
(DU PONT)

FIG. 5. PRODUCT ORGANIZATION (KENDALL COMPANY)

It shows a basic organization built about three major products. It also shows in an interesting way the provision of staff services to these line divisions, the operation of which is decentralized, while coordination and control are centralized.

3. *Location* (also called territorial or geographical division or departmentation). Under this type of arrangement, all activities performed in a particular area are brought together. It is found in companies serving customers on a national or international

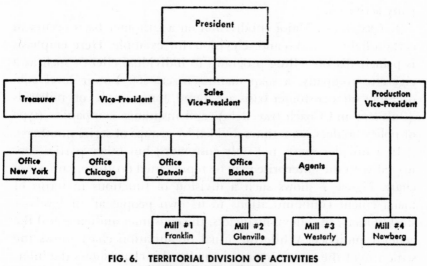

FIG. 6. TERRITORIAL DIVISION OF ACTIVITIES (AMERICAN FELT COMPANY)

scale—e.g., the liquor business, railroads, chain stores, life insurance companies, the overseas branches of motor car and oil companies. The product and locational principles may be combined, with different factories in different locations devoted to the production of different products (e.g., General Motors).

The major subdivisions of oil companies are often on a regional basis, since the natural unit of work centers around the major oil-producing fields. Production and selling or the selling function alone may often be subdivided on a regional basis. The advantage of such a division is that the power of decision-making is concentrated near the source of origin and is all-inclusive, with functional central control. It prevents the losses of efficiency that arise when a company spreads out too thinly. It ensures that careful account is taken of local conditions — an important factor, since the problems of selling may be different in different parts of the country. It makes it possible to take advantage immediately of favorable opportunities arising on the spot. It permits coordination on a manageable scale. It facilitates operation in times of emergency or war. Finally, it provides opportunity for training of lower executives in a wide range of activities so that qualified men will be available to fill vacancies in higher jobs.

Figure 6 illustrates territorial or geographical division of company activities.

4. *Customers.* Major subdivision on a customer basis occurs in certain fields — radio and television, for example. Here emphasis is principally on selling programs to individual clients, such as a cigarette company, a soap manufacturer, etc. Lower level subdivisions on a customer basis are found, for example, on railroads (Pullman and Coach travellers), and insurance companies (type of policy-holders, sometimes divided by groups of serial numbers).

In a broader sense, not only customers, but other parties connected with the enterprise may be represented on the organization chart. Figure 7 shows such a division of functions in terms of management communications to its own people at all levels — stockholders, suppliers, financiers, the consumer audience and the general audience. While the usual organization chart shows the structure of the management hierarchy, this chart shows the interrelationships (and their absence) between the various "publics" connected with the enterprise. It shows the functions which fall into natural groupings and the combinations of functions which are possible in various managerial activities. For instance, in preparing the company annual report, its uses and the varying interests of the different groups may be indicated by such a chart. (This chart was prepared by A. F. Arnold, designer and management consultant to industry.)

5. *Process.* In integrated textile concerns, major divisions may be made on the basis of operational sequence — e.g., spinning, weaving, bleaching, dyeing, inspection, boxing, shipping. In steel and men's and women's clothing subdividing is often based on the process.

6. *Equipment.* In certain fields, equipment determines major

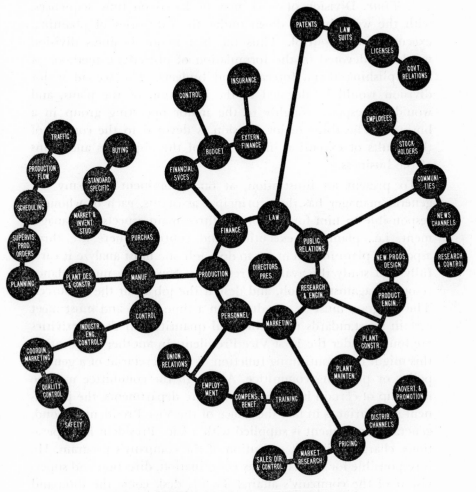

**FIG. 7. DIVISION OF FUNCTIONS SHOWN IN TERMS
OF MANAGEMENT COMMUNICATION**

subdivisions. In a secretarial school, for example, the subdivisions may be determined by the chief instruments whose operation is taught, such as the typewriter, the stenotyping machine, the comptometer, etc. (often identical with process).

7. *Time*. Division of work may be based on time sequences, with the work broken down under the categories of planning, execution and control. Thus the first major business division would be devoted to the formulation of objectives, methods of accomplishing them, forecasts and budgets. The second major division would be devoted to the execution of the plans, and would correspond roughly to the major operating group in a business. The third major division is devoted to the control of the results of execution in the light of the objectives and plans of the business.

To present an illustration, at one prominent company the general manager has three principal assistants, each of whom is responsible to him for one of the three main aspects of management, i.e., planning, execution, and control. There are three aspects of planning. In order to do a job one must analyze it carefully and study the available resources. Next, one must balance resources against the job, and design the job to fit the resources. The program must be scheduled on a time basis, and must meet certain set standards of quality and quantity. All these activities are found under the First Vice President. In another corporation this might be a continuing function of the secretariat of a general policy or planning committee. Although the committee may be made up of certain heads of subordinate departments, the permanent secretariat is in fact the Office of the Vice President. Second, general management is supplied with a Vice President for Operations, charged with the execution of the company's program. He is responsible for the day-to-day coordination, direction and supervision of the company's affairs. To his desk come the thousand and one issues which demand prompt decisions to expedite the efficient execution of any large and complex program. And, finally, in the jurisdiction of the Third Vice President is the function of controllership. His is the job of keeping the progress of the company under scrutiny, comparing it constantly with its program. One might say that this Third Vice President serves the other two. He serves the planner by making prognosticative analyses, and by analysis of past performance which can serve as the basis for future program activities. Obviously, he is a most valuable aid to the General Manager, because he is able to make decisions on the basis of *all* the facts — not merely those which happen to come to him in connection with specific problems.

8. *The "harmonious overlap."* Another method of work division may be useful, particularly in research work which must be speedily completed to meet competition or fulfill an urgent customer requirement. It can sometimes be applied to a variety of rush jobs.

This method of work division may be best explained by recounting Dr. Alexander Sachs' conference with the late President F. D. Roosevelt in 1939 on dividing the work on the atomic bomb construction:

> F.D.R. was worried whether an atomic weapon could be ready in time to decide the outcome of the war. Dr. Sachs had estimated the project might cost two billions, and honestly told the President that ordinarily, it would take 25 years to do the job. He explained to F.D.R. that he had searched the history of human thought for an example of how time could be telescoped.
>
> He found the example in music, he says. The composer of music has ways of making time three-layered. Remember the old round you used to sing: "Are you sleeping, etc?" Three tunes going at once, harmoniously overlapping each other. This, he advised, was what must be done with the atomic project.
>
> "When you start one part of the project, assume you have finished it successfully, and start the next as if you had." That is exactly what was done, probably for the first time with such a huge undertaking. It worked.[2]

9. *Coordination and balance.* An attempt has been made to bring together the various factors of organizational planning in such a way that each acts as a check or balance on the others. In his *Design for Industrial Co-ordination,*[3] Robert W. Porter set out a technique for coordinating the basic functions in the field of industrial organization. He set up seven major categories for

[2] From "How F. D. R. Planned to Use the A-Bomb," by Nat S. Finney, *Look Magazine,* March 14, 1950, page 25, copyright 1950 by Cowles Magazines, Inc.
[3] Harper & Brothers, New York, 1941.

classifying industrial activities, with three subsidiary classifications for each:

1. The problems of policy, performance and compensation, identified as technical problems.
2. The problems of planning, production and inspection, identified as functional problems.
3. The problems of administration, management and operation, identified as jurisdictional problems.
4. The problems of communication, cooperation and control, identified as organizational problems.
5. The problems of executive capacity dealing with intellect, volition and ethics, identified as leadership problems.
6. The problems of employee stimulation, application and discipline, identified as institutional problems.
7. The problems of expectancy, efficiency and economy, identified as measurement problems.

The author attempts, on the basis of wide practical experience, to bring out the inter-operation and relationships of the 21 elements of performance, so that staff needs can be reduced, while the coordination process is improved. It is claimed that this plan of division has the advantages of economizing staff services, improving communication, cutting down jurisdictional problems, and providing better balance in general.

The foregoing are some general guides for determining how the work of the organization may be subdivided, and what consequences may follow. Their specific application will depend upon the special needs of the enterprise. There is no indication from this list that any one way of grouping activities is better than another. If one basis is adopted, then other bases will have to be intermixed. Even when a proper primary basis of dividing work has been decided on, its specific limits must be determined. For example, suppose it has been decided that it will be best to divide sales activities on a territorial basis. This still leaves open the question as to how the territories are to be split up. It is not always practical to determine sales territories by geographical boundaries. The problem must be solved in terms of selling a particular article in a particular situation.

For these reasons it is necessary to develop criteria which are helpful in deciding which method of grouping to use. That method should then be chosen which satisfies best the criteria under consideration, and is best adapted to individual needs.

CRITERIA FOR DETERMINING THE DIVISION OF BASIC ACTIVITIES

In general, the various functions which must be performed to accomplish the objectives of the enterprise should be so assigned as to obtain the greatest possible advantage from the division of labor:

1. Work should be so divided that the incumbent of a position should be able to become a specialist and increase his knowledge on the particular job assigned to him.
2. Special abilities should be used to the full.
3. Groups of people (divisions, departments) should comprise a workable, homogeneous and separate field of activity. The nature of their work should be similar or complementary (the former is probably more important in the lower executive ranks, the latter more important in the upper ranks).

Three major criteria may be distinguished for dividing work — economic and non-economic criteria and the size of the company.

Economic Efficiency

Economic criteria relate to business efficiency. These in turn may be evaluated in terms of saving money, contributing more to the company's revenue, in the speed or accuracy of transacting business.

That particular grouping of activities should be chosen which will make the greatest contribution to the profitability of the enterprise. This may take many different forms, some of which are discussed below.

1. *Major contributions to survival and profitability.* In the early stages of a company's growth the fundamental problem is that of economic survival. This may require improvement of the production process so that goods will be turned out on time and within the proper cost limits. It may require successful acquisition of sources of raw materials, as in the timber industry and mining.

Or, most commonly, it may require acquisition of cash through sales to meet current expenses and to build up a reserve of working capital. These basic objectives tend to become the major function in the business, with the executive in charge becoming in fact the most important official in the business.

Once production or sales have reached satisfactory levels and have become more or less stabilized, they may well lapse into secondary activities, while research and control become dominant. The primary aim at this point may be technical superiority. If this is under pressure by competitors, or the company itself is forging ahead, this very instability will greatly increase the importance of the technical function — especially if the firm's competitive superiority rests on it. The development by the research or style department of innovations which will accelerate the growth of the company are likely to be primary functions. Or the primary activity, from the standpoint of profits, may be that of integration, consolidation and establishment of central control. Once the firm has reached its final stage of growth and is at the point of defending its share of the market, sales may again become predominant.

2. The company may wish to take full advantage of *specialization* and therefore may group together similar functions or specialties. Thus the selling function is often divided into groups of closely related products — in a food company, confectionery products, for example, may be grouped together so that salesmen can devote themselves to selling one product group well rather than dissipate their efforts over many products. Similarly, activities which serve the same purpose may be most efficiently grouped together—e.g., recruitment, interviewing, testing, hiring and induction may be handled by the employment department, while the employee benefit activities are handled separately by a welfare department.

3. *Lines of communication* may be shortened by a particular type of grouping. Thus specific functions in subsidiary plants may communicate directly with the corresponding headquarters function without going through the local plant manager—e.g., control and auditing.

4. *Duplication* may be reduced or abolished by consolidating a

particular function which was previously widely scattered, e.g., the consolidation of the personnel function into a headquarters department.

5. *Balance* may be improved and better operating results attained by combining different parts of a job under several men into one complete job under one man. Joseph B. Hall, President of The Kroger Company, describes such a change in operations as follows:

> Until the past few years, we operated on a functional basis with one man responsible for buying and another man responsible for selling. Sometimes there was friction between these men. If, for instance, merchandise failed to sell, the sales promotion man claimed that the merchandise was inferior; whereupon the buyer would intimate that the sales promotion man had missed his true vocation and should be farming or cleaning the streets. The situation was somewhat like that between the meat managers and the grocery managers; in both cases it was difficult to hold men responsible when each man handled only a part of the complete job.

Railroads have experienced similar cleavages between different parts of the system.

6. The extent of delegated authority may be widened so that lower executives have a greater *power of decision-making*. This has the advantage that people on the spot who are most familiar with the problems can make better and speedier decisions.

7. *Uniformity and consistency* of policy may be brought about. For example, if a personnel department is set up, there is likely to result greater uniformity in pay for similar jobs, more consistent policies with regard to merit rating and promotion, hiring and training.

8. *Control* may be improved. Work may be so divided that similar units are created so that there is better comparability of selling and production efforts. On the other hand, control may be improved by separating inspection activities from the group — e.g., separation of the financial or auditing function from a subsidiary plant, separating credit from sales for fear salesmen will be too easy on the creditors.

9. Activities may be grouped in the department which makes the *most effective use* of them. For example, a company might

consider having the production department take over the training function from the personnel department if this is the best way
to gain acceptance from foremen and hourly-rated employees.

10. *Competition* may be the criterion for dividing activities.
Accordingly, the work may be split up into different departments
or factories so that the results are fairly comparable. For example,
in cement companies the work is distributed to different plants
which are usually highly comparable. Sometimes it may be necessary to proceed on the opposite line of reasoning and join two
types of work in order to suppress competition which hurts the
total effort of the company.

11. *Job interest* may be severely impaired by over-specialization of individual jobs as well as of whole departments. Where
work is divided too finely, with little variation or change, the
monotony may obscure the meaning of the job and its relation to
the end product, and give rise to job dissatisfaction and quits.
Over-specialization is likely to require extra superiors (to deal
with the resulting discontent) and an elaborate system of formal
controls.

Non-Economic Factors

There may be important *non-economic* factors to consider in
the division of work. These frequently make for *autonomy* in a
particular activity. Thus a special division may be set up to look
after special interests connected with the enterprise, e. g., a division on stockholder relations or local community relations. Or
the division is created to arouse *attention* to the particular activity — defense work, governmental relationships, safety (Central
Maine Power Company), executive health, or salary evaluation.
At the National Biscuit Company, for example, the head of the
Sanitation Department reports directly to the president because
the company attaches primary importance to the maintenance of
sanitary conditions. Or a special division may be created for a
particular man—to feather his ego, to "kick him upstairs," to
take account of reduced abilities, or to retain some of his services
on retirement (e.g., the position of Honorary Chairman of the
Board). Division of work may have to be fitted to traditional
arrangements within the company. For example, both the produc-

tion and sales manager may have equal standing in a subsidiary and be given equal powers, but there may be no plant manager. Or the office manager may take over personnel work because there may not be enough of it to justify a full-time division. Or a particular division may continue to occupy an important position within the company simply because it has existed for a long time—e.g., in one company the engineer in charge of bridge-building (the oldest activity in the company) headed up a major division and reported to the president long after bridge-building had become a minor activity. *Preconceived ideas* and principles, and excessive reliance on formality may also be powerful factors in structuring a business enterprise.

Finally, the *personal interests* or hobbies of the chief executive may play a role. For example, Mac Fisheries were originally added to the Lever soap business in order to facilitate sale of the catch of fishermen of some islands on the West Coast of Scotland in whose development the first Lord Leverhulme took a private interest.

Obviously, not all the factors mentioned above are either rational or desirable determinants of the division of work within an enterprise. However, their existence should be taken into account and the reasons for their existence understood before any attempt is made to change the status quo.

Size of Company

The final major criterion for dividing the work of the organization is the size of the company. The importance of the chief problems faced by the top management varies as the company grows. Hence the major functions exercised and supervised by the chief executive are likely to change also. This may be illustrated by the Work Table which the great French industrialist, Henri Fayol, drew up (see page 48).

From this table the following conclusions may be drawn:

1. The most important ability of the head of the small industrial company is technical ability.

2. As one goes up the chain of command, the relative impor-

RELATIVE IMPORTANCE OF REQUISITE ABILITIES OF PERSONNEL
IN INDUSTRIAL CONCERNS[4]

	Requisite Abilities						
	Man-agerial %	Tech-nical %	Com-mercial %	Finan-cial %	Se-curity* %	Account-ing %	Total Evalua-tion %
One-man business	15	40	20	10	5	10	100
Small firm	25	30	15	10	10	10	100
Medium-sized firm	30	25	15	10	10	10	100
Large firm	40	15	15	10	10	10	100
Very large firm	50	10	10	10	10	10	100
State enterprise	60	8	8	8	8	8	100

* Safeguarding property, avoiding social disturbances in the broad sense and any influence endangering the life of the business.

tance of managerial ability increases and that of technical ability declines. Equilibrium between these two obtains in medium-sized companies.

3. The most important ability on the part of heads of large companies is managerial ability or skills, and the more important the company the greater the place occupied by this ability.

4. Commercial and financial ability play a relatively more important part in the case of heads of small and middle-sized companies than they do in the case of larger companies.

5. As one goes up the scale of industrial concerns the managerial coefficient increases at the expense of the rest, which tend to even out, approximating up to one-tenth of the total evaluation.

It is clear that the larger the size of the business the greater the emphasis on broad managerial functions, such as planning, forecasting, organizing, commanding, coordinating and controlling.

[4] From Henri Fayol, *General and Industrial Management*, Sir Isaac Pitman & Sons, Ltd., London, 1949, pp. 10-11. Translator Constance Storres.

CONCLUSION

The most important criterion for the division of work is that of economic efficiency. This should lead to specialization, full utilization of abilities and homogeneity between groups.

Where this criterion is paramount, the basic functions (i.e., those supervised by the chief executive) are those which make the greatest contribution toward profitability. However, the economic criterion, it should be remembered, must usually be modified in the light of non-economic needs. Both need to be fitted to the particular stage of the growth and the special requirements of the company.

Stage II: Delegating Responsibility: A Problem of Personality

As THE ENTERPRISE grows in size, the number of employees reporting to the owner-manager increases. He has charge of an increasing number of management functions, carrying the load of long-range planning and innovation, policy-making, execution and control. At this stage, it may become necessary that the owner-manager delegate a major management function, if he is to handle the others effectively.

The need to delegate responsibilities is the first major organization problem that arises with growth. This problem is one of personality—in part it is *personal,* in part it is *personnel,* as Lt. Col. Urwick has put it so well.

On the *personal* side, the owner-manager may find it extremely difficult to delegate any part of his work. He may feel that nobody can do it as well as he, and he may be right. Nevertheless, because his time is limited, he must concentrate on those matters which he alone can handle or which he can handle far better than anyone else. However, the owner-manager may be unable to delegate, because he does not trust his subordinates. He may not want to place anyone else in a position of any importance in the enterprise. Even if the owner-manager acknowledges the need to delegate, he may be unable to do so effectively. He may insist upon having *his* suggestions, *his* instructions, *his* way of doing things adopted by a new department head so that the latter is nothing more than a glorified clerk. He may be unwilling to give up the close personal relationship to his employees.

The *personnel* problem facing the owner-manager may also assume serious proportions. Present members of management, such as the foremen and the engineer, may have been hired originally because they were good at carrying out the chief executive's ideas. Now they may expect promotion to higher managerial jobs, because of long service and seniority, even though they are not qualified for them. If there is no policy of promotion-from-within, outsiders with production experience and familiarity with modern management methods may be hired instead. But this may cause friction among the existing personnel. There may also be the problem of rivalry between a new executive and the president, aggravated in cases where there is an overlap of functions — especially where capital has been supplied by the newly arrived executive.

ILLUSTRATIVE CASE

A case may be cited to illustrate the dominating effect of executive personality on small organizations. The following is the short history of a small enterprise (25 employees) which failed largely because of the chief's inability to delegate. Its organization chart is shown as Figure 1.

This company produced plastic novelties, which required aggressive selling if the public was to accept them. Accordingly, a supposedly able man was put in charge of sales. However, the title of vice president went to his head. He considered it his function to entertain prospective customers lavishly, and drew heavily on his expense account. He brought in little business.

The president of the company had planned to devote himself to production problems. He had much energy and spent almost all his waking hours in the plant. But he had confidence only in himself. Because of this, he interfered frequently with his production manager. He inspected the work of the employees regularly, and usually detected work methods which he considered

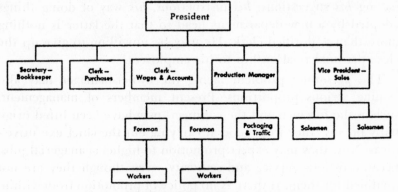

FIG. 1. THE PRESIDENT PLASTICS CORPORATION

faulty. So at times he took over the operator's job himself and worked at the bench. Then he decided that he was not satisfied with the packaging of the merchandise and so he took to wrapping the paper and tieing the strings himself. Because he did a poor job, the subordinates usually had to do the packaging over again. He distrusted his mail clerk, and so he affixed the stamps himself and carried the letters to the post office.

In the meantime, working capital was dwindling fast and was not being replenished through sales. So the president tried to take over the sales function in addition to his production work. He collected addresses of possible customers from the telephone book, compiling the mailing lists himself. He made up the promotion folders and spent a good deal of money on hit-and-miss advertising.

In the meantime, product and engineering design were neglected. No real effort was made to tap other sources of capital. There was no change in personnel. Machinery and raw materials which were urgently needed were not ordered on time. As things became worse, more functions were taken over by the chief executive. He believed that, because he was president, he could do everything, and do it better. As a consequence, he accomplished nothing. He lost the cooperation of his people, he lost customers, his sources of funds dried up. Being immersed in small details, he did not even notice the rapid and inevitable march of his business toward total destruction. In the end only he, the president, was left, presiding over a rubble of debt.

GENERAL ANALYSIS

Many organization authorities deny that personality should be taken into account in dividing up the company's work. They fear that such a consideration might vitiate what they believe is essentially an impersonal piece of engineering.

It would be a grave error not to pay close attention to the engineering aspects of organization and its principles. But it would be an equally grave error to imagine that a single type of organization, or a single slogan of organization, is the solution to every business problem. Organizations are no more than frameworks into which living people must be fitted. They are not, as executives interviewed complained, straight-jackets, which restrain flexibility, initiative and spontaneity, or an iron cast of rules which regulate every action and tell exactly what must be done on every occasion. Perhaps it may be said that, to the extent to which an organization is impersonal, its efficacy in unifying the activities of people will be impaired.

These considerations raise the question as to whether there is one best organization structure. Can we say that one type of organization is definitely superior to another? "Better" in terms of what — profits, satisfaction? And how do we isolate the effects of organization from other influences? Can we furnish scientific proof? Perhaps all we can say is that experience or the "logic" of organization, or a rough economic calculation would appear to make one way of organizing a particular activity better than another.

But even if organization were scientific, there would remain the problem of fitting all kinds of people successfully into that structure. It may be asked whether this is desirable, whether in fact organization is not merely a method of improving working relationships. Is organization master or servant?

Impact of Executive Personality on Organization

Apart from these very real problems, there always remains the question whether the dominating personality (or personalities) in the business will voluntarily fit into a set of working relationships which does not fit his or their conceptions. If not, the best planned organization structure will not work. Therefore, some authorities hold, if the organizational plan is to be accepted, we have to take some account of the personality of the key man (or men) in the company.

This is obvious when we look at some of the great industrial organizations of our time. One could hardly deny, for example, that the one-man organization which fitted Henry Ford, Sr. did not fit his grandson, Henry Ford II. The former built up the business from scratch and was familiar with its many aspects. He had his finger in every pie, often staying at the plant day and night. He boasted that his corporation had "no organization, no specific duties attached to any position, no line of succession or of authority, very few titles and no conferences." He made many personal decisions and for a long time delegated relatively little. There was a strict functional control from Ford headquarters, with little freedom permitted lower down the management echelons. Henry Ford believed in keeping free from anyone else's influence and concentrated the production of all his needs in vertical fashion in one place, River Rouge, as far as possible. At the end, the operations of his company became so widespread and his physical capacity declined so that adequate controls in some functions became impossible. With Henry Ford II there came a complete change in the organizational structure. His own knowledge of the business could not equal that of his grandfather to start with. The extent of decision-making and the sum of unsolved problems had increased to such an extent that delegation became imperative.

Henry Ford II is an advocate of human engineering and composite decision-making. He believes in the utilization of highly specialized and able talent, in a more precise formulation of a complex set of relationships, and an extensive delegation of decision-making. Accordingly, an executive vice president was appointed with great policy-making and administrative powers. A group of top functional specialists headed up large staffs of sales, finance, engineering, personnel, and organization experts. Various manufacturing divisions were set up on a semi-autonomous basis.

Again contrast such personalities as W. C. Durant and Alfred P. Sloan, Jr. at the General Motors Corporation, the one a great promoter, the other a great organizer. Or contrast the heads of large organizations, exercising a highly centralized control, with Robert E. Wood at Sears, Roebuck and Co., a highly decentralized and flexible organization. As General Wood describes his point of view: "While systems are important, our main reliance must always be put on men rather than on systems. If we devise too elaborate a system of checks and balances it will only be a matter of time before the self-reliance, and initiative of our managers will be destroyed and our organization will gradually be converted into a large bureaucracy." Many other great business leaders could be mentioned whose very names are associated with various types of organization.

Unfortunately, we cannot attempt to analyze in so short a space the impact of personality on organization (or, what is equally important, the reverse). We must confine ourselves to some aspects of personality as it affects organization, as follows: (1) Types of decision-makers; (2) the values of the chief executive; (3) the impact of the executive's environment; and (4) the impact of the informal organization.

1. Types of Decision-Makers

It may be possible to "type" the chief executive so as to deduce the kind of organization structure which he is in fact (not on paper) likely to have. The following "types" are taken from the work of the psychologist Erich Fromm.[5] Obviously, there are no pure types, but they are intermixed, with characteristics of certain types predominating. Dr. Fromm's five "orientations" and their impact on the company's organization structure may be summarized as follows (the quotations are from Dr. Fromm's book, the organization analysis ours):

a. *The receptive or defensive type.* "In the receptive orientation a person feels 'the source of all good' to be outside, and he believes that the only way to get what he wants . . . is to receive it from that outside source" (Fromm, p. 62). This type tends to lean heavily on the organization ideas of his most influential advisers and the people most affected by them. He likes to pass on responsibility to others. His organization structure is characterized by delegation.

[5] From *Man for Himself*, copyright 1947 by Erich Fromm, and reprinted by permission of Rinehart & Company, Inc., Publishers, New York, 1947, pp. 50-117.

b. *The exploitative or aggressive type.* His basic premise is "the feeling that the source of all good is outside" . . . but one must "take away from others by force or cunning" (Fromm, p. 64). The organization structure is built from ideas taken from others, used to manipulate others for personal ends. Manipulation is accomplished partly by a highly formalized and centrally controlled structure, partly by setting subordinates against one another and in this way combatting any potential threat. Whenever necessary, management is exercised by veto.

c. *The hoarding type.* "This orientation makes people have little faith in anything new they might get from the outside world . . . They have surrounded themselves, as it were, by a protective wall, and their main aim is to bring as much as possible into this fortified position and to let as little as possible out of it" (Fromm, p. 65). Organization structuring becomes a means of strengthening one's position. It is designed very economically, but what there is tends to be exact. Everyone knows where his place is and is assumed to be very self-reliant.

d. *The marketing type.* "The experience of oneself as a commodity and of one's value as exchange value" (Fromm, p. 68) . . . "Those qualities are developed which can best be sold" (Fromm, p. 77) . . . "He who wants to get ahead has to fit into large organizations, and his ability to play the expected role is one of his main assets" (Fromm, page 82). The organization structure is designed to be salable and acceptable to the people who matter (not necessarily those affected). It must look good to those persons whose judgment this type values most. The actual organizational relationships may be quite different and much less satisfactory than they appear on paper and in conversation.

e. *The productive type.* "Productiveness is man's ability to use his powers and realize the potentialities inherent in him" (Fromm, page 84). The organization structure is likely to be one which aids others in developing themselves to the maximum of their abilities, while integrating them successfully with the company's objectives.

It should be borne in mind that Fromm's typology has shortcomings for application to the analysis of organization, and that it was not intended for this purpose. The types themselves are

very broad and may encompass a considerable number of variations, each of which may be of significance for the nature of the
organization structure. The types are inter-mixed in real life and
we cannot predict how they will react in various situations. Moreover, the analysis does not take into account the interactions of
other personalities or suggest how the passive or active resistance
of others may modify the type and its behavior. Nor does the
analysis take into account the whole array of traditional and
institutional factors and their impact on the structure. Therefore,
we should regard these types as over-all categories, which are
necessarily loose, and, in using them, strive to avoid over-general-
izations.

2. The Values of the Chief Executive

It may be possible to deduce the kind of organization an executive is likely to need by studying his personal values. On the
basis of the studies of the psychologist Eduard Spranger,[6] we may
learn something about the personalities of men by examining
their values. Spranger develops the following types (note that he
stresses that almost all persons are mixtures of these six types,
though the degree varies greatly; the organizational inferences
are ours):

a. *The economic*—interested in what is useful and practical. Requires that the organization structure be utilitarian, adjusted
   to the objectives and purposes of the enterprise.
b. *The aesthetic*—his highest values lie in harmony, individuality,
   pomp and power. He may have a highly centralized structure,
   elegant rather than workable.
c. *The theoretical*—is chiefly interested in the discovery of truth
   for its own sake, is interested in diversity and rationality. This
   may result in brilliantly conceived and original structures,
   overly rational for irrational people.
d. *The social*—love of people; other persons are ends; he is kind,
   sympathetic, and unselfish. The organization is highly informal, built around and adapted to personalities.
e. *The political*—is interested primarily in personal power, influence, renown. Requires that the structure be highly controlled
   to retain power.

---

[6] *Lebensformen, (Types of Men)*, Haale a/d Saale, Germany, (1928). See also
Gordon W. Allport and Philip E. Vernon, *A Study of Values*, 1931, pp. 8-11.

f. *The religious*—his highest value is the greatest spiritual and absolutely satisfying experience; he is ascetic and looks for experience through self-denial and meditation. This may result in structure founded largely on personal and idealistic principles.

We find that Fromm's types relate to a person's *behavior* rather than to the specific *goals* to which he aspires. Spranger, on the other hand, focuses on the nature and quality of goals sought and analyzes major interests. Among other typologies which might be used in explaining *primary motivations* is W. I. Thomas' breakdown of characteristics in terms of recognition, response, security and new experience. Of course, there is considerable intermixture among the three typologies, and they overlap. For example, Spranger's theoretical man might be *driven* by one or another motive and at the same time might be receptive, hoarding or exploitative in his orientation.

For the purpose of organization analysis, Spranger's personality types, like Fromm's, are essentially subjective and take little account of the group in which they operate. Furthermore, it is difficult in practice to find out the personal values of a chief executive even though we may attempt to draw some conclusions from the goals which the executive consistently seeks. Therefore, these typologies are represented here chiefly because they are pioneer attempts to trace the impact of personality on others. They merit our attention because they may eventually be used to gain further insight into executive behavior and its effects on organization.

3. Impact of the Executive's Environment

The executive is obviously influenced by his environment, past and present, in his views on organization.

One such influence is his *early formal training*. A university education, courses at a good school of business, rigorous schooling in technical subject matter and management skills, a keen interest in current management thinking and writing — all these may result in a highly professional interest in organizational structuring.

His previous *experience in other organizations* and exchange of experience with other executives will also affect his views on organization. For example, a man "brought up" in a highly decentralized and successful organization is likely to perpetuate this type of management. He may also place emphasis on the particular management function in which he specialized, and this may affect other functions. For example, an executive who came up through sales may spend a major part of his time on this function, even after he has risen to the presidency. Furthermore, he may instill a "selling approach" into other management functions. He may over-expand the organization because he projects a favorable short-run trend in the past too far in the future. On the other hand, a former production executive may be too conservative in expanding the organization.

Finally, the chief's executive *experience in his own company* will be highly significant. The organizational weaknesses from which he and his associates might have suffered are likely to receive a lion's share of the attention when he is in a position to change them. Furthermore, the circumstances under which he became president are likely to play a part, at least in his first years. The extent to which the chief executive imitates his predecessor because he thought it wise to do so and because he had to do so may be a major influence in his structuring of the organization. For example, if he was brought in specifically to overhaul the organization structure, his attitudes would be quite different than if he were a family successor still dominated by the former head of the company.

4. Impact of the Informal Organization

Finally, there is the impact of informal pressures within the organization. It is well known that an organization is made up of small groups or "societies," formed by friendship, proximity, type of work, similarity of objectives, etc. These individual structures may not coincide with the groupings which have been set up formally. The imposition of a formal structure and formal channels of communications — even the mere possibility of a change in the small group and informal relationships — may gravely upset productivity and cooperation. The irrationality of informal group arrangements may be superior to the rationality of formal organization structuring for efficiency and morale.

For these reasons organization planning should take account of informal organization arrangements. This can be done by super-

imposing on the formal organization chart the informal or existing relationships. The chart shown as Figure 2 is of interest as an
example of one such attempt.[7] The formal organization relationships are drawn in solid lines. The checked lines show the two
persons with whom most time is spent. The arrow points in the
direction of the person named. For instance, the formal relationships of Executive 5 are with Executive 2, 51 and 52. Actually,
he spends most time with Executives 1 and 2. This, it should be
noted, may be quite consistent with the formal relationships of
line command, but other important relationships are revealed by
the informal lines.

In some companies the informal organization is so different
from the formal organization as conventionally established that
it is not published or is discarded after it has served its purpose.
Many companies are so small that the organization structure is
known to everyone and consequently need not be written up. In
this connection, the president of a medium-size company remark-
ed, "In an organization of this size where all executives have daily
intimate contact with each other and their associates, this kind
of material (organization chart, manuals, etc.) has not been
necessary."

Executives often do not speak in organizational terms: They
do not say "I am from the Manufacturing Department," but "I
am from Mr. Blank's office." Many report that they have been
successful for many years without "an iron-bound organization
chart." Their views are well summed up by A. S. Armstrong,
Executive Vice President, The Cleveland Twist Drill Co., when
he wrote to the AMA survey: "This is a rather difficult matter
to put on paper, for ours is a pretty closely knit and informal
organization which does not spell out such relationships in great
detail. By and large, one grows up with the company and after
a while he gravitates into a certain area of responsibility, and
finally he learns by instinct where he fits in and what is expected
of him."

Many feel that a formally established structure may eventually
result in an overly rationalized, bureaucratic relationship which
may stifle the very initiative which management originally be-

[7] From Carroll L. Shartle, "Leadership and Executive Performance," PERSONNEL,
March, 1949, p. 377.

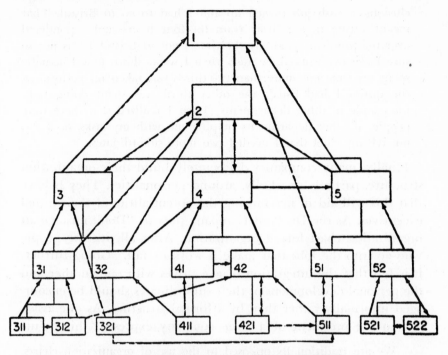

FIG. 2. INFORMAL ORGANIZATION SUPERIMPOSED
ON THE FORMAL ORGANIZATION

lieved would be nurtured. Overly precise organization structuring
may be economically wasteful, as the following observation by Sir
Geoffrey Heyworth, Chairman, Unilever, Ltd., suggests:

> We do not spend much time drawing up functional charts or
> writing definitions of duties. We believe that undue precision and
> definition can be—and often is—the enemy of flexibility, liveliness
> and effectiveness. I may perhaps be permitted to illustrate this
> with a personal reminiscence of 21 years ago. I had just read a
> book on organization and methods and been greatly impressed with
> what seemed to be the secret of efficient working, to define exactly
> what everybody was doing. So I started out one weekend to define
> my own job and those of my two chief assistants. When I finished
> there was one obvious and simple conclusion—I was overworked
> to the point of breakdown, and so were the two others. The remedy
> seemed clear; we must have at least two competent people more in
> our group to help carry our intolerable load. But I was lucky be-
> cause, before I had a chance to tell my chief of my weekend's con-

clusions, a rush job turned up and I had to go to Bristol. That meant sitting in a railway train for four hours and I pondered over the problem again. By the time I got to Bristol I was not so sure I *was* overworked, because when I wrote down how I actually spent my time not more than two-thirds was taken up performing the duties I had listed; the other third was spent doing tasks for people in other departments. Then I realized that there were people in other departments helping me with my tasks. So I did not tell my chief that I needed two more subordinates.

Finally, many companies deliberately build their organization structure, partially or wholly, around personalities. They believe that this will aid in maximizing the potentialities of their gifted executives. As the Du Pont Company puts it: "Don't mistake an organization chart for an organization. After all, it's the people who go into the jobs that make it work or fail." Going further, it is felt that the integration of executives with one another and the personal development of their subordinates should be encouraged informally rather than by a formal structure. As one assistant to the president of a large company expressed this point:

> We are traditionally opposed to the use of organization charts. Our reason is that no two individuals handle a given job in the same manner. In our view, it is unrealistic to create a well-defined spot on an organization chart, simply because the individual placed in that spot probably would not function in accordance with the specifications, or if he did so function he would not be effective. Moreover, we are committed importantly to the proposition that business cannot be conducted effectively through the lines of authority, but must be conducted via lines of communication. As an illustration, our factory and branch house managers deal directly with each other rather than through the general office, and generally throughout the organization individuals within a factory or a branch house communicate directly with individuals in the various central office departments, and in the factories and branch houses, without going through managers.

Informal relationships can be recognized to some extent by a study of "reference groups" and their inter-relationships. Reference groups are a kind of "inner circle" with which individuals seek association and approval for reasons of prestige, ego satisfaction, power, respectability, etc. They are groups or individuals whom executives strive to impress, whom they admire or fear, whom they wish to consult or to be consulted by. Thus their relationship with the members of the "inner circle" may play a major role in their happiness on the job. Formal organization can do much to contribute toward creating or destroying that happiness.

For formal organization structuring affects the sources of power in the company. By shuffling jobs and job responsibilities it affects status, prestige, technical competence, and important lines of communication. Formal organization may be opposed in an informal fashion — through deliberate "misunderstanding" and falsification; refusal to act in the spirit, if not the letter, of organization changes; and reluctance to yield to authority as it is established in the formal organization.

Perhaps most important of all, formal organization structuring must not destroy spontaneity or discourage original thinking. A good test of the new structure is whether executives whose responsibilities are of a creative nature are better or worse off than before. How much time is now required to introduce new ideas and to change existing methods?

The advantages of formal organization structuring must be carefully balanced against the possible loss of advantages obtained through the informal organization.

CONCLUSION

The influence of personality on the organization structure is obvious. It varies in importance from one company to another, but it is a factor that cannot be overlooked. Neither should it be exaggerated, however, and used to justify any form of organization or fancy. What is obviously needed is a judicious compromise between the canons of organization and the needs of personality. This may be provided by isolating the two from one another initially. First, the ideal formal organization structure may be drawn up. Next, an inventory of personnel may be made, emphasizing especially the informal and group contributions made by the executives. Finally, the formal organization structure may be modified in the light of personality, so as to make possible the greatest growth of the individual and his maximum contribution to the success of the enterprise. It is therefore essential that the best aspects of both the formal structure (skeleton) and the informal relationships (living personalities and their interrelationships) be considered in shaping the organization. The criterion for selecting the best features of both will usually be "least cost," modified by the conditions necessary for maintaining smooth working relationships. This will probably mean an increasingly formal structure as the enterprise grows in size, with increasing care necessary to preserve informal relationships.

This generalization may be illustrated by the following account of a judicious combination of formal and informal structuring. It shows how the two can aid in establishing a position in such a way that talents are fully utilized and shortcomings minimized. Thomas Roy Jones, President of Daystrom, Inc. tells how the comptroller's job changed constantly over a period of a few years. It remained the same on the chart and in the manual, but its incumbents changed and their personalities changed with the passage of time. The first comptroller, who was given the duties of chief accounting officer, was delegated an increasing number of the problems of the chief executive. He did so well that eventually his title was changed to that of assistant general manager. His successor was unable to fulfill the responsibilities assigned to him, and the scope of his job shrunk so much that eventually a new comptroller had to be appointed. This third man was able to fill the job of comptroller as it was originally designed, but also filled in some related gaps in the organization. If the president had insisted on a rigid adherence to the job description on the organization chart at the time of each of the major changes, he would have failed to acquire a competent helper, suffered a partial breakdown in his accounting division, and neglected to develop an able accounting officer. Many other examples could be cited, such as that of the sales manager who is a great success as long as he is actually selling, but flounders as a general administrator; the comptroller who has a special ability for solving production problems; and so on.

It is imperative that those charged with organization planning take account of the different personalities passing through the same position and the changes that take place in the same personality over time. To do so is to make the formal organization structure a means to an end — a useful servant rather than an imperious master.

Stage III: Further Delegation of Management Functions: Span of Control

ILLUSTRATIVE CASE

AT THIS stage in the growth of the company, the basic problem arises whether the chief executive can supervise effectively the expanded production and sales activities of the company. At the second stage he was trying to make too many decisions himself and so had to delegate some of them. At the third stage he is confronted with the problem of trying to supervise the activities of more people than he can successfully handle.

The Liverpool Machine Tool Company, whose case we shall now consider, was already highly specialized, producing metal-forming machinery. Its products were patented and trade-marked. The work was skilled and required technical competence of various kinds. The president began by working as a designer and sales expert for many years. Assisted by a few clerks and a salesman, he had the machines built elsewhere to his specifications. His was a typical one-man, owner-managed business.

But he lost several very good lines of machinery because of labor disputes in the plants which manufactured to his specifications. As a result, the manufacturing function was added in 1930. Though his aptitude lay in designing and selling, the owner-manager did all the necessary production work himself, assisted by a few skilled employees. Despite the Great Depression, he secured a major order from the Mexican Government. It was of such dimensions that he had to expand his little workshop to an acre-size plant. He hired clerks to help on production and accounting, and foremen to supervise employees. He had to divest himself increasingly of the production function, partly because design and selling occupied all his time, partly because he was not temperamentally fitted to handle painstaking and minute tasks. He had six foremen reporting to him (some with the power of superintendents), four sales supervisors and several production (scheduling) clerks and accountants. This stage is shown in Figure 1. It indicates that the number of subordinates had reached 13.

In an average workweek of 60 hours, the chief executive spent 20 hours on designing and 15 hours on personal selling— the strategic functions of the business. Over-all financial problems took another 10 hours of his time; relations with outsiders, such as suppliers, bankers, auditors, and government officials, took 10 hours. This left only five hours which the chief executive could spend on supervision, or roughly 20 minutes per week for each subordinate. And this limited time for supervision had to be fitted in at odd moments, into a workload of 10-12 hours a day, which was clearly excessive.

The number of subordinates had obviously become too large at this stage to be supervised effectively by the chief executive. His first step was to delegate the supervision of the production function (in which he was relatively least expert) to a production manager, and the acquisition of supplies to a purchasing manager. Next he delegated much of the financial function to a treasurer, who relieved him of many of the burdensome details in a field in which he had never been very happy.

The chief executive's sales went so well that he delegated this responsibility to a sales manager. Finally, he appointed a chief engineer, a designer, and a products manager. Now he had time for other matters: he participated in international conferences, wrote books and articles, and traveled widely. The company continued to expand and eventually there were nine executives reporting to the president. He decided to delegate to an exec-

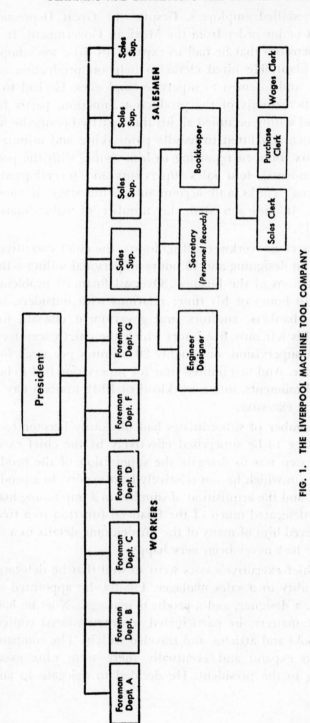

FIG. 1. THE LIVERPOOL MACHINE TOOL COMPANY

utive vice president, who was also general manager, all responsibilities except personal participation in major decisions when
he himself was on hand and approval of long-range plans. (As
is the case in many small companies, the new general manager
was also the treasurer; he was very competent in his own field,
was excellent in implementing and modifying plans, and had
acquired a good all-around knowledge of the business.)

With only one man to supervise, and this man highly trained
in the ways of the chief, the president now spends only four or
five months out of the year in his plant. He is able to devote the
rest of the time to his personal interests. Both management and
the workers are doing extremely well financially, and the company is known for its cooperative relationships. Such is the power
of judicious delegation!

THE SPAN-OF-CONTROL THEORY: A GENERAL ANALYSIS

In organizational theory, the optimum "span of control" — that
is the number of subordinates who can be effectively supervised
by one man — is generally set at between three and six. For
example:

"The number of subordinates whose tasks are interdependent
who can be directed immediately and effectively by one individual
is strictly limited. . . . It should not exceed five or six. The ideal
number of subordinates for all superior authorities appears to be
four."[8]

"The average human brain finds its effective scope in handling
three to six other brains."[9]

"It is generally agreed that if the functions that are being co-
ordinated are interdependent and dissimilar, the span of control
should not exceed five."[10]

While it is conceded that the number may be considerably
larger for first-line supervision, most authorities on organization
believe that the theory should be applied above that level, and

[8] Lt. Col. L. Urwick, "Executive Decentralization with Functional Coordination,"
THE MANAGEMENT REVIEW, December, 1935, pp. 356, 359.
[9] General Sir Ian Hamilton, *The Soul and Body of an Army*, Arnold, London,
1921, p. 229.
[10] R. E. Gillmor, *A Practical Manual of Organization*, Reading Course in Executive Technique, Funk & Wagnalls Company, New York, 1948, p. 12.

that the higher up in the management hierarchy the superior, the greater the need for a small number of subordinates. Thus General Sir Ian Hamilton wrote in an often-quoted statement: "The nearer we approach the supreme head of the whole organization, the more we ought to work towards groups of three; the closer we get to the foot of the whole organization, the more we work towards groups of six."[11]

Reasons for and Against a Small Span of Control

Three reasons for limiting the span of control are most commonly advanced: (1) As subordinates are added, there is not only an increase in direct relationships, but also an increase in the number of cross-relationships among members of the group; (2) human beings have a limited span of attention, which makes it impossible after a certain point to do an adequate job of supervision; (3) the larger the number of subordinates, the more likely it is that they will be dispersed geographically, and hence be more difficult to supervise.

The need for a definitely limited span of control was cogently put by Henry L. Stimson, one of our great administrators:

When I last held the post of Secretary of War under Mr. Taft, who was a very good administrator, there were only nine Cabinet officers or 10 persons at the Cabinet table including the President. Barring the Interstate Commerce Commission, and perhaps one or two other minor quasi-independent commissions, every administrative function headed up in one of the nine Cabinet officers and went to the President through the departmental head. Mr. Taft dealt with his departments through his Cabinet, and that gave you a sense of responsibility and security that could not otherwise be obtained. Today the President has constituted an almost innumerable number of new administrative posts, putting at the head of them a lot of inexperienced men appointed largely for personal grounds and who report on their duties directly to the President and have constant and easy access to him. The result is that there are a lot of young men in Washington ambitious to increase the work of their agencies and having better access to the President than his Cabinet officers have. The lines of delimitation between these different agencies themselves and between

[11] Op. cit., p. 229.

them and the Departments [are] very nebulous. The inevitable result is that the Washington atmosphere is full of acrimonious disputes over matters of jurisdiction. In my own case, a very large percentage of my time and strength, particularly of recent months, has been taken up in trying to smooth out and settle the differences which have been thus increased.[12]

On the other hand, there are continuous tendencies toward increasing the span of control. These are:

1. The desire of executives to have access as high up as possible, as a means of advancement and a sign of status.

2. The need for keeping the chain of command as short as possible. The shorter the span of control, the more layers of supervision there will be and the longer the lines of communication, with corresponding disadvantages.

There are small companies of 1,000 employees where there are as many as 10 levels of supervision—as many as in the AT&T Company! Thus a man may be the proud manager of the third production sub-district of the Suffolk division of the Eastern Area in the Northern Region of the so-and-so company. The red tape created by such organizational channels can be comparable to that of the government. One company plotted the number of persons through which an order for a durable instrument went from receipt to shipment—it touched 15,000 people, and the chart plotting its meanderings was 30 feet long!

3. A natural tendency on the part of executives to take a personal interest in as many aspects of their job as possible, the lack of trust in the ability of subordinates, the fear of possible rivals, and the desire for power (as shown by the number of people reporting).

4. The political argument that as many interests as possible should be represented.

5. The danger of overly close supervision which may discourage initiative and self-reliance.[13]

The need for a wider span of control is evident in a number of companies. Detailed studies on the span of control at Sears,

[12] Henry L. Stimson and McGeorge Bundy, *On Active Service in Peace and War*, Harper & Brothers, New York, 1947, pp. 495-496.
[13] James C. Worthy, "Organizational Structure and Employe Morale," *American Sociological Review*, April, 1950, p. 178.

Roebuck and Company very definitely showed superiority in operating efficiency of a large span of control, provided subordinates are of high competence and self-reliance. Sears' regional vice presidents now have full authority over everything in their territories, except purchasing, of course. These vice presidents report to the president. As a result, Sears' president now has 13 executives directly under his supervision. These territorial vice presidents, in turn, have even more people reporting directly to them. In addition, other executives down the line have direct access to the president.

Similarly, at IBM one level of management was eliminated entirely between 1940 and 1947, the job requirements of foremen and plant managers enlarged, and those of middle management reduced. "Within this simplified organizational framework, the company has apparently found it easier to build teamwork and morale."[14]

Criteria for Determining the Span of Control

The optimum span of control may be determined by weighing the advantage of retaining managerial responsibility as against the gains to be realized by delegating it. The span of control should be extended to the point at which the advantages of delegation (e.g., unburdening of executives so that they may have time for more profitable work) are outweighed by the costs of extra staff, additional supervision, and added difficulties of communication. It should be noted that an increase in the span of control is interpreted here to mean an increase in the delegation of responsibilities.

When the optimum span of control is reached and still additional responsibilities need to be delegated by the executive, it may be wise to add a new link in the chain of command. Thus, if a chief executive has ten different men reporting to him and is overloaded, he may find it advantageous to appoint two men under him to supervise the ten. In this way the span of control is reduced by adding another layer of management. Such action would be advisable, of course, only if the cost of the additional

14 F. L. W. Richardson, Jr. and Charles R. Walker, *Human Relations in an Expanding Company*, Labor and Management Center, Yale University, New Haven, Connecticut, 1948, p. 49.

two men and the possible increased costs of communication are outweighed by advantages gained by freeing the chief executive's time.

In the following discussion we shall merely examine the optimum span of control in terms of the gains and costs of increasing delegation of responsibilities. We shall ask: "Under what circumstances is it worthwhile for the chief to increase his span of control (supervise *more* executives) by increasing delegation of responsibilities?" In each case it is necessary to examine the alternative to the problem—i.e., reducing the number of executives supervised and adding another chain of command.

The *gains from delegation* of an executive's responsibilities to a larger number of subordinates depend on the contributions he will be able to make to the company's earnings or profits, and indirectly on the degree to which such delegation furthers better relationships. These gains may result from devoting more time to top management work—e.g., developing new ideas, planning, policy-making, looking at company problems as a whole, being available for advice and for help in emergencies, improving governmental and community contacts, and having time to think.

The following factors seem to increase the gains of delegation:

1. The greater the executive's capacity in top managerial work the greater will be the gains. If his abilities tend to lie in supervision only, the gains will be correspondingly smaller.

2. The less time previously devoted to top management work the greater the gains of delegation. (For confirmation of this observation see the work tables of Henri Fayol in Stage I of this study which show the proportion of time spent on various aspects of management at different management levels and in companies of different sizes.)

3. The less complex the type of work supervised (and the management functions), the greater the gains of delegation. For example, in personnel work, personal attention must be given to many matters, and therefore the span of control must necessarily be small. This holds true for many types of research. However, factory workers are not in need of such close attention from their superiors, and hence the span of control can be larger. Again, in some types of activity, such as marketing through large numbers

of wholesale and retail branches, under uniform policies with specific delegations of responsibility, the span of control may be quite wide. The same holds true for department heads of general services (building operation, motor vehicle maintenance, purchasing, engineering) where as many as ten may report to a single officer or member of top management. Delegation depends on the type of business; for instance, in a stable business like banking a much larger span of control is possible than in the volatile automobile industry.

4. The fewer the number of different functions supervised by one man and the less diverse these functions are, the greater the gains of delegation. Thus, if an executive supervises seven people, all doing the same things—even salesmen, for example—the gains of further delegation will be greater than if he supervised such different functions as finance, personnel, traffic, office management, public relations, and law.

5. The more "mature" the relationships between the superior and his subordinates—that is, the higher the degree of initiative and independence permitted by the superior and possessed by the subordinate,—the greater the gains of delegation. Also, the better the mutual relationship.

6. The better trained the subordinates, the wider their experience in different parts of the company, and the longer their service, the greater the gains of delegation, for each of these conditions reduces the amount of direct supervision required.

7. The more competent the aid of "staff assistants" to members of general management, the greater the gains of delegation. (See Stage IV.)

The costs of increased delegation, expressed in terms of the increased cost of supervision, may be summarized as follows:

1. The greater the number of additional subordinates reporting to one executive, the greater will be the direct cost of supervision. Thus, if an executive has 10 men reporting directly to him, it is obvious that the cost of supervising them will be considerably greater than if he had only five immediate subordinates. But it should be remembered that the direct increase in the number of subordinates may lead to a reduction in the chain of command and in this way may reduce the total cost of supervision.

2. The greater the additional number of individual relationships between the supervisor and his subordinates, the greater the number of group relationships between the supervisor and groups of subordinates, and the greater the number of cross-relationships involving two and more than two subordinates, the greater will be the cost of supervision. As R. E. Gillmor, Vice President of the Sperry Corporation, points out: "The number of cross relationships rises geometrically as new subordinates are added. With a span of five the number of direct, cross and group relationships requiring coordination is 41; the relationships rise geometrically with increased span until at 10 there are 1,068 direct, cross and group relationships."

3. The greater the degree and extent of delegated authority, the greater will be the cost of supervision. Also, the smaller the capacity of the subordinates and the greater the possibility of errors on their part, the greater will be the cost of supervision. Finally, the smaller the span of control which the subordinates are able to manage effectively, the greater will be the supervisory cost. As an example, take a sales manager with 12 sales offices reporting directly to him.

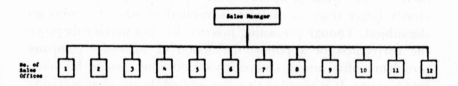

After delegation to three assistant sales managers, the delegating situation is as follows:

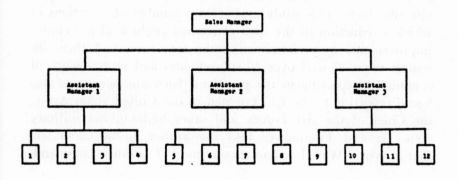

In the case of this delegation, the sales manager must weigh the time he gains against the cost of three additional assistant sales managers, the extra cost of supervising them, and the additional costs of longer communication channels (longer time of communication, less accurate transmission of ideas and messages, loss of direct contact, etc.).

A Survey of the Span of Control in Industry

For purposes of organization planning, it may be worth while to know the extent and nature of the span of control as it is actually found in industry—in large and medium-sized concerns.

Table 1 shows the number of executives reporting to the president in 100 large companies (over 5,000 employees) surveyed recently by the AMA. The companies selected were all known to have good organizational practices.

The median number of subordinates supervised by the president is between eight and nine. To this responsibility should be added the president's contacts with the Board of Directors, a more or less large number of company committees, important customers, suppliers, financial interests, government, local community, etc. The number of executives reporting to the president is clearly larger than the number advocated by several writers on the subject. Though prevailing practice does not necessarily prove the correctness of a policy, the action of successful company presidents, often under competitive conditions, should be taken into account. It is possible that the limited degree of supervision which can be given to a large number of subordinates makes for greater independence and self-reliance on their part.

However, there are definite limits to one man's ability to supervise effectively. This study uncovered a number of situations in which a reduction in the span of control might lead to definite improvements in performance at the top; several of these instances revealed well over 30 subordinates and several score of committees reporting to the president! Such numbers were also found reporting to the Chief-of-Staff of the United States Army, the Chief of the Air Forces, and other high-ranking military men. General Eisenhower told the author in an interview that in World War II he had at one time 150 battalion commanders *reporting* to him, and that through his personal, though brief, contact with them he was able to influence the men to such an extent that a superb supply job was performed. Now it would

Table 1

NUMBER OF EXECUTIVES REPORTING TO PRESIDENT IN 100 LARGE
COMPANIES (over 5,000 EMPLOYEES)

No. of Executives Reporting to President	No. of Companies
1	6
2	—
3	1
4	3
5	7
6	9
7	11
8	8
	Median
9	8
10	6
11	7
12	10
13	8
14	4
15	1
16	5
17	—
18	1
19	—
20	1
21	1
22	—
23	2
24	1
Total	100

be physically quite difficult even to receive reports from 150 people or, to express it in organizational language, "effectively supervise" so many. What the General had in mind is that accessibility of the chief executive and personal inspiration can make important contributions. Actually, the number of people he *supervised* was small, while the number who had access to him was large.

In this connection, it is important to note that interpretations of the term "reporting to," made by different companies range from occasional access to the superior to direct and constant supervision. Our findings seem to indicate that instead of close supervision by the president of a few executives the trend is toward *access* to him by a considerable number, with more or less intensive supervision of a few.

In six out of the 100 companies studied, the president has only one subordinate whom he supervises. This individual usually carries the title of executive vice president. In such a case, the president may devote himself largely to policy-making, long-range planning, areas of special urgency, or functions which are particularly important to the profit or loss of the company. The executive vice president concerns himself with implementing the policies and plans by means of directives and administrative procedures. Thus one of the president's functions might be to chart the broad organizational objectives of the company — for example, decentralization. The executive vice president would then work out the means of accomplishing these objectives. It should be noted that in a number of instances one or more executive vice presidents, as well as a number of vice presidents, report to the president. Though there may be an executive vice president, it is usual for the president to supervise directly those executives whose activities involve such important long-range factors as finance, industrial relations, or government.

This leads to the second basic question covered by the AMA survey, namely the type of activities which are supervised by the company's president. The findings for the 100 large companies are shown in Table 2:

Thus, in all except six companies (which have executive vice-presidents), the head of production (operations or manufacturing) reports to the president; even in these six companies considerable operating supervision may be involved. Marketing is second, with the marketing executive reporting directly to the

Table 2

TYPES OF EXECUTIVES REPORTING TO THE PRESIDENT

Function*	No. of Companies
Production, Operations, Manufacturing	94
Marketing, Sales	88
Industrial Relations, Personnel Administration	64
Legal Counsel, General Counsel	55
Controller, Comptroller	46
Treasurer	45
Finance	42
Purchasing	38
Research, Development, New Products	38
Plant Managers	37
Assistant to President	37
Engineering	37
Secretary	37
Public Relations	34
Executive Vice President	29
Advertising	15
Overseas Operations	13
Traffic	13
Organization	9
Economic Research	7
Quality Control	4
Patents	4
Special Assignments	3
Government Relations	3
Maintenance	2
Office Management	1
Safety	1
Claims	1
Production Control	1
Coordination	1

* The functions listed in Tables 2 and 4 are as described in the companies' organization charts. Their importance and content is obviously not the same in all cases. When two functions were combined, each was counted as one-half. In the case of plant managers and heads of subsidiaries, the function itself was counted once in the case of every company, even though there were several of them.

president in 88 per cent of the companies. Industrial Relations is third, reporting directly to the president in 64 per cent of the companies. The Legal or General Counsel is fourth with 55 per cent. The Controller, Treasurer, and the head of Finance are fifth, sixth and seventh respectively. While the titles assigned to the executive handling the finance function vary in different companies, this executive reports to the president in almost all the companies surveyed. Also noteworthy is the relatively high ranking of Purchasing and Research.

For a partial comparison, the same problems may be studied in the medium-sized companies (500 to 5,000 employees) participating in the AMA survey:

Table 3

NUMBER OF EXECUTIVES REPORTING TO THE PRESIDENT IN 41
MEDIUM-SIZED COMPANIES

No. of Executives Reporting to the President	No. of Companies
1	3
2	—
3	2
4	2
5	4
6	8
	Median
7	7
8	5
9	2
10	4
11	1
12	—
13	1
14	1
15	—
16	—
17	1
Total	41

The median is somewhat lower than in the case of the larger companies, with between six and seven reporting to the president. The range between the lowest and highest number of executives reporting is also less. The reduced median and range reflect the lesser volume of important problems faced by the smaller companies and the smaller number of people required to assist the president in coordination and control.

At the top again are Production, Sales, Finance, and Industrial Relations, though Sales and Finance report to the president in only three-quarters of the companies surveyed, and Industrial Relations in only half the cases. There are relatively more plant managers reporting to the president. Engineering occupies an important fifth place. Again, in many companies a number of plant managers report to the president (on the average, two), but only one was counted in the enumeration of functions.

Table 4
TYPES OF EXECUTIVES REPORTING TO THE PRESIDENT IN MEDIUM-SIZED COMPANIES

Function	No. of Companies
Production, Operations, Manufacturing	38
Marketing	32
Treasurer	21
Industrial Relations	20
Engineering	17
Executive Vice President	14
Purchasing	14
Controller	13
Plant Managers	13
Finance	12
Research	12
Secretary	12
Assistant to President	10
Legal Counsel	6
Overseas Operations	6
Organization	3
Public Relations	3
Advertising	2
Economic Research	2
Transportation	2
Production Control	1

A Tentative Conclusion

In concluding this analysis of the span of control theory, it may be well to summarize our major findings. As has been pointed out, some authorities on organization hold the number of men who can be effectively supervised to a number from three or four to seven or eight. In actual practice, the span of control tends to be larger than in theory, both in terms of "supervision" and certainly in terms of "access to," principally because the longer the chain of command, the less satisfactory are communication and efficiency. An ill-advised plan to reduce the span of control can defeat its own objective by the creation of too many links in the chain of command. This is one of the most paralyzing features of a large organization. The most economical and generally satisfactory solution is one which avoids both an over-long, complicated chain of command resulting in a predominantly "vertical structure" and disproportionately extended organizational units which would eventually result in a "horizontal structure."

Of course, a formal limit on the number of subordinates supervised is necessary to make the executive aware of the limitations of time and ability. The span of control may be determined by weighing the advantages (additional revenue) of increasing delegation to a greater number of subordinates against the disadvantages (additional costs). This process of setting limits to the span of control, together with the actual limits which will result, will help each executive realize that he cannot live forever as a managerial superman, continuously operating beyond his physical and intellectual capacity. As a result, he will be better able to replace an able and trusted subordinate who suddenly leaves, or to cope with an expansion to unfamiliar fields. He will also have a margin of safety, or a reserve capacity.

Stage IV: Reducing the Executive's Burden:
The Staff Assistant

INCREASE in a company's size magnifies its problems so that the chief executive may find it difficult to handle all his former duties. Once a company has several hundred employees, some formal planning is usually required to handle its growing personnel problems, to diversify its product line, to uncover new sources of supply and new markets for its products, to streamline production, to meet the increasingly complicated problems of finance. Rules of thumb, personal experience and hunches are no longer adequate. The problems arising with increased company size require the services of specialized, technically trained personnel.

The technical responsibility may be delegated by establishment of a separate function for the exercise of the technical specialty. However, in some cases it may be advisable to appoint an "assistant to" the delegant. The "assistant to" has no power to act on his own. Instead he furnishes his chief with information and recommendations which the latter is free to use as he pleases.

The position of the "assistant to" may have the advantage of introducing a new function "under the wing" of the boss. Thus the incumbent of the new function is given a chance to show what he can do. If put on his own, he might fail because of opposition from those in the established functions, particularly if the other top management men felt the new function legitimately

belonged to them. Thus, the head of the new production department might well feel that the personnel function should be his,
that successful operations require unified control. The separation
of these functions might incur the bitter hostility of the production man, who might never give the personnel man a chance to
demonstrate that he can succeed. But if the new function remains
part of the chief's responsibility, his own position protects it.
Furthermore an "assistant to" the president can learn a great deal
more about the company, and more quickly, than if he were on
his own. Once in possession of company know-how and accepted
as a personality, he can be invested with personal responsibility.

ILLUSTRATIVE CASE

Let us consider, in this connection, the case example of the
Kalamazoo Company, an owner-managed organization employing
approximately 500 persons. When the chief executive found his
burdens increasing with the size of the company, he appointed a
general assistant to himself, while the company secretary took care
of many operating problems and public relations matters. By the
time the secretary became executive vice president, the assistant
had been accepted by everyone and could become secretary.

Next the chief executive was eager to avail himself of the best
thinking in economics as well as the analytical ability that often
accompanies such training. He appointed a second assistant with
an economics background to help him standardize the production
line, set up a marginal costing system, and introduce a price
system geared to the existing competition. After a few years, the
second assistant headed an economics department. The third
assistant to be appointed worked on the problems of estimating
the potential sales 25 years in the future; later he was made head
of a market research department.

In each of these instances, as the assistant assumed responsibility, he of course ceased to be an assistant and assumed direct and
personal responsibility for a department. Thus the chief executive was able to get highly specialized work done under his
supervision and later to establish that work as a separate function.
This organizational method was of real help to the company in
gaining an edge on its competition.

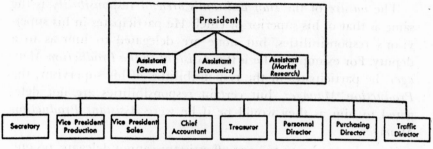

THE KALAMAZOO COMPANY

GENERAL ANALYSIS

A widespread complaint on the part of top executives interviewed in the AMA survey was that of excessive pressure of affairs
on them. They are working long hours—from eight to 12 hours
a day—some staying until midnight in the office, many taking
work home at night and over weekends, and most having short
and inadequate vacations. Almost all the time of top executives
is spent with other people, an increasing proportion with others
than company executives—such as government officials, trade
association officers, local community contacts, and non-working
directors. The result is lack of time on the part of the top executive for adequate contact with associates and subordinates, for
rest and recreation, for reading—particularly of a non-business
nature—and, most serious of all, lack of time for reflection, for
developing long-range plans, for thinking up new ideas.

Perhaps this grave situation could be relieved by resort to the
staff assistant, a device often used, for similar reasons, by the
military. In our interviews with General Eisenhower, he stressed
the opinion that business men made too little use of the staff
assistant. He reported that his own practice was to have at least
four or five such assistants, able men closely trained by him
and completely familiar with his decision-making habits. They
were able to relieve the General of an enormous burden, leaving
him free to see anyone with a really important problem—from
the journalist with a hot tip before the invasion of Europe to a
group of university professors with a grievance.

Similarly, when the job of an executive begins to exceed his
capacity, he may consider appointing an "assistant to" himself.

The *nature* of the *staff assistant's area of responsibility* is the same as that of his superior or chief: He participates in his supervisor's responsibilities, but none are delegated to him as to a deputy. For example, if he is the *Assistant to the Production Manager,* he participates in the responsibilities of his supervisor, the *Production Manager,* but certain responsibilities are not delegated to him as they would be if he were *Assistant Production Manager.*

Since the "assistant to" or staff assistant cannot delegate, no one owes any responsibility to him.

The assistant helps his chief in his work. He has been well described as "an extension of his chief's personality," whose job it is to "worry about the problems which worry the boss." The "chief" may be a line executive or a staff specialist. Or he may be the company president. In this discussion, we shall deal principally with the functions of the assistant to the chief executive, i.e., the president.

His status is below that of other executives reporting to his chief or supervised by him. It cannot be overstressed that there should be no dilution of responsibility through the assistant. As one top executive describes his function: "We believe that the chief executive officer should not surround himself with any assistants who in any way diminish the responsibility of the other chief officers of the company. The assistant should not presume to pass judgment in any way on any of the principal officers, since it discourages them and makes judgment on their promotion difficult. If he criticizes his chief's subordinates who are his superiors in status, it is the assertion of an authority which he does not possess; and if he criticizes any of their subordinates, he is criticizing them. Further, he is interfering with his chief's authority."

To sum up, in Lt. Col. Urwick's remarks to the AMA survey, "The 'Assistant to' is . . . essentially a man who *represents* his chief in matter of administrative detail. His functions are limited to study, research, analysis, recommendation and, above all, to helping his chief to get things done by handling the publication of instructions, etc., watching the organization, and foreseeing and forestalling any failure in coordination between the specialists and the 'line.' He has no executive duties."

Qualifications for Successful Staff Assistants

In the AMA survey we found that the staff assistant requires technical competence, discretion, high analytical powers, and ability to present his material effectively in speech and in writing. He must unfold his activities slowly to begin with and win confidence. He should be free from organization politics and give his views on the basis of the merits of the problem. He must gain top management support so that his efforts may bear fruit. He must be able to "live with" his superior successfully and have a good sense of timing. On their part, line executives must learn how to use staff assistants. This requires, among other things, the ability to listen.

Possible Activities of Staff Assistants[15]

The activities of staff assistants may vary in importance from the equivalent of those of an office boy up to activities of a vice presidential character. Major activities may include, in rough order of importance:

1. Coordinating work by bringing together the parties concerned, clarifying misunderstandings, collecting and disseminating information, acting as secretary for coordinating committees.
2. Collecting, analyzing, writing up top management policies, plans and procedures.
3. Economic and market research, study of competitive conditions, governmental regulations.
4. Screening visitors and requests to the chief executive or top management.

Minor activities may include:

a. Design of management control reports.
b. Design and installation of inter-departmental procedures, leaving intra-departmental procedures to be handled by departmental staffs.

[15] This discussion is partially based on interviews and on E. W. Reilley's "Why Short-Change the Chief Executive on Staff Assistance?" PERSONNEL, September, 1947, pp. 85-88. See also Henry E. Niles and M. C. H. Niles, "Assistance in Coordination," PERSONNEL, August, 1938, pp. 35-36, in which they discuss what the staff assistant may do and what the staff assistant should avoid.

   c. Plans for reorganization analysis, preparation of recommendations, preparation of organization manuals and charts, and keeping them up-to-date.

   d. Part-time functions like public relations or personnel activities in smaller firms. The staff assistant may not exercise these functions himself, but may merely see to it that they are properly carried out.

   e. Working out and suggesting methods of office improvement; control over internal reporting systems, forms, space and office equipment. (These functions are, of course, frequently performed by the controller, purchasing director, office manager, or industrial engineer.)

In connection with these activities, two different types of "assistants to" must be distinguished. One type performs a function not performed anywhere else. The other type performs a function which is being carried out elsewhere. For instance, if a company officer has an assistant to do economic research, with no such work being done anywhere else in the company, there is no problem of duplication. However, if there is a department of economic research in the company and the president has an assistant to go over the material produced by that department, dispute and confusion may result from the lack of clear-cut responsibility.

Advantages

The advantages to the chief executive or a top vice president of having an assistant include:

   a. Reduction of the burden of work. This may make it possible for the chief executive to see people, to do some quiet thinking, to extend his span of control (if necessary) or to supervise his present subordinates more satisfactorily, to supplement his technical competence with administrative and human relations competence.

   b. An improvement in planning and coordination.

   c. Better utilization and continued application of outside counsel.

   d. Training for the assistant so that he may acquire an over-all point of view of the company's affairs; learn how to persuade others; have the opportunity to observe and to be observed; and ultimately, perhaps, be in a position to take over a managerial function.

Staff assistants may be particularly helpful (though this is not necessarily the case) in small firms, under rapidly changing conditions (increase in company size, seasonal and erratic fluctuations), in geographically dispersed enterprises, in organizations having long chains of command, in situations in which the line executive is newly appointed—especially if he is revitalizing an established company. At his best, the staff assistant develops analytical ability, practical application, sincerity and enthusiasm for the company to a point where all his actions make him an asset to his superior and to the company.

It is General Eisenhower's belief, as he told the author, that business has overlooked an important opportunity to increase the effectiveness of the chief executive through a larger and abler staff of assistants to reduce his load, making it possible for him to devote himself to broader issues and closer contact with his men and with others. The experience of business men with the armed forces seems to show that this is the principal lesson they have learned from the military.

Disadvantages

Among the disadvantages of having "assistants to" is the confusion which frequently occurs regarding the nature of their responsibilities. There is also the danger that the assistant may substitute his personal opinions instead of representing his chief's views—for example, he may put obstacles in the way of the chief's seeing individuals whom he really wants to see. Line men may resent advice from someone who is their junior in status (and probably age). Such matters as executive job evaluation and reorganization cannot be wholly entrusted to the "assistant to," if he is at all involved in or susceptible to company politics. Moreover, there is a danger that the assistant may have more access to the boss than the "doers" or line executives who are out performing their jobs. Worst of all, perhaps, a business man may be deluded into believing that his capacity for decision-making is multiplied in proportion to the number of assistants working under him.

Some feel that the training afforded by service as a staff assistant can be better provided through rotation, staff meetings and personal development plans. The opposition to the "assistant to" centers especially on the objection that the assistant too often becomes the executive's interpreter, confidant, companion, errand boy, paper dispatcher, informal contact man, spy, whipping boy, or assumes the role of the "grey eminence behind the throne."

For these reasons a number of companies avoid the appointment of an "assistant to" or even an "assistant manager" (who takes over some of the responsibilities of the manager) unless the appointment is clearly temporary and made primarily for training purposes. Some maintain that a good secretary can render most of the services performed by the "assistant to" without giving rise to many of the problems of relationship mentioned above.

The issue between the proponents and opponents of the "assistant to" is sharply drawn. The choice depends on the individual case, with due consideration to past company experience, economic feasibility, and the personalities involved.

Distinction Between Staff Assistant and Staff Specialist

The word "staff" is derived from the organization terminology of the military. In its broadest sense it refers to the non-combatant elements of military organization, set apart from the *line* or fighting sector of the armed forces.

The staff was created when the commander-in-chief delegated the planning function to the "general staff," headed by the chief of staff.[16] The general staff was to assist the commander-in-chief in the more effective exercise of his command through planning.

The functions of the chief of staff, as head of the general staff, are as follows: to plan operations, to consult with and advise the commander regarding field operations, to issue the commander's orders and promulgate supplementary orders to insure their proper execution, to see that all orders are carried out.

Staff officers are of two kinds—staff assistants and staff specialists. The distinction between these two types of officers is described below.[17]

Staff Assistants. The "general staff officers" in the United States

16 The concept of staff was used on a systematic basis for the first time under Gustavus Adolphus in the Thirty Years War 1618-1648; Frederick the Great in the middle of the 18th century delegated his planning functions to a Quartermaster General. The "General Staff" was created by the Prussian Army just before the Battle of Jena in 1806.

17 This material has been adapted from some of the unpublished studies of Lt. Col. L. Urwick.

Army ("staff officers" in the British Army) are extensions of the commander who aid him in carrying out orders, e.g., by interpreting his directives to subordinates. These men are almost invariably of lower rank than the commander's direct subordinates but are closer to the commander personally.

In business the equivalent function is that of the staff assistant. He is the representative of his chief, acting purely in an advisory capacity with no personal authority. Even if, in his chief's absence, he makes decisions, they remain his chief's decisions.

Staff Specialists. The "technical and administrative staff officers" in the United States Army ("specialized fighting troops and services" in the British Army) have an indirect "advisory" or "functional" authority in relation to the combat forces, the line. Their specialized responsibility is to prepare the plans, e. g., medical, legal, intelligence, technical, etc. In business the staff specialist is found in three major activities: (1) He advises operating departments, i.e., the "line," on his particular specialty; (2) his advice may apply to all parts of the business; (3) he has line authority in his own department. For example, the personnel director advises various departments on personnel procedures; his influence extends to all departments because the personnel function is all-pervasive; he exercises line authority in his own department.

There is some difference of opinion as to the extent of the difference between the two functions of "staff assistant" and "staff specialist." General Eisenhower told the author he thought the two functions were distinct but not diametrically opposed. Organization authorities such as Alvin Brown and Lt. Col. L. Urwick believe that the two functions are quite different. However, in discussing specific activities, it is not always easy to identify the functions definitely. Thus Lt. Col. Urwick, speaking of a personnel function in the Army, states, "Personally, I do not regard the G-2 Personnel as a staff specialist. In the British Army he is called a Deputy Assistant Adjutant General and is definitely regarded as a staff assistant. But the whole question of the correct placing of personnel work is a most complex one." The answer depends on whether or not the personnel function is a delegated responsibility. If it is, then its head is a staff specialist and carries responsibilities. If it is not, then the person concerned with it is a staff assistant, and has no responsibilities inherent in his position.

Stage V: Establishing a New Function (Functionalization): The Staff Specialist

ILLUSTRATIVE CASE

AT EACH stage of its development, a business needs specialized technical aid. Business management is a complicated affair, and the pressure of day-to-day operations makes it difficult to deal successfully with many of the managerial problems which arise. Even the one-man grocery business, described in Stage I, requires technical advice. Someone has to keep books, make an audit, and prepare a tax return. Occasionally legal or financial services will be required. Or the company may frequently need merchandising counsel on what items to buy, what quantities to purchase, how to meet competition, how to push a slow item, how to keep an inventory, how to arrange a display, etc.

The small business and especially the medium-sized firm (employing generally from 500 to 5,000 workers, with annual sales from $2 to $25 million annually) must rely to a considerable extent on outside help by specialists of various kinds. Frequently, such outside help does not appear on the organization chart, even though its influence on major decisions is substantial. The Wisconsin Paper Board Company, a medium-sized firm, is an example of such a company.

It employs a large, reputable firm of auditors to run quarterly audits. In addition, the accountant in charge of the audit acts as a consultant to the management on a large variety of questions, from tax matters to organization problems within the company. Not only has his advice become more important to the management than the advice of the company's own treasurer and chief accountant, but the auditors are frequently called in to carry out specific jobs which should be performed by the line organization.

The company retains a lawyer, who consults with the management once a week on current problems. In major legal cases and contract negotiations, it utilizes the services of a large law firm. In addition, it frequently requires the services of a patent lawyer to protect its research developments.

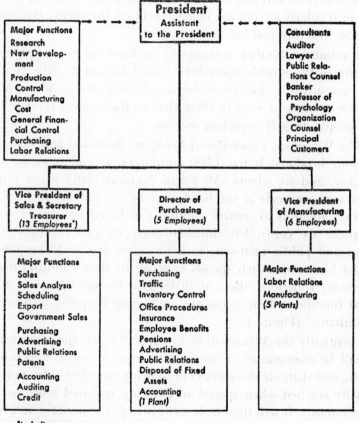

Major Functions
Research
New Development
Production
Control
Manufacturing
Cost
General Financial Control
Purchasing
Labor Relations

President
Assistant to the President

Consultants
Auditor
Lawyer
Public Relations Counsel
Banker
Professor of Psychology
Organization Counsel
Principal Customers

Vice President of Sales & Secretary Treasurer
(13 Employees*)

Director of Purchasing
(5 Employees)

Vice President of Manufacturing
(6 Employees)

Major Functions
Sales
Sales Analysis
Scheduling
Export
Government Sales
Purchasing
Advertising
Public Relations
Patents
Accounting
Auditing
Credit

Major Functions
Purchasing
Traffic
Inventory Control
Office Procedures
Insurance
Employee Benefits
Pensions
Advertising
Public Relations
Disposal of Fixed Assets
Accounting
(1 Plant)

Major Functions
Labor Relations
Manufacturing
(5 Plants)

*Including
2 Accountants
2 Auditors
2 Head Bookkeepers

**FIG. 1.   THE WISCONSIN PAPER BOARD COMPANY
TOP MANAGEMENT DUTIES AND RESPONSIBILITIES**

A public relations firm is charged with developing community good will and handling the customary public relations activities. The company also deals occasionally with an advertising firm.

Several of the principal customers have financial interests in the business, and their counsel is often required on major decisions. In many instances, the management will seek the advice of these customers before proceeding with certain projects.

The company has very close bank relationships, developed over many years. While the banker has no place on the organization chart, he is nevertheless an important factor in the business.

Further, a university professor of psychology gives advice on tests, selection, and employee morale, while an expert on organization regularly advises the management on improving the organization structure and methods.

A number of other services are utilized on a regular basis. Owing to the outside specialists' initial lack of familiarity with the company, the chief executive may be required to devote more time and effort to some of these than to the services rendered by the people directly reporting to him.

The Wisconsin Paper Board Company is owned and managed by four brothers. It has 1,500 employees, a head office in Milwaukee, and six plants. All major decisions (and many minor ones, too) are made at the head office by the four brothers. Each brother attempts to control a number of functions, though some of these are controlled simultaneously by two brothers—e.g., labor and public relations; each has from five to 13 employees under him. Since each spends most of his time handling major operating functions, there is little time for specialized or technical functions. This is the reason for the frequent recourse to consultants. (Figure 1.)

Eventually the Wisconsin company will reach the stage where it will be economically more advantageous to appoint specialists to the staff than use the services of so many outsiders. This point is usually reached when special services are required more or less continuously. It will then be less costly to put a specialist full-time on the payroll than pay him for his time and overhead expenses on a per-diem basis. Another argument for a specialist is that at various points during the growth of the enterprise, different aspects of the same specialized or technical function may be exercised by different executives. For example, various parts of the personnel function may be exercised by the chiefs of production, sales, and finance. This may result in major inconsistencies in personnel policy.

At this point, the chief executive may well decide to undertake a "functional analysis" to discover which of the major executives are engaged in various specialized types of work. The kind of breakdown for making a functional analysis which has been suggested by Lt. Col. Urwick is illustrated on the next page.

On the basis of this analysis, the chief executive may decide that it is now necessary to "functionalize," that is, to combine the different aspects of any one function under one executive. The problem of introducing functionalization is comparable to that of initial delegation from one-man control, for the chief executive's willingness and ability to delegate are involved. However, if he has taken the first step and changed from a one-man business to one controlled by several men, this additional delegation may not be difficult.

The personnel problem will be more serious. A primary obstacle may be those members of management who, because of long service and experience, may feel that they are entitled to a major functional position even though they may lack the necessary educational and technical background and be otherwise unfitted for the jobs.

Second, the major line executives, who are accustomed to handling certain questions, may resent having some of their functions taken away from them. One possible solution to this difficulty might be the appointment of an "Assistant to" the President, who would aid him in carrying out the particular function. When, as a result of presidential authority and guidance, the new function and the incumbent are more fully accepted by the rest of the organization, this individual might be set up as a functional specialist in his own right, or, if necessary, an experienced functional specialist from another company may be appointed.

The foregoing discussion indicates, to some extent, the complexities of functionalization. For the purposes of analysis, let us now consider separately three aspects of the subject: (1) nature of functionalization, (2) organizational problems created by functionalization, and (3) reconciling staff specialists and line operators.

FUNCTIONAL ANALYSIS

Function (partial enumeration)	Chief Executive	Vice President Manufacturing	Vice President Finance	Vice President Sales
GENERAL MANAGEMENT Planning Budgeting Capital Expenditures Organization Hiring and Dismissal				
PRODUCTION Planning Production Inspection				
DEVELOPMENT Technical Research Process & Product Devel. Manufacturing & Methods Development				
PURCHASING Buying of Goods, Materials Materials Control				
PERSONNEL Employment Training Wage & Salary Administration Union Relations Welfare				
MARKETING Selling Advertising Marketing				
TRANSPORT Shipment Assembling Warehousing Packaging				
CONTROL Accounting Costing Statistics				

NATURE OF FUNCTIONALIZATION

Line activities are those functions which follow one another as stages of major operations. These are sequential activities. One such activity is production[18] In addition, there are services common to line, which are grouped under major functions (hence "functionalization")—e.g., finance and personnel—and which are handled by staff specialists. These specialists are distinguished from line executives in that their authority is indirect, not direct; functional, not operating; and their responsibility specialized, not general.[19]

Marvin Bower, Partner, McKinsey & Co., explains this distinction cogently: "The executive with line authority says 'do'; the executive with functional authority says 'if and when you do, do it in this way.' The line executive determines the need, time, and place for action, while the executive with functional authority determines the method."

Activities of the Staff Specialist

The possible types of staff specialist activities vary greatly among companies. They may be summarized as follows: (1) staff advice, (2) operating service, and (3) direct command. (It should be noted that not all these activities are considered proper staff specialist functions in all companies. These are merely the staff activities found in the majority of companies surveyed.)

1. *Staff Advice.* Staff specialists prepare plans, procedures, and standards and provide counsel. These activities may be highly technical, and are often described as the exercise of "functional authority." They involve such steps as the following:

a. Gathering facts about managerial and technical problems of concern to the line.
b. Exchanging information on various company problems.
c. Drawing up policies, programs, plans and procedures.
d. Discussing these with other staff specialists, staff assistants, and line executives, for advice and criticism.

[18] In the small and medium-sized company and at the plant or operational level of the large corporation, selling is frequently considered another line activity. However, it tends to be a staff specialist's activity at the headquarters of many large companies.
[19] Another class of activities which may be sequential, common to other activities, or a mixture of the two may be purchasing.

e. Obtaining approval for the plan from all concerned.

f. Preparing written orders and making arrangements so that the plan is put into action.

g. Helping to install, explain, and interpret the plan, developing interest and enthusiasm and advising line executives on overcoming difficulties.

h. Watching the operation of the plan and following up on progress.

i. Setting standards and establishing necessary controls, such as company standards, systems, procedures and implementing policies to assure that major company objectives and policies are carried out.

j. Measuring performance through reports and reviews.

k. Collecting and analyzing results.

It is clear, from this list of activities, that the work of the staff specialist is of a facilitating nature. The planning department exists, not so much to tell the foreman what to do, but to aid him in obtaining a more efficient flow of work by relieving him of the task of planning his activities. Authority to act is assigned solely to the line operator and should be commensurate with his responsibility for the results; if this authority were assigned to several individuals, it might be more difficult to place responsibility. Usually, only one man should give orders to a subordinate. The personnel department, therefore, should not possess the authority to direct the line department to hire employees it sends; its function is to relieve the line men of the task of recruiting, interviewing and selecting new employees. Similarly, an inspector should in no case except an emergency have the authority to halt production, even though he can reject products. Finally, if the safety precautions prescribed by a safety engineer are violated by an operator, it is best to make the operator's superior responsible, not the safety engineer. The supervisor, being closest to the operator both physically and organizationally, is in the best position to take the required disciplinary action.

Staff specialists are often available for advice and consultation to other staff specialists under the direct command of line officers. For example, the head office personnel department may always be available to aid the personnel director in one of the company's plants—e.g., in labor negotiations—at the request of the latter's line superior, usually the plant manager. The headquarters personnel staff may furnish plant personnel managers with up-to-date information on personnel developments in other parts of the company and in the field generally. Finally, such programs as executive development, job evaluation, and employment stabilization, which are highly specialized and require uniform application, may be outlined and offered to the line units by the headquarters staff specialists, who may also aid in their installation.

2. *Operating Services.* A number of the staff specialists operate special service units to aid other activities. For example, the personnel staff specialist may have some of his subordinates run a cafeteria or be responsible for recreational facilities, a company magazine, safety work, and training. (The relationship of the personnel director to the cafeteria manager is one of direct command or "line.") Such separate service functions may include the handling of legal problems, public relations, taxes, office management, real estate and right-of-way, building design and construction, engineering, product acceptance, purchase and stores, traffic, and research, to cite examples of direct, centralized functions performed for the company as a whole. Other staff specialists, often at headquarters and concerned with such activities as finance, industrial relations, manufacturing, sales, and advertising, may perform certain direct services for the entire company, but act primarily as agencies responsible for performing "functional supervision" over the line.

The establishment of a service function is advantageous only when separating a unit is more economical than attaching it to another activity. A separate service function *must* involve full-time work for one man if it is to be worth while; otherwise, the activity can be assigned part-time to a regional line or staff man or be performed by headquarters. A separate service activity also raises the problem and additional expense of coordination. If it is decided to establish a service function, it usually best to place it in the department which makes the most use of it—e.g., special statistical services might be placed in the accounting department.

3. *Direct Command.* Under certain conditions, the staff specialist may issue direct orders, either in his own name or in that of his superior or chief executive. He may give orders to his immediate

subordinates in his department—e.g., the director of industrial relations may issue requests or orders to the assistant director of industrial relations and to the director of personnel research. In certain exceptional cases, he may give directions to the line executives in order to (1) install new technical methods, such as job evaluation; (2) ensure uniformity—e.g., in the installation of a benefit plan; (3) speed up action without reducing the quality of a decision—e.g., hire a labor gang of unskilled workmen, more or less equal in ability; (4) improve quality of performance— e.g., participate in difficult labor negotiations which the line is unable to handle; (5) take necessary action in the absence of the immediate supervisor—e.g., a safety supervisor may order a man to leave a machine which is not operating properly and which may injure him.

AUTHORITY ENFORCEMENT BY THE STAFF

A serious organizational problem which may result from the creation of staff specialist functions is the assumption of command or line powers by the staff. It must be recognized that in actual practice staff specialists do at times exercise command powers over the line executives, in addition to those powers cited earlier, in order to get the results of their work accepted and thereby justify their continued activities. The following are some of the ways in which staff specialists require line executives to apply their suggestions (it should be noted that such authority enforcements by the staff are widely opposed, not only by the line, but also by many organization specialists).

Command Through Superior Articulation

Staff men are generally articulate and skilled in persuading others to accept their ideas, while the line executive is often less vocal. A classic example drawn from another field is perhaps the success of Florence Nightingale in persuading the Army authorities to accept the nursing function during the Crimean War:[20]

It is easy to imagine the kind of disgust and alarm with which the sudden intrusion of a band of amateurs and females must have

[20] Lytton Strachey, *Eminent Victorians*, London, 1918, pp. 141-143, (quote from 1948 edition).

filled the minds of the ordinary officer and the ordinary military sur-
geon. They could not understand it; what had women to do with
war?

Miss Nightingale's position was, indeed, an official one, but it
was hardly the easier for that. In the hospitals it was her duty to
provide the services of herself and her nurses when they were asked
for by the doctors, and not until then. At first some of the surgeons
would have nothing to say to her, and, though she was welcomed
by others, the majority were hostile and suspicious. But gradually
she gained ground. Her good will could not be denied, and her
capacity could not be disregarded. With consummate tact, with
all the gentleness of supreme strength, she managed at last to
impose her personality upon the susceptible, overwrought, dis-
couraged, and helpless group of men in authority who surrounded
her. She stood firm; she was a rock in the angry ocean; with her
alone was safety, comfort, life. And so it was that hope dawned at
Scutari. The reign of chaos and old night began to dwindle; order
came upon the scene, and common sense, and forethought, and
decision, radiating out from the little room off the great gallery
in the Barrack Hospital where, day and night, the Lady Superintendent was at her task. Progress might be slow, but it was sure. . . .

On one occasion 27,000 shirts, sent out at her instance by the
Home Government, arrived, were landed, and were only waiting
to be unpacked. But the official "Purveyor" intervened. He could
not unpack them, he said, without a Board. Miss Nightingale
pleaded in vain; the sick and wounded lay half-naked, shivering
for want of clothing; and three weeks elapsed before the Board
released the shirts. A little later, however, on a similar occasion,
Miss Nightingale felt that she could assert her own authority. She
ordered a Government consignment to be forcibly opened, while
the miserable "Purveyor" stood by, wringing his hands in departmental agony.

Command Through Technical Competence

Since the staff specialist has technical skills and knowledge not
possessed by the line department, his advice, like legal counsel,
may have to be accepted. Also, renowned scientists and techni-
cians in staff research departments may obtain acceptance of their
ideas (or refusal of others' ideas) on the basis of their reputations
alone. Finally, recommendations on such technical matters as staff

training, quality control, and safety are difficult for the non-professional to dispute effectively and may, on that account, be accepted by the line, even though interference with operations sometimes results.

Command Through Status

Many staff specialists are considerably higher in the management hierarchy and in the salary scale than the executives they advise and are able to obtain acceptance on that account as well as because of their technical competence. Staff specialists may be fortified by such titles as "director," "manager," "vice president," and, occasionally, "member of the board." The kind of influence resulting from a combination of status and technical competence exerted by the staff specialist on the line is shown in Figure 2.

Though this chart is not necessarily representative, its basic trends are confirmed by such an outstanding production authority as Glenn Gardiner, Vice President of the Forstmann Woolen Company, who feels that staff specialists have taken so many functions away from the foreman that the latter's authority and ability to meet his responsibilities have been impaired.[21] This was also confirmed some years ago in an AMA survey of 100 companies, which showed that in 30 per cent of the companies foremen have no right to hire, and in 80 per cent of the firms they do not participate in policy-making.[22]

Multiple influences on the line—that is, instructions from several sources rather than one—are found in many other fields. On the railroads, for example, the engineer is subordinate to the conductor, but he also obeys instructions of master mechanics, station agents, yard masters, and station masters.

The danger of staff command may be illustrated by an example drawn by military history. In World War I, German staff officers assumed field command. The fateful retreat of the German First Army behind the Marne was directed by an emissary of the Chief of Staff, who obviously lacked the line commander's first-hand knowledge of operations. Its surprised commander, who wanted

[21] Glenn Gardiner, "The Operating Executive and the Personnel Department," *Personnel Series No. 121,* American Management Association, 1948, pp. 3-12.
[22] Ernest Dale, *The Development of Foremen in Management,* Research Report No. 7, American Management Association, 1945, pp. 16-21.

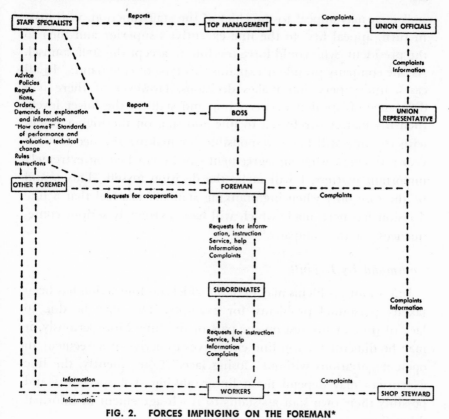

FIG. 2.   FORCES IMPINGING ON THE FOREMAN*

to move forward and take Paris, was not even consulted! Some authorities believe that this false step lost the war for Germany. Other failures have resulted from the attempt of general staffs to engage in major planning for the line with the result that line men became automatons.

Command Through Sanctions

Line acceptance may be forced through the threat or use of sanctions. Staff sanctions may be so influential as to lead to demotion and removal of opponents, with the final result a hidden state of warfare between staff and line.

If a line executive does not agree with the staff proposals, the

---

* Adapted from Fritz J. Roethlisberger, "The Foreman: Master and Victim of Double-Talk," *Harvard Business Review,* Spring, 1945, p. 286.

staff men may appeal to the chief of the staff function, who may, in turn, appeal first to the line executive's superior and then to the president, who could force the line to accept the staff counsel. As one company president explains this type of command: "In all cases, line supervision makes decisions. However, if there is a difference of opinion between line and staff on the lower levels, then the matter is referred to line and staff on the higher levels, with the line still being responsible for making the decision. In very rare cases, when no agreement can be reached on extremely important matters, I will make the decision myself. This would be the case only when high-ranking staff officials feel that a line decision has been made which will have extremely serious consequences for the company."

Command By Default

Important problems may exist on which no line action has been taken—personnel problems, for example. This may be due to lack of time or interest on the part of the line. More seriously, it may be difficult for top line executives to arrive at agreement in open negotiations without "losing face." Consequently, the line executives may depend upon lower-ranking staff specialists and possibly their own staff assistants to reach agreement in informal discussions.

For example, a personnel director in one company with a number of plants believed it would be advantageous to have all plants begin to work out pension agreements with the union at the same time. The research director of the personnel department contacted the production planning staff specialists in the different plants and the staff assistants to the various plant managers, convinced them of the value of his superior's idea, ironed out difficulties with them, and got them to persuade their superiors. At the formal meeting of the plant managers, the personnel director, and manufacturing vice president, the agreement was formally ratified. With this really united front, the union locals were approached. Such efforts on the part of younger staff and line executives to get agreement on technical problems are quite common in large corporations.

RECONCILING STAFF SPECIALISTS AND LINE OPERATORS

The following are a number of general proposals for integrating the activities of staff and line executives and for improving their relations. These may best be examined in terms of the successive stages of reconciliation involved in solving a typical staff-line relationship problem.

Integrating Staff and Line Activities

1. *Familiarity with Line Operations.* It is desirable that the staff specialist have some experience in the line so that he may know its problems and understand the kind of organizational relationship necessary to its successful operation. A number of companies make line experience a pre-requisite for staff work. Where such an arrangement is not possible, an apprenticeship as "assistant to" a line executive might be arranged. In most instances, it will be desirable for the staff specialist to spend some time in getting acquainted with the line executives and in finding out their problems *before* making any recommendations.

2. *Persuasion Rather Than Command.* The staff specialist should get line executives to accept his ideas by using argument and negotiation rather than by forcing his authority upon them. His advice, therefore, must not only be sound; it must be tactfully presented as well. This requires much diplomacy on part of the staff specialist. Suggestions should be integrated with line operations and with other staff proposals and should be carefully considered and tested. Informal checks might be made with the line before the ideas are formally presented to assure that they are practical and thus forestall any possible resentments. The ideas should be presented at the right time and in language understandable to the operators. There should be scope for amendments. Finally, the staff specialist's proposal should not be introduced until it is approved in its final form by the joint superior of the staff specialist and the line executives affected (many companies insist on the agreement of all line executives). Though credit for success often goes to the operators, staff specialists must remember that success is often as much dependent on them as upon the man on the line. Exceptions to the rule of staff consul-

tation and coordination with the line should be made only under extenuating circumstances.

3. *Use of Informal Approach.* Lt. Col. Urwick advises us from his long experience:

> Officially speaking, authority must be exercised only *through* the line superior—that is, with his approval and agreement. This does not mean, however, that all action must climb wearily up one chain of command, across the top, and down the other chain. Once a specialist has won the confidence of a line executive and has no intention of infringing upon his authority over his subordinates, he can do 90 per cent of his work direct, provided he is meticulous in observing two precautions: (1) He should *always* have the common courtesy to inform a line executive of any action he has taken affecting any of his subordinates. (2) If there is the least chance of disagreement about any action, he should consult the line superior first.
>
> It might be thought that this careful observance of "official channels," with all the resulting paper work, must necessarily slow down business. But this conclusion rests on a misunderstanding of what this paper work is for. It is "for the record," a safeguard in case personal relations break down, *not* a primary means of getting work done. All the real work of the world in good organizations is done by men who trust each other. They agree on decisions on the telephone, using first names. Then they merely tell their secretaries to "file the confirmation when it comes through." If there is the least chance of misunderstanding or disagreement they try to meet each other face to face; if you can't see the other fellow's eyes, you can't really tell "what's biting him."

4. *Resolving Disagreements.* If the line should disagree with the staff specialist, the latter should continue his attempts to obtain agreement rather than enforce his ideas by assuming authority himself or exercising it through others. Though staff promotion may gain verbal acceptance of a program, its successful execution can be sabotaged in many ways.

Should an accepted policy be violated, the staff specialist should call this to the attention of the line executives concerned. If no agreement is reached, the matter might be carried to the head of the specialist function or to the joint superior of the two parties. In extreme cases, the dispute may be carried still higher up—

eventually to the president or the board. The process of carrying out a staff policy (or gaining its acceptance) through persuasion, technical competence, or appeal to a joint superior is a broadening of functional authority requiring very good judgment on the part of the staff specialists.

Long friendship and, if necessary, a more tolerant interpretation of the rules can usually aid in settling disputes. If that is not possible, a written (or oral) statement of the recommendations not followed by the line may be given by the staff specialist to his superior and possibly to the joint superior. This would place on record the staff specialist's position and prevent him from being blamed for failure to recognize shortcomings. It is usually best to leave matters there rather than arouse animosity. However, if the disagreement between the staff and line may hinder the staff's work in the future, the matter may be carried further.

Occasionally, the problem of disagreement is solved by giving the staff specialists "concurrent authority" requiring the line executives to obtain staff agreement to carry out a proposed action. However, the line would still remain free to reject staff directions.

RECONCILING STAFF AND LINE IN LARGE COMPANIES

In the large company, a number of special procedures may be required to reconcile staff and line executives. These procedures are divided into those which concern lower-ranking line executives and those which deal with higher-ranking line executives.

Reconciling Lower-Ranking Staff and Line Executives

The first type of reconciliation concerns chiefly the relationship of supervisors (assistant foremen, foremen and general foremen, and possibly superintendents) to the staff specialists. The procedures involved in this relationship should be kept relatively simple so that they can be easily understood and followed. Outstanding for its treatment of the line-staff relationship at the supervisory level is the *Leader's Guide* prepared by the Training Department of the Ford Motor Company. It should be remembered that the procedures described below apply to a very large company and therefore may not be as flexible as those required by other, smaller concerns.

The following principles, which should govern the relationship between line management and the staff, are outlined to supervisors at special training sessions. Printed summaries are later distributed to the manufacturing supervisors participating in the training program:

First: *You Have Only One Boss.*

Note that you have only one boss on the line. There is only one spot in this whole organization chart from which you receive your assignment of responsibility and from which you receive a delegation of authority. As a subordinate, recognize only one immediate supervisor.

Second: *As a Supervisor, Give Equal Support to Equal Subordinates and Only to Your Subordinates.*

You are the supervisor on the line to the subordinates below you. When it is necessary for you to transmit orders or policy statements, or give instructions and directions, you should do so only to your immediate subordinates—that is, to those on the line just below you. As a boss, you may have several subordinates. You may find it necessary to define the assignment of responsibility and the delegation of authority to each man individually, according to the merits and abilities of each.

Third: *Directions Flow Down the Line, Reports Flow Up the Line.*

Directions, orders, instructions, etc., flow *down* the line. It is necessary for each supervisor to make interpretations to his subordinates. These should be stated clearly and understood by both the supervisor and subordinate. Reports flow *up* the line. Recommendations, suggestions, and ideas are often submitted by a subordinate to his supervisor. Many of these will be of interest to the supervisor only. On the other hand, it may be advisable for him to make further report on certain matters to his own supervisor on the line above him. Just how much he should keep and how much he should pass on up the line calls for the exercise of discretion and good judgment on *his* part.

Fourth: *Keep the Line Open.*

We should also keep the line open. As a supervisor, your subordinate may have submitted to you a recommendation on which you have taken no action. Your subordinate may feel that you have not used good judgment in doing this. He may feel that it is important enough to warrant passing up the line for further consideration. If he discusses the problem with you, you may openly admit that, although you see certain difficulties that may prevent adoption of his recommendation, you have no objection if your subordinate goes above you on the line and presents his recommendation direct. Not only this, but you may go so far as to arrange for your subordinate to present his proposal to your supervisor with or without your presence and participation [some companies prefer both men to go together]. This does not violate the principle to keep in line, because you have given your consent. If the proposal has merit, see to it that your subordinate gets the credit. If it has no merit, you will be given credit by your supervisor for having foreseen the difficulties that were involved. (In addition to keeping the line open, a line supervisor should serve as a buffer for his immediate superior to prevent obviously unnecessary or wasteful demands on the latter's time.)

Fifth: *Keep the Line Advised.*

Sometimes a break occurs in the line. It may be that one of your subordinates is at home, sick; or if you have pulled him off his regular job temporarily for a special assignment, it may be that you do not wish to have him disturbed. In transmitting directions down the line, it may be necessary for you to skip him and give those directions to the person next on the line below him.

Similarly, if your supervisor cannot be reached or is out of town, and you must report on some matter, it may be necessary for you to skip him and make the report to the supervisor next on the line above him.

Whenever a line supervisor skips an echelon of supervision above him in passing on information or below him in giving instructions, he should advise the supervisor concerned as soon as practicable.

Sixth: *Associates Support Each Other.*

Associates working together should support each other. If we support the associates we work with, they, in turn, will tend to support us. We shall get each job done more quickly and at the same time pave the way for close cooperation in future jobs.

Seventh: *An Associate on the Line Has No Authority over an Associate on the Staff, and Vice Versa.*

Ordinarily the staff has no authority to command or direct that certain action be taken on the line. Their suggestions may or may not be accepted by the line.

If a staff recommendation is made to a member of management on the line, and it is not accepted, there is a possibility that later the same recommendation may be accepted by your supervisor on the line. In this case, he may transmit the decision as a directive down the line to you. You as subordinate will be responsible for carrying out the directives of your supervisor. Responsibility for acceptance is *his,* not yours.

If you feel that there are valid reasons why the proposal should not have been accepted, you still have the privilege of discussing the matter with your supervisor. But, until he has changed his decision, you are bound by your line responsibility to carry out that directive as it was originally given to you.

It should be noted that at the Ford Motor Company, staff personnel may be delegated specific authority to act in certain matters on behalf of line management, and in such cases the staff, as representatives of line management, may exercise "functional" supervision over the line. In any large, complex operation, such flexible lines of demarcation between line and staff are mandatory if line management is to be relieved of part of the burden of handling details.

Reconciling Higher-Ranking Staff and Line Executives

In the large company, the relationship between the higher-ranking staff and line executives within a branch, as well as their relationship with staff headquarters, constitutes a serious problem.

This problem may be most clearly studied when a company shifts from direct supervision of headquarters staff over the branch or regional staff to supervision by a newly appointed regional general manager. In the following example, the regional staff men, who had been directly responsible to the headquarters staff men, became responsible to the regional general manager after decentralization took place, retaining an advisory relationship with their former headquarters staff. The regional departmental managers' reaction to the change varied all the way from an attitude of complete severance of connection with headquarters ("I don't know what headquarters will do now that I do all the work"; "Maybe they'll have to play golf to keep busy now," etc.) to a conviction that no change had taken place in the relationships ("I have a continuous pipe line to headquarters"; "Whenever I need any help I call headquarters"; "There is going to be no change in my job.") A minority thought the regional general manager "would continue as coordinator," "was too busy," "did not have experience and knowledge of headquarters," "could be sold easily," "was just a formality."

The general attitude which prevailed among the regional departmental managers was one of perplexity and apprehension regarding the staff-line relationships. For the most part, they were concerned about personnel increases, specific operating decisions, and their own promotions. Who would have the major say—their former headquarters staff superior or their new superior, the regional general manager?

In the large company with a number of plants, a basic problem in line-staff relationships is whether the staff specialists are to be independent of the plant operating executives or responsible to them. Independence would mean that headquarters staff specialists would advise line operators at the plants directly from headquarters (and possibly also through subordinates in the plants). This procedure has the advantage of saving the expense of duplicate staff units in the plants and avoiding the dangers of parasitic growth at every level of command. It would make possible the full advantages of large-scale specialization. It would encourage uniformity of policies and procedures as well as coordination from the center. Auditing control in financial matters (e.g., accounting methods) might be more reliable if the plant financial specialists report directly to headquarters.

However, the centralization of staff specialists might also entail serious disadvantages. For example, it might undermine effective leadership at the operating unit (the plant). If a plant manager is subject to a variety of regulations, which may often be too insensitive and too rigid to be applicable to local conditions, his initiative and leadership may suffer, especially if headquarters is out of touch with the "feel" of the local plant situation. Serious conflicts may result between the staff specialists, who may have to act strictly to enforce headquarters thinking, and the plant manager, who may wish staff specialists to have merely an advisory relationship.

One way of overcoming this difficulty might be to set up the operational unit as a separate entity, as far as possible. The plant manager would receive all the decision-making powers necessary for the most successful possible day-to-day operations, and obtain from staff specialists any aid necessary to that end. Should the suggestions of local staff specialists, who are responsible to the plant manager, prove more applicable to a particular situation than advice or action from headquarters staff specialists, the former would be adopted. For example, though concentration of toolmaking or purchasing at headquarters may result in considerable economies and advantages, these may be offset by the frustration and delays at the local plant level.

For purposes of classification, a staff-line relationship is outlined in Figure 3. This has been adapted from a suggestion by Sir Charles Renold, Chairman of the British Institute of Management and Chairman of the Renold and Coventry Chain Co., Ltd. In this chart, the activities of a large corporation are broken down into manageable areas. A large number of separate plants are held together by headquarters, which exercises a kind of federal authority. Here the top staff specialists of the various functions assign general spheres of activity, help to provide financial support, make long-range and highly specialized plans, review results, and are available for advice to the second tier, the Regional or Group Level. The Regional Level again provides all the specialist services necessary to operate the region as a rational and, as far as possible, self-contained unit. The third tier is the Division, which consists of several plants and again is operated on a self-contained basis. The fourth level, the Plant, has its own set of plant specialists directly responsible to the plant manager, who, at the same time, accept advice from the staff specialists of the Division. The plant is still subject to overriding uniformities in such matters as personnel policy (accounting, operating and capital budgets and other top management functions (discussed in Stages VI and VII), but it operates with considerable freedom. Its size may vary from a few hundred to a few thousand employees.

Such a rational operating unit in industry may, in some ways, be compared to a single ship in the navy, as has been suggested by Sir Charles Renold. The ship is a self-contained unit, and all its

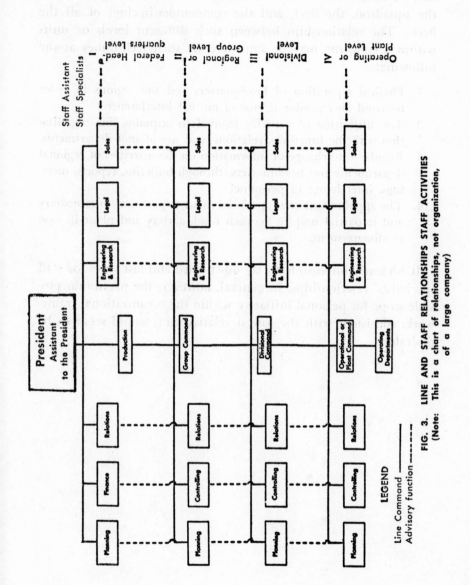

FIG. 3.   LINE AND STAFF RELATIONSHIPS STAFF ACTIVITIES
(Note: This is a chart of relationships, not organization,
of a large company)

LEGEND

Line Command ——————
Advisory function - - - - - -

major relationships are handled by the captain, even though he may be subject to certain overriding influences by larger units— the squadron, the fleet, and the commander-in-chief of all the fleets. The relationships between such different levels or units within a company may be improved by such techniques as the following:

1. Physical separation of headquarters and the regions in order to avoid an excessive degree of mutual interference.
2. The utilization of a policy manual to acquaint line organization with the functions, relations, and use of staff departments.
3. Regular interchange of information on the activities of regional departments and headquarters, through bulletins, reports, meetings, interchange of personnel.
4. The appointment of a top official to act as part-time intermediary and impartial umpire between headquarters and plant in case of disagreement.

It is clearly impossible to lay down hard and fast rules for staff specialists' relationships. In general, however, the maximum possible scope for personal initiative within the organizational framework, consistent with the lowest relative cost, would seem to be desirable.

Stage VI: Coordination of Management Functions: Group Decision-Making

ILLUSTRATIVE CASE

LUKENS STEEL COMPANY[23]

Ownership: Joint stock company (60 per cent publicly owned, 40 per cent family holdings)

Control: Nine-man business (The top organization consists of a Chairman of the Board, President, Vice President in Charge of Operations, Vice President in Charge of Sales, Treasurer, Secretary, Controller, Director of Industrial Relations, and Purchasing Agent)

Size: 5,000 employees (originally with two subsidiaries).

Nature of Business: Semi-integrated producer in the steel industry, manufacturing steel plates, steel plate specialties, fabricated parts, and machinery made primarily from steel plates.

As the number and complexity of delegated functions increase, misunderstandings and conflicts of authority may arise among the different functions. The chiefs of the various units tend to think largely in terms of the welfare of their own units and not of the

---

23 This discussion is based partly on an interview with Charles L. Huston, Jr., President of the Lukens Steel Company, and partly on his article, "The Management Committee: Co-ordinator of Policies and Practices," *Dun's Review*, March, 1951, pp. 16-18.

enterprise as a whole. Every such point of intersection may give rise to possible misunderstanding, increasing the need for coordination and for the integration of diverse opinions. To overcome these difficulties and accomplish the objectives of the enterprise as a whole, it becomes necessary to hold formal or informal meetings regularly among the unit heads concerned. The Lukens Steel Company's "Management Committee" provides a valuable illustration.

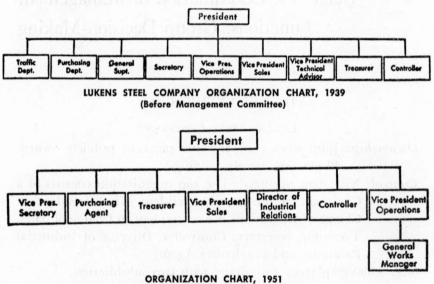

LUKENS STEEL COMPANY ORGANIZATION CHART, 1939
(Before Management Committee)

ORGANIZATION CHART, 1951
(After establishment of Management Committee, showing all members)

The Lukens Management Committee was set up because the individual formulation of sales and operating policies by the two subsidiaries and the parent company was causing difficulties. It had become obvious that increased and broader cooperation was necessary in establishing policies and practices of the parent company and its subsidiaries. The establishment of the Committee made it possible to reorganize the company and to allocate fewer responsibilities, especially in operations, thus shortening the span of control of the president.

When first appointed by the president of Lukens in 1940, the Management Committee consisted of the parent company's general manager as chairman, the parent's operating superintendent, and the presidents of the two subsidiaries. The committee was directed to concern itself with matters of policy, labor relations, wage systems, time studies, and, in general, development of an improved operating balance among the three plants.

The committee could call on the sales, finance, purchasing, industrial relations, and other divisions of the company for such information and consultation as it might need. It was given full power to act on all matters except those that should come before the Board of Directors, and was given the right to put into effect such plans as its members agreed upon, subject to approval by the president of the parent company. Eighteen months after establishment of the committee, the Lukens vice president in charge of sales, the controller, director of industrial relations, and purchasing agent were added to its membership.

Changes in the Committee

Within the last few years the two subsidiaries have been dissolved as corporate entities and have been made divisions of the parent company. Lines of responsibility have reflected the change; the vice president in charge of operations now is directly responsible for all three plants and the vice president in charge of sales is responsible for all marketing activities.

The make-up of the management committee has also been changed. Today it consists of the vice president in charge of operations as chairman, the vice president in charge of sales, the company treasurer, controller, secretary, director of industrial relations, purchasing agent, and general works manager. The chairman of the committee is appointed by the company president.

Work of the Committee

From the committee's experience to date, the following major advantages are considered to justify its establishment and continuance:

It offers consultative supervision. This results in uniformity of direction throughout the organization; it helps to provide coordination of long-term and short-term programs toward established objectives; it allows for flexibility in emergency situations, should they arise, without interference with basic schedules. Finally, it provides broader experience for executives and greater interchangeability of management personnel.

Free discussion by members of this group concerning proposed general policies and practices makes for better understanding, improved coordination, and closer cooperation among divisions and departments of the company.

When a recommendation to the board of directors is made by the management committee, the proposal carries much more weight than if it were submitted by an individual executive. The directors know that the recommendation has come to them only after it has been examined and approved by management committee members representing all the important divisions of the company.

The management committee at Lukens has functioned primarily as an advisory body. Line responsibility of division heads is retained for decisions that affect only one division. Decisions affecting more than one division are developed by the committee as a whole.

Scope of Committee Meetings

Every Monday morning the committee reviews such vital matters as current operating and sales performance, the company's financial position, cost developments, proposed capital expenditures, current manufacturing expenditures, inventory and procurement problems, customers' claims or complaints and their handling, and occasionally, requests for charitable or civic donations.

In addition, each committee member reviews important projects either contemplated or under way in the departments under his supervision. Such projects may include progress of the company's plan of cost improvement, company patent applications, developments concerning pensions or social insurance, consideration of annual or semi-annual reports from divisions, handling of quarterly reports to stockholders and employees, public relations projects, divisional budgets, proposed national and state legislation likely to affect the company, research and development engineering projects, litigation involving the company, important contracts and agreements, plant visits and tours, and projects affecting health and welfare of employees.

This may seem like a heavy program for a four-hour meeting. The work is facilitated by presentation of brief reports, followed by action where committee members can reach substantial agreement. Where the committee is divided, the matter is either postponed for further study or discussion or is submitted to the president to decide.

On specific matters of particular importance, subcommittees are appointed to study the problems and report their findings to the main body. Brief minutes are taken during each meeting and distributed to the various committee members for permanent reference.

Several disadvantages may be ascribed to the operation of the management committee. It offers an opportunity for sharing in policy-making but with the risk of diffusing and possibly clouding what otherwise would be a clear-cut responsibility. There is also the danger of slowing down decisions and actions on company matters. Nevertheless, Lukens firmly believes that the advantages far outweigh the disadvantages and become increasingly apparent as management faces new and more difficult problems.

GENERAL ANALYSIS

Strategic Factors in Successful Committee Work

Group action is increasingly characteristic of American management, especially in the larger corporations. Of the 150 companies surveyed by AMA, 110 reported that they have one or more committees meeting regularly. More than half of the companies studied have a general management committee to discuss problems of over-all company significance. Sometimes this general committee consists of full-time working directors. In most cases it is composed of working directors of the board and the heads of the major functions of the business. Meetings are held at regular intervals and committee duties are only part-time obligations.

In addition to the general management committees, many companies have functional committees with limited authority over a particular aspect of the business, such as production, sales, or personnel. In addition, frequent informal group meetings are held.

The major requirements for success of committee operation may be summarized as follows: (1) Work of committees should justify their costs. (2) The principles of effective group action should be applied. (3) Committee mechanics should be arranged so that meetings will not be hampered by procedural difficulties. (4) Only subjects that can be handled better by groups than by individuals should be selected for committee discussion.

1. Work of Committees Should Justify Their Costs

The aim of committee work is to get a more comprehensive view of a given problem than can be obtained from any single member. If one member of the group gets his particular view accepted by dominating the rest, he might just as well have made that decision outside the committee meeting. Similarly, a compromise can often be reached without a committee meeting. If we accept profit maximization as the company's over-all objective, then the purpose of a committee meeting is to obtain a result that contributes more to company revenue than the expenses it entails.

Positive committee contributions to company revenue may include:

a. *Problem-solving.* Many problems of management are complex and affect different functions; often their impact is company-wide. Decisions must be made on questions to which there is no clear-cut answer, but where feeling, "instinct," and personal opinion play a vital part. Some decisions require the counsel of experts in various fields. Since the view of each is somewhat different, the synthesis of their opinions should be better than those of any one person involved. Moreover, long-run considerations are more likely to be emphasized in a group decision. Other problems require the consultation of two or more departments for proper balance and an over-all view, e.g., determining levels of output on the basis of probable sales. Individuals are safeguarded against the danger of thinking too long alone. The stimulation of participation may lead to better ideas and their more wholehearted acceptance.

b. *Coordination of related functions.* Committee work makes an important contribution when its members meet in order to determine what parts they shall take in a pre-determined course of action in order to avoid overlapping or working at cross purposes. This function of the committee is especially important when there is no other means of coordination. The committee also may serve as a means of communication among the representatives of large groups.

c. *More complete acceptance of a decision already reached.* Making a decision does not, of course, ensure that it will be carried out effectively. If those affected by the decision disagree with it or are aggrieved because they were not consulted, they may oppose its execution in many ways. The committee offers an opportunity to air arguments against a proposed action and clarify its advantages.

d. *Training.* Participation in committee meetings may be used to help to train younger executives and give top management a chance to observe them in action.

Against these possible contributions to company revenue must be set the following gross costs (which should be compared to the revenue and cost of handling the problem through individuals):

a. *The direct cost* of the committee, such as the time of the committee members in preparing for the meetings and at the meeting itself, the expenses of the committee staff and secretary, the cost of office space and clerical work, the time spent traveling to and from meetings (important in large companies where executives may have to travel some distance).

b. *Additional expense* may arise from committee work because of the lack of responsibility for results on the part of committee members. Since a group of persons cannot be held responsible in the same sense as an individual, decisions may not be properly carried out.

Neither the committee as a whole nor any individual member can be criticized effectively. If the group takes action which is not well received, no individual can be blamed. Unpleasant questions or problems can easily be shelved. Committees also are expensive because they tend to be bad employers. The individual subordinate finds it hard to know whom and how to please. If he does take action, some member of the committee may disagree with it; if he does not, he may be charged with negligence. This complaint, familiar among employees of club committees, was given prominence when Carroll L. Wilson resigned in July, 1950, as general manager to the Chairman of the Atomic Energy Commission, warning that the five-member Atomic Energy Commission was drifting toward a policy of "management by committee": "I have serious apprehension that the ultimate projection of this trend will result in a cumbersome, slow-moving administrative machine which is incapable of giving the country the kind of direction needed to maintain and increase our leadership in the atomic field." More recently, a scientist charged that the members of the A.E.C. Advisory Committee were acting like the passengers in an automobile where each had control of the brakes; no progress could be made until all the advisors agreed.

If these criteria for cost and benefit appear too complicated, it might be possible to estimate regularly for each committee the total number of man-hours involved in a year of meetings, as follows:

1. Multiply the number of meetings per year by the average number of hours per meeting by the average number of executives attending a meeting.
2. Add the number of hours spent by the secretary and his staff in planning meetings, distributing agenda, writing minutes and recommendations, etc.
3. Multiply the total man-hours in a. and b. by an average hourly salary cost figure.
4. Estimates might be made for the past and the coming 12 months.
5. List past accomplishments and estimate their possible monetary value.
6. Attempt to determine how the functions assigned to the committee would be carried out, if the committee were abandoned.

The study should conclude with a recommendation as to the committee's future. (For the details of a "Committee Data Sheet," compiled by the Standard Oil Company of California, see Appendix B.)

c. *Personality factors and internal policies.* The committee may meet merely to satisfy the chairman's ego. Free discussion may be curtailed for fear of offending others. The committee may operate as a rubber-stamp for an individual or a clique. Agreements may be made for agreement's sake, as a result of horse-trading or logrolling, entailing undesirable compromises. Certain individuals may have blind spots or may be overly articulate, may fail to express themselves adequately, or to carry their share of the work and responsibility entailed. Committee decisions may be slow; they may not be carried out or may be inadequately followed up. The tactics of "agreement" may be bulldozing, withholding facts, maneuvering a prior majority, falsification of data, "guiding" agreement, intrigue, sabotage, or giving only the semblance of democracy by letting everyone talk and then forcing agreement to a decision reached before the meeting began. Individual contributions to discussion may be irrelevant or designed only to impress a superior. The committee may exceed its authority or, at the other extreme, be lax in exercising it.

2. Principles of Group Effectiveness Must Be Applied

It is an erroneous assumption that anyone can be a good committee member. Assuming the proper role in a group is a difficult art, mastered by relatively few. Although almost everyone spends much of his working (and social) life with formal and informal groups, only rarely is there systematic training for effective group behavior at any stage of a person's career. One of the few companies that have supplied informal training in committee management is the Standard Oil Company of New Jersey. In general, however, knowledge of and training in committe work have been acquired largely through experience, which has often been costly.

Successful committee action requires selection of members who are able to express themselves in the presence of a group. It is surprising how many otherwise able individuals find themselves completely tongue-tied when confronted by a small audience. The objectives and limitations of the group must be considered. The committee requires only those contributions which will advance group thinking (without necessarily advancing the individual). Conflicts must be resolved by integration rather than by domination and compromise. Group work calls for emphasis on concrete considerations and practical actions rather than undue preoccupation with theoretical matters.

Some of the elements of effective group participation have been systematically studied in the course of the human relations research sponsored by the United States Navy.[24] Some of the hypotheses and findings (as a rule based on small examples) may be adaptable to management committee work:

    a. *Productivity of the committee* is said to vary with:

      1. The urgency of the problem (pressure to show results may lead to concentrated and economical committee work or to impressive accomplishments on paper only).

      2. Power to make decisions. (Delegation of responsibility may move participants to exercise it, but collective responsibility to make decisions does not necessarily mean that they will be made or that, if made, they will be superior to individual decisions.)

      3. Ease of communication, degree of mutual understanding and freedom to participate. Freedom of expression is vital in getting results. (However, if consideration is not shown to the feelings of others, it may be a mixed blessing.)

      4. Orderly treatment of problems. (However, treatment may be too orderly with consequent loss of flexibility.)

      5. Intelligence and originality on the part of individual group members.

    b. *The extent of agreement* among the members of the group is said to be the greater:

      1. The stronger the attraction among individual participants in the group;

      2. the more personal friendship there is among members of the group, for opinions can be more easily changed;

      3. the greater the uniformity of the group;

      4. the fewer dissenters present;

      5. the more readily each reacts to another's action;

      6. the greater the cooperation and the less the competition.

Comment Based on the AMA Survey

There is little disagreement with these propositions. Most of them are self-evident, though it is valuable to have had them tested. The point that needs to be questioned is the desirability of agreement for its own sake—for if everyone agrees, what con-

[24] Harold Guetzkow, Editor, *Groups, Leadership and Men,* Carnegie Press, Carnegie Institute of Technology, Pittsburgh, Penna., 1951.

tribution does the meeting make? There is no advantage to the company or to the participants from meetings that merely satisfy the ego of the top executive present. Sessions held to bring about agreement may have some value. But the real test of the committee it its effect on company revenue. Its contribution to "morale" (whatever this vague term actually means) may be important, especially in relations between the management and other parties in the enterprise, such as labor. But, over all, the economic test would seem the most important one.

3. Committee Mechanics Should Eliminate Procedural Difficulties

a. *Definition of function and scope.* The first step in successful committee action is definition of the function and the scope of the committee. Appendix B lists objectives and areas of discussion of a number of typical company committees deliberating on major management problems.

b. *The size of the committee.* Next, the proper size of the committee needs to be determined. With less than five or six members, it may not realize the advantages of group work. On the other hand, if there are more than 15 or 16 members, the group becomes a crowd. Generally speaking, the larger the committee, the greater the areas of disagreement; and the harder it is to reach a decision, the greater the expenses involved. On the other hand, a larger committee is usually a more representative group, draws upon broader and more diversified experience, and makes it possible to reach more people. By bringing in experts where needed and through the use of sub-committees, it may be possible to obtain the advantages of a large group without making the group unwieldy. The specific size of the committee depends on many factors: the type of problems to be discussed, the competence of participants, the homogeneity of the group, the degree of integration of its members, the nature of the participation required, the amount of face-to-face contact that has existed in the past, the clashes of interests that may be expected.

c. *The chairman.* Perhaps the most important aspect of the mechanics of committee work is the choice of the proper chairman. The man who presides exercises great influence. His age, experience, or status in the company often enables him to make or break the committee, even though in theory he may be merely "the first among equals." This strength of position also imposes grave responsibilities—he must avoid imposing his own opinion or relinquishing his powers to other members. As an example of an "ideal type" or chairman, the scientist Carl Alsberg may be cited:[25]

He was an intermediary, marshaling expert advice and cooperation from whatever department they were needed. When he sought information or assistance, he was scrupulously careful to drop in on his informant and never to request anyone, even his juniors, to come to him. Alsberg never tried to make an impression. His simplicity was disarming. The delightful informality of the man, the total absence of selfishness, the complete reasonableness, and the understanding of the other person's point of view instilled confidence. The sincerity with which he could place the welfare of an institution, of science, or of any worth-while endeavor above minor considerations inspired cooperation. "No scheme of cooperation can work better than the cooperators are willing to permit," he observed. The task of creating the will often fell to him. Yet in these dealings with others there was never a trace of personal ambition, or insincerity, or a desire to wield power, but only an eminent reasonableness in behalf of ends to which he had a fair-minded attachment.

*   *   *

In meetings he was informal and casual but adroit. He would at times appear to ramble far from the subject, in order to bring out forcefully and effectively in the end some relevant point. He knew how to intercede. By taking a recalcitrant committeeman's side and stating for him a generous version of his views, and then by showing the basis on which agreement might be reached, Alsberg could often win the recalcitrant over, maintain harmony in the group, and earn the gratitude of his confrères.

Committees were to Alsberg more than a way of reaching group decisions. They were a medium of communication, helpful if not essential to understanding and cooperation in any large organization.

    25 The quotations were taken from Robert D. Calkins, "University Professor and Administrator," in Carl Alsberg, *Scientist at Large*, Edited by Joseph S. Davis, Stanford University Press, Stanford, California, 1948, pp. 76-78, 94-95, 99-100.

d. *The secretary.* The decisions of a group of executives usually are recorded and communicated to others in writing. Oral communications may be misunderstood and may not reach all those concerned. In theory the secretary has no influence on the committee's deliberations. His task is merely to record what has occurred in the meetings. But that task involves a selective process that imparts much power. The secretary also may influence the committee if he asked to prepare data and investigate material for the committee's consideration or to formulate the agenda. His power is enhanced when the chairmanship is rotated frequently. As in the case of the chairman, an appreciable difference between the secretary's nominal and actual authority may cause jealousy and dissension.

e. *Getting action.* To insure accomplishment of desired results, committee members should give some advance thought to the deliberations. In many committees the problems to be considered are broken down into manageable portions and analyzed well in advance; relevant documents and reports are sent to participants several days before the meeting for study. During the meeting the basic problems are broken down into their major components and all points of view are presented. Committee meetings may end with a summary of proceedings to unify the main points of the discussion. Definite action may be decided on and assigned to special committees or subcommittees. Provision is also made for follow-up on these committees' activities. Many who are experienced in committee work are opposed to formal voting because it tends to split the group. They prefer adoption of a solution corresponding to the "sense of the meeting"—i.e., the concensus of the group—if this can be arrived at. However, votes are useful in establishing a firm decision for the record. Voting has been used successfully by a number of committees that operate informally. The division of the vote is not communicated outside the committee.

f. *Scheduling the meetings.* Many feel that committee meetings should be bunched together to leave plenty of uninterrupted time for work. For example, General Motors groups all committee meetings into two periods each month, with two meetings on consecutive days in New York and two or four consecutive days in Detroit.

4. Only Subjects That Can Better be Handled by Groups Should be Selected for Committee Discussion

For every group action leading to a decision there is the alternative of individual action. The basic issue is whether group decision-making (through a formally established committee or conference or through informal meetings) is superior to individual action.

To make the comparisons necessary, management activities may be broken down into such categories as planning, control, organization, etc., and the respective merits of individual and group action for each management activity analyzed.

In the course of the AMA survey, we attempted to find out, through interviews with executives and inspection of records in

PERCENTAGE OF CASES IN WHICH MANAGEMENT FUNCTIONS CAN BE EXERCISED BY A UNIT OF ORGANIZATION IN COMMITTEE FORM

MANAGEMENT FUNCTION	A Can be exercised by committee effectively	B Same as A, but can be exercised more effectively by individual	C Individual initiative essential; may be supplemented by committee action	D Individual action essential; committee ineffective
Planning	20	20	25	35
Control	25	20	25	30
Formulating Objectives	35	35	10	20
Organization	5	25	20	50
Jurisdictional Questions	90	10	—	—
Leadership	—	—	10	90
Administration	20	25	25	30
Execution	10	15	10	65
Innovation	30	20	20	30
Communication	20	15	35	30
Advice	15	25	35	25
Decision-making	10	30	10	50

a score of companies, the relative merits of individual and group action. A rough estimate was made of the proportion in which different management activities: (a) can be exercised effectively by committee (group) action; (b) can be exercised effectively by committee action, but more effectively by individual action; (c) can be exercised by individual action, though supplementation by committee action may be helpful; (d) require individual action because committee action is ineffective.

The table on p. 128 shows an approximate breakdown of management functions into these four categories of effectiveness (suggested to AMA by Lt. Col. Lyndall Urwick, who also discussed with us at some length the relative effectiveness of individual or committee action in performing the major management activities.)

To summarize these rather rough breakdowns of our sample of 20 companies, committee action seems to be definitely superior in settling questions which may give rise to jurisdictional disputes within the company; individual action seems to be superior in providing leadership, in organization structuring, in execution, and in decision-making. Committee action is slightly superior in communication, but slightly inferior in planning, formulating objectives and administration. Committee action is approximately equal to individual action in control, technical innovation, and advisory activities.

GROUP VS. INDIVIDUAL DECISION-MAKING

The really vital question is, *under what circumstances* is group decision-making superior to individual decision-making and vice versa? The following general analysis represents an attempt to clarify this question.

If committees were to be grouped by the names they carry, there would be an excessive number of classifications. Furthermore, the names may be misleading: they sometimes suggest a good deal more (or less) than the committees actually do. To get some idea of the committees' real activities and scope, their variety should be reduced to a small number of categories. Such a division should make it possible to compare the relative merits of committee and

individual work. One method of comparison might be a classification of committee (and individual) work as follows:

1. Policy-Making
2. Administration
3. Execution
4. Innovation

and the degrees of authority with which the committees operate:

a. Informational
b. Advisory
c. Decision-Making

1. Policy-Making Committees

Policy-Making Committees at the Directors' Level. Policy-making committees are found particularly in larger companies. At the
directors' level there are, in addition to the board of directors,
subsidiary committees such as the executive committee and/or
the finance committee. In a National Industrial Conference Board
study of the distribution of these committees in 286 companies,[26]
415 directors' committees were reported as follows:

Name of the Committee	Number
Executive (general direction of company affairs between full board meetings)....	241
Finance	49
Salary	22
Bonus, profit-sharing and pension	11
Audit	11
Others	81
Total	415

Salary and bonus committees are more common than the table
indicates. Moreover, it should be noted that these directors' committees overlap considerably.[27]

[26] *Prevailing Practices Regarding Corporation Directors, Studies in Administrative Control No. 2,* National Industrial Conference Board, New York, 1940, p. 16.
[27] Directors' committees require a separate study, and the reader is referred to
the bibliography in the Appendix on problems such as the selection of board
members and interest representation, the organization and procedure of the
board and its committees, etc. This study is limited to the management functions which the board may exercise.

The principal subjects dealt with at the directors' level are the following:

Reports on major company developments, with possible approval (often perfunctory)

Determination of fundamental business concepts

Review of financial operations

Distribution of profits (amount paid in dividends and amount to be retained as surplus)

Provision of capital

Major capital expenditures

Executive compensation, salary, bonus, and pension payments to major executives

Appointment of new directors

Hiring and dismissal of the chief executive

New issues of securities

General Management Committees. Many companies have one general committee of top-management working officers and executives for basic policy deliberation. It may be called the "Policy Committee" (Ford Motor Company, General Motors Corporation, Penn Fruit Company); "Management Committee" (Continental Oil Company); "Planning Board" (The Chesapeake and Ohio Railway Company); "Operating Committee" (Phillips Petroleum Company, Chain Belt Company, Packard Motor Car Company); "Planning Committee" (Westinghouse Electric Corporation); "Administrative Council" (Caterpillar Tractor Company); "Executive Staff" (The Cleveland Electric Illuminating Co.). Occasionally in a very large company there may be a special management committee of top executives to make most or all major decisions and initiate, approve or veto actions. Examples are the Coordinating Committee of the Standard Oil Company of New Jersey, the United States Steel Corporation (parent company); and the United States Steel Company (formed of four major subsidiaries and also furnishing service to other producing and distributing companies). At the duPont Company the "Executive Committee," made up of the president and eight vice presidents, is an active approving and coordinating body, meeting weekly. The daily meetings of the executive committee of the Standard Oil Company of New Jersey (composed of working directors) exercises an active coordinating control over subsidiary companies.

Subjects dealt with by general management committees include:

Scope of operations (products and markets)
Operating budgets
Capital budgets
Selection and dismissal of major executives
General supervision of executive activities and basic decisions on major functions such as production, engineering, research, sales, pricing, labor relations

These over-all committees meet weekly or bi-weekly. Membership varies from four or five to 14 or 15. Each member may report on his activities and make recommendations. The committee's decision-making power is usually one of three types: (1) the committee may act as adviser to the chief executive and to the board of directors; (2) it may initiate decisions subject to acceptance by the chief executive; (3) it may actually make decisions in conjunction with the president.

Functions of Policy-Making Committees

The policy-making committees concern themselves chiefly with one or more of the following major aspects of management (listed roughly in order of time spent on each):

       a. Planning
       b. Control
       c. Formulation of objectives
       d. Organization, and
       e. Jurisdictional questions

How competent is a committee likely to be in these areas as compared to an individual?

a. *Planning.* In over-all planning, a committee can be helpful in rounding out the picture by contributing important facts and integrating divergent views, especially if its members have different backgrounds. It can provide valuable criticism of proposed activities. On the other hand, the initial conception, the painstaking analysis entailed, the technical implementation, usually must be the work of an individual who can devote much time and thought to the project. Forecasting, for example, requires care in collecting, analyzing, checking, and weighing facts; it requires intuition and imagination in drawing and presenting conclusions—qualities more likely to be shown by an individual than a group.

b. *Control.* The purpose of control is to determine whether objectives and policies have been carried out. Tremendous improvements have been made in the scope and techniques of reporting through the media of accounting, costing, statistics, ratio analysis and graphic presentation, making it possible for a committee to review extensive and up-to-date information. However, the reports themselves are usually compiled by an individual or a group under an individual's direction, rather than by a committee, because use of committees for purposes of investigation sometimes proves cumbersome and costly.

c. *Formulating Objectives.* In the absence of a committee, executives tend to be tied down by their day-to-day problems and to overlook basic principles and goals. In these all too frequent cases the operating executives need group meetings for contact with each other, with those more directly concerned with policy formulation, and with non-working directors representing various interest groups. Such meetings, by reason of the group's composition and authority, can determine basic objectives and guiding principles and can thus establish a general constitutional framework within which executives can act more purposefully and more effectively.

However, there may be serious difficulties in group formulation of objectives. The framework of basic principles may be formulated in such broad terms that it offers little guidance. Perusal of company statements of objectives in policy or organization manuals will confirm this opinion. Note, for example, the vague and lofty language with which they sometimes treat such subjects as "maintenance of confidence," "teamwork," "profits," "goodwill." Such generalities conceal rather than resolve differences of objectives, for each executive is left to rely on his own interpretation. Such vagueness results when cooperation in committee is forced and no one is allowed to get too far out of line. Unclear statements may be accepted in the hope of modifying policies as they are executed. Or the vagueness may be deliberately designed to give the strong members of the committee a chance to do as they please. On the other hand, if the committee directive is clear, those who are affected by it (and did not participate in the meeting) may refuse to accept it. Thus committees can direct the general formulation of objectives, but the task of casting them into policy statements is better assigned to individuals.

d. *Organization.* A group can study different plans of organization, review their merits, criticize details, and approve or recommend a final plan. But it is hard to see how a committee can draw up the plan itself. Organization is an intricate subject, requiring intensive thought, analysis, and evaluation—sustained labor ill suited to a committee. Committee organization work has the added drawback that some of the persons to be affected by the reorganization are likely to be members of the committee. Different personalities and vested job interests may impede the evolution of the ideal structure. However, some cooperation in developing the plan facilitates its acceptance.

e. *Settlement of Jurisdictional Questions.* Committees make ideal arbitrators in jurisdictional disputes within the company—over, for example, the degree of decision-making power in one function as against another. The weight of collective judgments carries more prestige than does that of a single arbiter and is more likely to be accepted as an impartial determination.

2. Administration

The "formation of policies" and the "administration of policies" are distinct functions. The former is concerned with the establishment of broad principles by which administration is to be guided. The latter, in the narrow sense of the word, is concerned with the daily conduct of the company's affairs—setting standards and procedures to guide and govern execution of policies, establishing controls to insure adherence to the standards, solving inter-divisional disputes, improving inter-divisional coordination, and meeting various emergencies as they arise. As a company grows in size and complexity, administration tends to be divorced from policy-making, because the broad problems and their technical ramifications become too numerous for one man to handle both.

Thus the larger companies develop administrative committees, chiefly concerned with the work of the staff specialists, to initiate decisions for approval in various management areas, such as employee and labor relations, engineering, research, distribution, manufacturing, public relations, foreign operations, safety, construction, productivity, etc. These committees have such names as "Administrative Committee," (General Motors Corporation); "Steering Committee" (Penn Fruit Company); "Subcommittee" (Ford Motor Company); "Administrative Council" (Caterpillar Tractor Company); or "Coordination Committee" (Carrier Corporation). An example of a committee administering policies is the Coordination Committee of the Carrier Corporation whose functions are described in Appendix B.

It should be noted that since these functions involve highly technical and continuous tasks requiring the contributions of experts, committee administration of them may be less effective than administration by an individual.

3. Execution

A committee can execute only when its members act as a team in carrying out policies or enforcing administrative standards by explaining policy, allocating tasks, following up assignments, reviewing work or motivating action. Such teamwork is difficult for a group of people to achieve.

One area in which a committee may often function better than an individual is in the appointment of personnel. Appointment committees to fill a vacancy are not uncommon. (On the supervisory level they may concern themselves with rating and promotion.) The combined judgment of several persons is usually considered sounder and more objective than that of an individual acting on his own. In addition to interviewing applicants and making a selection, a committee also may be of value in determining job qualifications.

4. Innovation

Perhaps the most important management function is that of innovation. It is the mainspring of profitability, of flexibility, and of over-all industrial progress.

Many believe that a committee, as such, cannot innovate. It is true that a new idea is usually the product of a single mind. But a committee can evaluate it, point up omissions, suggest improvements, and help to integrate the new idea with existing ideas. Out of the committee discussions a completely new conception may emerge. Innovations resulting from group efforts are especially important and widespread in technical research.

Stage VII: Delegation of Decision-Making: Decentralization

ILLUSTRATIVE CASE

THE larger the company, the more urgent is the problem of decentralization, for an increase in size increases the number and difficulties of decisions faced by top management. Since the time and abilities of a company's top executives are necessarily limited, it becomes essential to pass on to others certain powers of decision-making.

However, it should be noted that the need for decentralization does not necessarily increase in proportion with size. Other factors play an important role, such as complexity of operations, variety of products, and geographic dispersal. Thus a very large company manufacturing a single, simple item might have less to gain by decentralization than a considerably smaller company manufacturing diverse types of complex technical products which it sells in diverse markets.

GM—An Outstanding Example of Decentralization

One of the companies with outstanding experience in decentralization is the General Motors Corporation. It has consciously followed such a policy for about 30 years. Today it is the largest manufacturing company in the world and has been the most successful in terms of total profits. While these results cannot be directly ascribed to decentralization, a study of this one element of its success may be of interest.

Because of its tremendous size, it is impossible to explain adequately the nature of the GM organization within a few pages: As of 1951, GM had 469,000 employees, 34 operating divisions; 103 plants in 52 cities, ranging from 1,000 to over 20,000 employees; scores of branches, warehouses and service stations; and a large variety of products. It would be impossible for the company to centralize all decisions without becoming hopelessly topheavy and unwieldy. Accordingly, operating decisions are left to the General Motors divisions, subject to broad company policy. While the basic plan of decentralization was established as an over-all company policy, it was put into effect in a flexible, pragmatic fashion.

General Motors' decentralization involves the following major features: (1) the determination of top management policy through widespread executive participation; (2) a high degree of delegated decision-making; and (3) centralization of control.

The Nature of the GM Program

The General Motors Corporation in the early years after its foundation in 1916 was largely a collection of independent companies, assembled by the promoting genius of W. C. Durant. Some of these companies were doing well, others were doing poorly. They had a high degree of authority but lacked coordination and unity of purpose. There was little in the way of central control, and independent action on the part of some plant managers, contrary to the advice of the central financial officials, led to considerable inventory losses in 1920-21.

Then a new management under Pierre S. du Pont, Alfred P. Sloan, Jr., Donaldson Brown, John Pratt and others, formulated basic policies and goals for all the General Motors holdings. This work has been ably continued under the leadership of C. E. Wilson and his associates. Because of the size and complexity of the enterprise, the basic feature of the new GM organization model was decentralization. Alfred P. Sloan, Jr. likens it to the free enterprise system. Each constituent unit is independent, save for the basic rules of operation. It is an outstanding example of what Peter F. Drucker terms the *federal principle* in which the component parts of the enterprise are autonomous within the framework of a uniform policy. Within this framework each unit competes with the others. Unit labor costs and other costs are carefully controlled to meet competitive prices successfully. Each part is judged on the basis of its performance, by such criteria as the percentage of sales of the potential market and other measurable performance factors. Executives' pay is linked to net contributions to company revenues. This evaluation is not carried out in accordance with a rigid mechanical formula. Judgment and careful weighing of factors other than those cited play an important role. The new organization was set up to permit as large an area of free decision-making as far down the management hierarchy as possible. Thus a divisional general manager is given wide latitude in decision-making, and is not subject to daily direction from the central organization, provided he continues to produce the results that are desired.

The nature of decentralization at the General Motors Corporation has changed as the nature of managerial functions and outside influences have changed. In the early days, the engineering work of each division was conducted independently, and without the benefit of the central engineering staff's consulting and coordinating services which are now available. The divisional engineering departments still operate on a decentralized basis and the chief engineer of each division is responsible to the general manager of that division. However, they now operate within the framework of broad engineering policy established through the Engineering Policy Group, which is composed of the corporation's top operating executives.

Over the years, institutional changes in the United States have changed the nature of decentralization. The development of labor unions has led to a central determination of the conditions of work. Not only do all the plants have to operate under a uniform labor contract, but the local managements' personnel and production decisions have to be shared to some extent with outside groups, as determined in the collective bargaining process. Technological and political developments have also led to a greater degree of centralization in the determination of hours, wages, and working conditions. However, it should be noted that General Motors has agreements with 18 international unions, and these vary in important respects. Moreover, there are local agreements under the national agreements which make for further diversity.

Policy-Making and Administration

Top management policy is formulated by the board of directors and by the Financial and Operations Policy Committees; the responsibility for administering these policies rests with the presidents, to some extent through the Administration Committee and the Policy Groups. (See Figure 1.)

1. *The board of directors represents* the interests of all the stockholders through centralized control. It is largely a reviewing and judicial body. The board of directors in turn delegates broad authority to two governing committees to act on its behalf when the board is not in session, subject to its review and approval. These are the Financial Policy and the Operations Policy Committees.

2. *The Operations Policy Committee* is composed entirely of members of the board of directors who are working officers of the corporation. The president is chairman of this committee. Its members formulate specific operating policies in order to establish the fundamental directives for administrators and executives for determining the activity of any or all departments and their interrelationship—for example, establishment of production schedules and price lists for the automobile divisions. Where no board policies have been laid down, the committee deals with problems as they arise.

3. *The Financial Committee.* This committee consists of members of the board of directors who are not closely connected with the corporation as officers, as well as those who are. This committee determines financial policy. Its chairman is the Executive Vice President in Charge of Finance.

This committee and the Operations Policy Committee pass on all major policy and administrative decisions. They receive reports on all major phases of the business. And they serve as a last

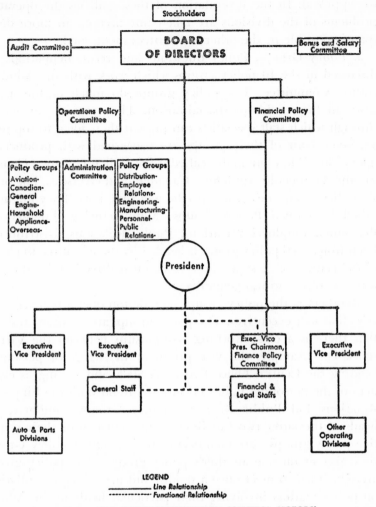

FIG. 1.   TOP POLICY FORMULATION (GENERAL MOTORS)

appeal in case of major differences. They have a decision-making as well as an integrative function.

4. *The Administrative Committee* is chaired by the president. Some of its members are drawn from the Operations Policy Committee, but it also includes the general managers of the Car, Truck, Body, Allison and Overseas Divisions. This committee deals with problems of administration and develops policies which are subsequently submitted to the Operations Policy Committee

for approval. In the formulation of these policies the operating problems of the divisions are taken into account in more detail than is possible in the other committees mentioned.

5. *Policy Groups.* Policy questions and recommendations are discussed in the 10 policy groups which work with the Administration Committee. The policy groups do much of the actual work in their fields of specialization. They provide an avenue through which staff specialists can present their ideas to top management. Four of these groups are concerned with products or operations. They might be called *Line* Policy Groups—General Engine, Household Appliance, Canadian and Overseas. The other six policy groups deal with specific staff functions. They might be called *Functional* Policy Groups—Manufacturing, Engineering, Personnel, Employee Relations, Public Relations, Distribution. Each functional policy group is headed by the executive in charge of the central office staff whose function is directly related to the interests of the group generally.

Members of the policy groups include top operating executives as well as staff executives. The policy groups are so interconnected that there is a close working relationship between the various staffs. For example, the vice president in charge of personnel, heading the Central Office Personnel Staff, and serving as chairman of the Personnel Policy Group, sits in on both the Employee Relations and Public Relations Policy Groups. Similarly, the heads of the latter two functions—and chairmen of their respective policy groups—are members of the Personnel Policy Group; they also sit on one another's policy groups. The policy groups are scheduled to meet once a month and make recommendations on policy matters involving their particular fields to the Administration Committee, which in turn passes them on to the Operations Policy Committee for final approval.

GM Committees in Action

The two major committees, Operations Policy and Financial, were created to bring the best available thinking to bear on the two major phases of management responsibility, policy formulation and administration. In large companies it is possible that board members, however competent, do not know enough about some important internal problems of the business itself which they are to supervise in a broad sense. A bank president could pass on a question relating to the provision of funds, but he might not make much of a contribution to a problem regarding the advisability of introducing a new product or expanding a particular plant. Therefore, the Financial Policy Committee, like other such committees in large corporations, was staffed with some operating directors as well as with some directors representing large stockholder interests, rather than staffed entirely with outside directors. Similar reasoning led to the creation of the Operations Policy and Administration Committees staffed entirely with operating people.

The Operations Policy and Financial Policy Committees meet from time to time in conference so as to integrate possible divergencies in their points of view. The Financial Policy Committee usually has among its membership a few retired operating people to whom present operators must offer convincing arguments for a proposed course of action. This committee, with its jurisdiction over financial and accounting matters, can serve as an important and effective check and balance over the operating side of the organization.

Administrative Management

General Motors' central office organization includes two major groups of "staff activities"—the General Staff and the Financial and Legal Staffs, each headed by an Executive Vice President.

The General Staff includes: Distribution, Styling, Engineering, Research, Employee Relations, Public Relations, Personnel, Manufacturing (each headed by a Vice President); Business Research (headed by an "Executive in Charge"); and the General Motors Holding Division (headed by a General Manager). The headquarters General Staff is held down to a relatively small size, considering the scale of General Motors operations. It operates on an advisory basis, in a fairly informal fashion.

The Financial and Legal Staffs are headed by an Executive Vice President who reports directly to the Financial Policy Committee, with a functional relationship to the President (a device which has been adopted by some other companies to increase the Board's financial control). He also has general supervision over the Finance and Insurance Group.

Operating Levels

There are two operating parts of the business at General Motors—the Automotive and Parts Division and other operating divisions. Each is headed by an Executive Vice President, reporting directly to the President. The Executive Vice President in Charge of the Automotive and Parts Divisions has under his direct supervision the heads of the following units:

1. The Group Executive in Charge of the Car and Truck Group, which includes the following divisions:

Buick	Chevrolet
Cadillac	GM Truck and Coach
Oldsmobile	GM Parts
Pontiac	United Motor Service

2. The Group Executive in Charge of the Body and Assembly Divisions Group (Fisher Body, Ternstedt, Buick-Oldsmobile-Pontiac Assembly Division)
3. The Group Executive in Charge of the Accessory Group (12 divisions), some of which sell important parts of their production to other industrial producers

The Executive Vice President in charge of the other operating divisions (22) has reporting to him the Group Executives of the following three groups:

1. Engine Group comprising the Diesel Engine Divisions at Cleveland and Detroit, the Allison (Aircraft Engine) Division, and the Electro-Motive Division at LaGrange, Illinois
2. The Dayton and Household Appliance Group (seven divisions)
3. The Overseas and Canadian Group (three divisions)

The two operating Executive Vice Presidents, as well as their subordinates, the Group Executives, have no regular staff except a few assistants. They utilize the services of the Headquarters General Staff.

The Group Executives represent top management to the divisional managers of their groups and act as their advisors. In turn, they keep top management abreast of divisional viewpoints and problems, through participation on many of the policy committees. An important part of their function is to maintain the two-way flow of information and authority that is essential in the formulation of over-all policy by top management, and its implementation at the operational level. The Group Executive can counsel with the divisional general managers of his group to interchange views and ideas.

These top management relationships are clarified in Figure 2.

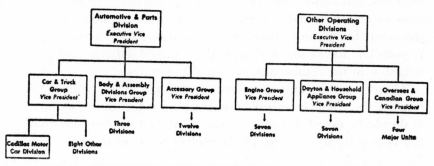

FIG. 2.   ORGANIZATION CHART, OPERATING LEVEL (GENERAL MOTORS)

As an illustration of the organization of a particular division, the top echelons in the Cadillac Motor Car Division and its Cleveland Tank Plant are graphically shown in Figure 3.

The divisions range in size from one plant with less than 1,000 employees to Chevrolet and Fisher Body with some 40,000 employees—equal in size to some of our largest businesses. Each division is headed by a general manager. He has almost as much of a staff as if he were heading an independent enterprise—including a production manager, controller, purchasing director, chief engineer, personnel manager, sales manager, etc. Thus each division designs, develops, manufactures, merchandises and advertises its own products. Staff functions at the plant level vary largely with size and product. Generally speaking a plant manager has a resident comptroller, a personnel director, an inspector, a purchasing agent and a manufacturing superintendent who report to him. He would not be apt to have a sales manager, since distribution is usually controlled by the Division. Since there are only a few staff layers, communication with headquarters staff is simple and direct.

Each division makes its own purchases of materials and component parts—both from other divisions as well as from outside sources. Where it buys depends on the source which is able to furnish the most suitable product or service at a reasonable price.

Purchasing is largely decentralized except in certain areas where volume is a factor or where allocation may be necessary due to restrictions of material.

Each division develops its own manufacturing processes and methods, hires and trains its own employees, develops and maintains its own staff and operating organization—including its own specialists for various phases of its business. Each division is also responsible for being a desirable industrial citizen and good neighbor in the community in which it operates.

There is no attempt to enforce a uniform organizational pattern on the whole company. There are no organization manuals. It should be noted that all executives engaged in operations have the responsibility to concern themselves with organization.

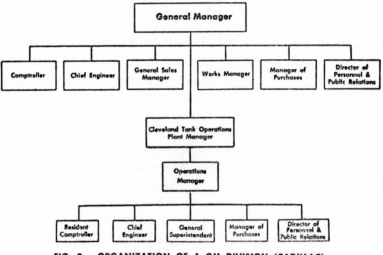

FIG. 3.   ORGANIZATION OF A GM DIVISION (CADILLAC)

The degree of autonomy prevailing at GM is seen in the fact that each division and each plant has its own personnel executive. The personnel set-up at the local level varies in size, depending on the operation. In some instances the same man may handle labor relations, training activities, safety, etc. In other cases, if the situation warrants it, each of these functions may be the job of a specialist working under the supervision of a personnel director. His responsibility is clearly defined, even though much of his work is done through informal contacts with higher line and functional authorities. The divisional personnel director is responsible to the divisional general manager. His relation to the Central Personnel Staff is functional, though in fact he will consult the Central Staff frequently and be guided by over-all corporation policy as it affects labor relations.

Unlike the manager of an independent small business, however, the general manager of a General Motors division has available to him the financial resources of the Corporation as well as the staff facilities and "know-how" of the central organization.

It should be noted that, even where there is centralized decision-making, as on job classification, some scope for independent action is left to the divisional management. National agreements leave room in certain areas for local bargaining. Thus for example, over 100 local wage agreements have been worked out between local managements and local unions which govern the application of pay scales in individual divisions or plants.

Another example is seen in the company's system of position classification for salaried employees. These classifications were worked out in the Central Office and are used by all GM divisions and plants. But the system does not tell a General Manager how much to pay a specific employee or in which classification to put him. It also permits local management to recognize ability and merit through merit increases up to a maximum rate within a given classification.

The benefits which General Motors has claimed from its long-standing policy of decentralization include especially the speed and improvement of decision-making; the successful development of executive talent; a relative absence of conflict between the operating divisions, staff and top management; comparability of the efforts and results achieved by the various divisions; and independence of action for profit-making.

Centralized Control

It is clear that decentralization is the basic organization policy of the General Motors Corporation. But it has always been tied to "centralized control." As stated in Donaldson Brown's classic paper, "Centralized Control with Decentralized Responsibilities,"[28] it is required that "the activity of all departments be controlled so that they coordinate with the needs of the business, and with the requirements of policy."

Centralized control is provided for in a number of different ways:

1. *Centralized programming.* Top management establishes overall goals for production, in consultation with the various divisions, in order to maintain logical relationships to sales, inventories carried and purchase commitments, and return on investment. Performance standards are set for each division. Each must fit into the general plan and operate in accordance with the dictates of four basic economic factors—long-term growth, business cycle variations, seasonal fluctuations and competition. Long-range goals are planned centrally in consultation with the divisions. The aim is to eliminate uncertainty.

2. *Authority limitations* are imposed on divisional managers with regard to such basic decisions as the following: capital expenditure, price ranges of products, salary changes above a certain level, bonuses, union contracts.

3. *Provision of services* through the general staffs at headquarters regarding new methods, techniques, future policies, uniform practices—all on an advisory basis (that is, division managers are free to decide whether or not to take the advice), through personal contacts, meetings, bulletins, periodic corporation-wide conferences.

4. *Accounting control* through (a) a central auditing staff; (b) measurement of cost efforts of the various divisions on a comparable basis, eliminating extraneous factors as far as possible; (c) measurement and comparison of the rate of return on invested capital; and (d) market standing through study of the division's sales as a percentage of the market.

Each division has a Comptroller at the head of its financial department, who, besides being responsible to the General Manager, also reports to the Comptroller of the Corporation. He sends in a monthly balance sheet and income statement on a standard form. Each division has an accounting department which sends monthly reports to the Central Office. In addition there are travelling auditors who make annual audits of all the operating units and send

[28] American Management Association, 1927.

reports to the divisional general managers as well as to the Central Office. Detailed operating results are regularly shown in chart or other visual form to all concerned. Informal controls are also maintained through frequent visits and exchanges among General Motors executives.

It is seen clearly, even from these few examples, that the GM organization is a classic combination of decentralized responsibilities and centralized control.

GENERAL ANALYSIS

The Nature of Decentralization

The term "decentralization" is interpreted in a number of different ways. Frequently it is used to denote the physical separation of production or sales activities away from the head office. But physical decentralization—as distinct from *managerial* decentralization—does not necessarily imply a change in the nature of management. For example, one medium-sized paper company which was studied in the course of the AMA survey proudly reported that it was completely decentralized. Why? Because it had set up five separate manufacturing plants. Upon examination of the nature of decision-making, however, it was found that not only were all major decisions made in the New York head office, but the plant managers had to check with New York on quite minor decisions—on any matter that diverged at all from established procedure. Thus managers had to get permission from the president to make small purchases, to pay an operator for a holiday when he was absent part of the day before on account of a death in a family, etc.

Another type of decentralization—and that with which we shall be primarily concerned here—refers to the nature of the company's management. More precisely, it implies the delegation of responsibility and authority from higher management to subordinates down the line.

We may say that the degree of managerial decentralization in a company is the greater:

1. The greater the number of decisions made lower down the management hierarchy.

2. The more important the decisions made lower down the management hierarchy. For example, the greater the sum of capital expenditure that can be approved by the plant manager without consulting anyone else, the greater the degree of decentralization in this field.
3. The more functions affected by decisions made at lower levels. Thus companies which permit only operational decisions to be made at separate branch plants are less decentralized than those which also permit financial and personnel decisions at branch plants.
4. The less checking required on the decision. Decentralization is greatest when no check at all must be made; less when superiors have to be informed of the decision after it has been made; still less if superiors have to be consulted *before* the decision is made. The fewer people to be consulted, and the lower they are on the management hierarchy, the greater the degree of decentralization.

The acid test of managerial decentralization is therefore the degree to which executives participate in decision-making. Or it may be put in this way: How far has the company moved away from one-man control of all major decisions? Traditionally, many of the early economists and business writers described the average enterprise of their day as a one-man business, run by the owner-manager. Thus the great economist Alfred Marshall spoke of the employer as "himself exercising a general control over everything and preserving order and unity in the main plan of the business." And this description seems to have fitted the typical 19th century business decision-making rather accurately. Since then, of course, the locus of decision-making has moved from the owner-manager to the professional manager. It is no longer true that "where the risk lies there also lies the control." As a matter of general practice provision is frequently made, either by statute or charter, for the delegation of the direction of the company from the owners or stockholders to a specially selected board of management, commonly known as the board of directors, designed to act on behalf of the owner.

In addition to the delegated framework for the exercise of the powers conferred upon the board of directors to act on behalf of the corporation, there are the statutory corporation law, the charter and certificate of incorporation, as well as the by-laws drafted and accepted by the stockholders. These are the articles which govern the conduct of the business in a broad sense. The board of directors usually has wide grants of power, including the power to amend or enact the by-laws.

The board of directors in turn usually delegates a major part of its powers to the company's chief executive, who is the president or—less frequently—chairman of the board of directors, or a combination of the two. The chief executive possesses very great powers, as a rule. One important question in decentralization, therefore, is this: Which powers does the chief executive reserve for himself and which does he delegate to his subordinates? The actual degree to which major decisions are delegated in a particular company may be determined by use of a questionnaire, such as is shown in Fig. 4, which also provides for information regarding the role of various major executives in decision-making. (AMA's survey of company organization practices indicates that there is little general agreement regarding the extent to which authority delegation should be spelled out. On this question, the majority of companies were rather flexible and informal, except in regard to capital expenditures and salary changes.)

Fig. 4. Questionnaire on the Delegation of Authority in the Company

I. Gross Annual Sales $_____ (millions) Total number of employees _____ Number of management employees, including foremen and corresponding levels _____ Number of plants _____ Total number of foremen (approx.) _____ Number of members of Board of Directors _____ Number of Directors (in the company) working full-time _____ In how many locations are plants _____

II. Please state type of authority and dollar amounts for each of the following management decisions or authority limits. For the sake of brevity, please use symbols to indicate the type of authority exercised as follows:

> A—Full authority; B—Full authority, reporting action to superior; C—Full authority after consulting; D—Committee action; E—No policy; F—Flexible policy, depends on circumstances; G—No authority

	Board of Directors	President or Chief Executive Officer	Executive Vice President or Equivalent	Division, Departmental Vice Presidents or Equivalent	Division Managers or Equivalent
Control over basic expenditures					
1. Purchase of capital equipment					
2. Sale of surplus equipment or materials					
3. Maintenance or repair of equipment					
4. Operating expenses					
5. Settlements of claims by Company					
6. Settlements of claims against Company					
7. Credit arrangements					
8. Purchase of materials					
9. Major sales prices (state whose authority)					
Control over miscellaneous expenses					
10. Expense accounts					
11. Donations and gifts					
12. Books, periodicals & subscriptions					
13. Employing professional services					
Personnel actions affecting salaried employees					
14. Salary adjustments					
15. Salary progression schedule					
16. Organization changes					
Personnel action affecting hourly-rated employees					
17. Hourly wage rates ⎫ State merely type of authority					
18. Employee benefits					
19. Paying overtime					
20. Changes in job classifications					
Approving the labor contract ⎭					

DECENTRALIZATION AS A CRITERION OF
ORGANIZATION

In and of itself managerial decentralization is neither desirable nor undesirable. We must apply certain criteria in order to evaluate it. One such criterion is economic efficiency: At what point in the management hierarchy and by what individual is a particular decision made most efficiently? Is a particular function exercised or a service performed more cheaply if it is "centralized" or "decentralized"? It is impossible to say in general that either centralization or decentralization is more efficient. It depends on the type of decision involved. The more costly a mistaken decision, the higher up it should be decided (provided the higher-ups make fewer mistakes in the matter under question). Obviously, the price to be paid for a major raw material purchase would be better decided by top management than by a foreman. On the other hand, the less costly a mistaken decision, and the greater the need for a speedy decision, on the spot, the nearer to the source of origin it should be made.

It should also be borne in mind that the same degree of decentralization need not apply to men doing the same work or having similar status. For example, in a textile plant, certain decisions regarding the quality of finished goods can be made at the point of operation, since the disadvantages of a wrong decision to the company's reputation might not be sufficiently important to warrant control at a higher point in management. However, in quality control of pharmaceuticals, an error may be of such consequence to the company's reputation that every safeguard must be imposed to prevent a wrong decision. In such a situation, the quality control director should probably report to the president or at least to a senior officer.

Finally, the same degree of decision-making power may be given to two men doing the same job and the economic result may be entirely different. Different personalities may have completely dissimilar abilities to exercise judgment when on their own. This will be obvious to any reader who considers the decision-making ability of those about him—how some cannot be trusted to do anything right unless they check each time before they make a move, how others unfailingly come up with the right answers by themselves and would merely be hamstrung if they were more closely controlled.

Just as decentralization is not necessarily good or bad from an economic point of view, the same holds true from a non-economic standpoint. It is widely believed that even if decentralization cannot be justified on economic grounds, it is worthwhile because it is "democratic." But the term "democracy" is a concept of political science. It is based on the premise of man's equality. In business, men are not equal in every sense—for, obviously, their salaries, status and power differ. Therefore, it would seem inappropriate to apply this term to business relationships. Nor is decentralization necessarily advisable because it involves participation. Participation may be desirable, but it may not be practicable under existing circumstances. Moreover, some executives do not wish to assume the responsibilities that participation entails; they may prefer an authoritarian relationship. And even where executives desire participation, extra expenses entailed for additional staff and the slowing down of decision-making may not be offset by the benefits to be derived.

Knowledge of the locus of decision-making within the company at best provides only a partial answer to the nature of its decision-making. To have a more complete picture, one must also know how decision-making is divided between owners and management hired by the owners, the impact of outside forces (government, consumers, financial interests, labor unions) on the company's decisions, and the relative emphasis given decisions involving short- and long-run questions.

FACTORS AFFECTING THE DECISION TO DECENTRALIZE

Since decentralization is not of itself a criterion of a good organization, on either economic or non-economic grounds, we must apply certain criteria in order to determine whether, and to what degree, decentralization is advisable in any given situation.

In this connection, the following factors may serve as tools of analysis: (1) Size of the company, (2) nature of the company's business, (3) economic trends, (4) political trends, (5) management philosophy, (6) personality, and (7) nature of the individual management functions.

The basic standard underlying this analysis will be profitability —i.e., to what extent will delegation of decision-making lead to a reduction in unit costs by lowering salary expense on given decisions? To what extent are profits increased through improved decision-making?

1. Size

The cost of making decisions generally tends to be higher the farther away they are made from the point at which the problem arises. Moreover, the decision itself may be less satisfactory. The larger the size of the firm, the more numerous the decisions that will have to be made, the longer it takes to make them at the top where they accumulate. Similarly, the greater the time and the physical distance involved, the more extensive and complex the process of communicating accurately the decision to everyone concerned. And finally, the larger the size of the company, the harder it will be to have the decision carried out as effectively and expeditiously as might be desired. To cite one instance, at a large company a study of the evolution of several policies showed how difficult it was to arrive at a decision. It was found that decisions made at the top, often reached the foreman in a very garbled form and their application was quite different from what was originally intended.

The big firm may well be a series of wheels within wheels, an elaborate hierarchy in which every decision requires the consulting of this man, the referring to that man, the permission of a third, the agreement of a fourth, and informing a fifth—so that decisions may become endlessly delayed. Where decisions must be reached frequently and quickly, such an organization, unless despotically controlled, may find itself paralyzed—and, if it is in fact a despotism, much of the benefit of specialist services and advice may be lost. The small firm, on the other hand, may be more often and more successfully despotic. The decisions are those, as a rule, of a single individual, made quickly and decisively.

To illustrate, contrast the process of decision-making in a small and a large firm. An oil company, we will assume, is considering whether to undertake the heavy expenses of drilling a series of oil wells. The opinions of the departments affected are sampled. The exploration department may be convinced that it will be a highly profitable venture. The production department has estimated the cost and determined the probable yield of the investment. The treasurer has the funds, but may be doubtful about the returns as compared to those obtainable through other uses of the funds. The sales department may not be certain about the possibilities of selling the additional refined products profitably. The personnel director may not be sure about the availability of the necessary skilled personnel. In some way or other the chief executive and the board of directors will have to weigh these different considerations against one another and reach a decision. How much simpler is the decision where the chief executive is just a wild-catter! He decided by "feel, hunch and hearsay," superimposed on highly specialized technical knowledge.

Reducing the Size of the Decision-Making Unit: Advantages

A reduction in the size of the decision-making unit, by splitting an existing large unit into several units, each smaller, and delegating to each decision-making powers, may bring about considerable increases in efficiency, in such ways as the following:

a. *Executives will be nearer to the point of decision-making.* Delays of decisions, caused by the necessity of checking with headquarters and/or top officials, are reduced by managerial decentralization. Since people on the spot know usually more about the factors involved in the decisions than those further removed (by physical distance and authority), and since speedy decisions may often be essential (competitors may move in otherwise), such a delegation of decision-making is advantageous. It also saves the considerable expenditure of time and money involved in communication and consultation before the decision is made. These savings may increase as the geographical dispersion and the volume of company activities increase. (A notable example of a chief executive who believed in the delegation of decision-making was Samuel Zemurray, former President of the United Fruit Co. who made his division managers' autonomy real by his stock message, "You're there, we're here.")

b. *Efficiency may be increased because there may be a better utilization of the time and ability of executives,* some of whom may formerly have shunned responsibility as much as possible, "going to headquarters" automatically, as soon as any problem came up.

c. *The quality of decisions is likely to improve* as their magnitude and complexity is reduced, and as major executives are relieved of possible overwork. The top men will be able to concentrate on the most important decisions. As General Eisenhower points out "full concentration on the chief problem at hand makes it possible to solve it; the details should be handled lower down the line. I never fired a man for delegating responsibility, but I did fire men who held the reins too tight and irritated others by their preoccupation with minutiae."

d. *The amount and expense of paperwork by headquarters staff may be considerably reduced* by delegating decision-making. For example, in a medium-sized company the regional managers formerly had to check most of their major decisions with headquarters. It took from 10 to 30 days before a decision was obtained. The transfer of a clerk from one division of regional headquarters to another required eight signatures. Now, only three are needed—all from the same regional headquarters. As an over-all result, headquarters staffs have been cut considerably.

e. *The expense of coordination may be reduced because of the greater autonomy of decision-making.* This requires the establishment of a clear-cut framework of general company policy within which the subsidiary units can make their decisions. For example, at Sears, Roebuck and Co. the establishment of such a policy has resulted in a considerable reduction of the coordinating staff, with greater freedom of action on the part of the individual stores. Sears, Roebuck has emphasized adaptability and ability to carry out simple procedures worked out at headquarters. In this way risks are considerably reduced. A store manager cannot go far wrong on merchandise selection, for example, because this is done for the most part by top experts at the head office. All he has to do is a good selling job, for which he has much incentive.

Disadvantages

On the other hand, the division of a large decision-making unit into smaller ones may have certain disadvantages:

a. *Lack of uniformity of decisions.* A major obstacle of decentralization is the lack of uniformity of decision from one location to another—e.g., payment of different wage rates and salaries for similar jobs, more liberal holidays and vacations, greater leeway in capital expenditures. However, this factor must be not overemphasized. A careful appraisal should be made of the advantages of uniformities as compared to the cost of achieving them and the possible deterioration of interest and capacity in independent decision-making. Perhaps the advantages of delegation can be enjoyed without loss of uniformity by holding of regular "integrating" meetings between headquarters and regional personnel performing the same function, and between the heads of various functions at headquarters and within each region, with the president presiding at headquarters and the regional general manager presiding at the regional level.

b. *Inadequate utilization of specialist advice.* The highest-priced and best talent of many companies is often assembled at headquarters. When decentralization is introduced, men in the field may feel that they no longer need to utilize headquarters advice. They may be glad to escape such counsel as they consider unwarranted and time-consuming. The result may be that headquarters staff is only partially utilized and its effectiveness is thus impaired. It is essential, therefore, that management carefully define relationships between headquarters and the field so as to strike an optimum balance between the advantages of waiting for superior advice and of action on the spot.

c. *Lack of proper equipment or executives in the field.* Headquarters staff is only partially utilized and its effectiveness is thus etc.) frequently feel that as long as they are in fact responsible for results (regardless of formal delegation), they must have the authority to achieve the desired results. Accordingly, they may be reluctant to delegate much authority—in which case decentralization will remain a fiction. Such opposition can be traced in part to the nature of the function exercised. Certain functions may

not lend themselves to delegation, because highly technical problems must be resolved or expensive equipment must be carefully
allocated. But perhaps the major reason for reluctance to delegate
is the lack of qualified executives in the field. The old ones may
be unaccustomed to taking on new responsibilities and the young
ones may not have adequate experience. There is a great deal of
difference between recommending action and actually making the
decision and assuming responsibility for it. In switching from centralization to decentralization, therefore, provision must be made
for training. Perhaps the best way is through the gradual allocation
of additional responsibilities, with regular checks on performance
to make sure that existing responsibilities have been absorbed
successfully before new ones are added.

2. Nature of the Company's Business

There are a number of cost factors peculiar to the particular
company which, when present, tend to increase the delegation of
decision-making.

a. *The flux of company growth.* There may be an early period
of widespread freedom of decision-making when the chief executive has to wrestle with the problems of growth and change and
is forced to delegate many of his decisions. Once a state of equilibrium is achieved, or a considerable body of tradition has been
built up, the chief executive may have time to devote himself to
the policies and problems of a more stable business. At this point
formalization and central controls may be imposed.

b. *Growth by acquisition of properties.* When a company's
growth is brought about by consolidation of several previously
independent units or acquisition of additional units, the newly
acquired properties may be left alone—especially when the ac-
quiring company is profitable and makes it a practice to let everyone go on as before, working out coordination and controls
gradually.

On the other hand, the first tendency on the part of the acquir-
ing company may be to impose an increased degree of centralization in an endeavor to reap the economies of increased scale of
operation. Here the process toward decentralization may be

worked out only gradually as the executives become overburdened and find it more economical to divest themselves of details.

c. *Geographical dispersion.* The more widely apart the location of company branches, offices and warehouses, the greater the need to delegate decisions, because of the difficulty, expense and delay of centralized decision-making. Such dispersion of some of the company units may be required because of the need for proximity to sources of raw materials (mining and oil companies, steel producers) or proximity to customers (retail stores). It should be emphasized that geographical dispersion does not necessarily result in delegation of decision-making. For instance, in a number of overseas operations studied in this AMA survey, head offices in the United States formulated in great detail working hours, employment standards, etc., even though local customs and manpower resources were quite different from those in the United States. In some instances, even small expenditures could not be incurred unless checked with United States headquarters.

d. *Diversity of production.* The small decision-making unit tends to be more economical and hence characteristic of industries in which fashion and design changes are frequent. Again, there are important decision-making delegations in those industries in which conditions of production vary so much that important decisions must be made at frequent intervals, as in coal mining, building, and some segments of the textile industry.

e. *Standardization.* Conversely, decision-making can be delegated more readily where manufacturing and selling specifications are standardized. Within the framework of centralized policies, administration and execution may well be decentralized. A degree of centralization is frequently maintained through central coordinating committees or central control to check on the efficiency of operations.

f. *Legal factors.* In many forms of legally permissible combinations, broad-scale powers of decision-making may have to be delegated in order to induce participating companies to agree to the combination, with the centralized decision-making confined merely to central price or output control as in export combinations or central quota allocations. On the other hand, there may be a good deal of centralized control over a subsidiary company, even though it is set up as a separate legal entity (e.g., to facilitate trading in some other country).

3. Economic Trends

There are two major types of economic trends which may lead to decentralization:

a. *Expansion of business activity.* The expansion of company activities, because of the general upward movement of the business cycle or the company's own long-term growth, tends to lead to decentralization. For the rise in activity increases the number of decisions with no direct effect on the decision-making capacity of top management. Paralleling company expansion, there tends to be a continuing delegation of the less important decisions.

b. *Decline of competition.* There is a tendency to decentralize as the degree of competition is reduced and the company dominates particular markets, for this is usually accompanied by an increase in company size. Further, the increase in company security and prosperity may make "experimentation" more feasible —and decentralization is often regarded in just that light.

The reverse tendencies may be noted in times of business decline and as competition becomes sharper. Top executives tend to feel that their personal influence and experience are especially needed in such emergencies. As a result, centralized controls are imposed to obtain cost reductions, uniform standards, improved methods of operation, fewer mistakes, checks on expenditure and follow-ups on execution. Staff specialist positions created to provide staff services to local branches are often cut in times of depression. Thus many organizations revert gradually to centralization in periods of retrenchment. Examples can be cited of many companies that alternately centralize and decentralize with depression and prosperity.

4. Political Trends and Philosophy

Political considerations involving important monetary and social costs may be factors in decentralization for such reasons as the following:

a. *Avoidance of "over-concentration."* There is a pronounced trend in corporation policy to avoid overly heavy concentration in one particular area. Originally such policy was promoted by the fear of the consequences for local communities when local branches were forced to make heavy employment cutbacks. Thus the General Electric Company, for example, limits its employment in any one community to a certain percentage of the employable population.

Another motive in escaping over-concentration is to avoid labor-relations problems. In this category falls the attempt of some companies to split up and move away parts of their large plants from areas where management believes that union leaders are potential and sometimes very active disturbers of the peace.

At the present time *fear of war* is leading to plant dispersion, largely in heavy goods production, but also in the dispersal of head office personnel.

Another major barrier to over-concentration is, of course, the *anti-trust legislation*.

It should be noted that these dispersals of plants and activities are usually accompanied by some delegation of decision-making.

b. *Economic concessions* may be obtained by opening up branches in certain states and foreign countries and some decentralization may follow from the attempt to gain local cost advantages.

c. There may be a long-run underlying trend toward a return to small scale units and autonomy because of the failures and heavy social costs of bureaucracy; this may have a powerful influence on business thinking and action.

5. Management Philosophy

In many companies the nature of top management philosophy has a profound influence on the nature of decision-making. Over the years an increasing number of companies have adopted decentralization of decision-making as a basic method of organization. These companies include very large units like General Motors, Ford, Sears, Roebuck, du Pont, International Harvester, General Electric, and others, and medium-large companies such as Sylvania Electric Products, Inc., Sperry Corporation, and American Brake Shoe Company. The top-management philosophy of these financially successful companies has done much to convince other executives that the adoption of decentralization may be helpful to the economic position of their company. Typical of this thinking is the statement of General Wood, Chairman of the Board of Sears, Roebuck and Co.: "We complain about government in business, we stress the advantages of the free enterprise system, we complain about the totalitarian state, but in our industrial organizations, in our striving for efficiency, we have created more or less of a totalitarian organization in industry—particularly in large industry. The problem of retaining efficiency and discipline in these large organizations and yet allowing our people to express themselves, to exercise initiative and to have some voice in the affairs of the organization is the greatest problem for large industrial organizations to solve."

Deeply ingrained in this top management philosophy is the belief in the efficacy of the small society, where there is close personal understanding and teamwork. This was stressed by the president of a large company in an answer to a question by the author as to the optimum size of the industrial unit, from the standpoint of good industrial relations. He declared that it should not be larger than 2,500 people. Such a small unit may make possible a better accomplishment of the company's economic and social objectives.

The small semi-autonomous unit also gives a much better opportunity for all-round executive development. Many of the present leaders of industry got their management training in small companies. To provide this training for leadership and initiative for their successors many high executives favor small units of operation. It is said that some large corporations maintain several small plants at least partly for the purpose of executive development. Similarly, "Multiple-Management" and "Bottom-up Management" stem from top management's belief in continuous executive development through participation. As L. F. McCollum, President of the Continental Oil Company, put it, in explaining his company's plan for decentralization (1950): "Probably the best part of the entire plan centers on the opportunity which will be given to all of you to do the job which you know best how to. It will give you more latitude, and it has always been my intention to do that."

There is also a desire to link managerial efforts more closely to results, as in the days of the small, independent entrepreneur. These conditions can be reproduced more easily in small, semi-autonomous units. At the same time, this makes possible greater comparability of results from one unit to another.

Finally, there is a growth of social responsibility in which many recognize the desirability of some kind of participation on the part of employees and perhaps consumer and financial interests.

6. Personality

The personalities in a business enterprise are an obvious factor in determining the degree of decentralization. Foremost, of course, is the personality of the chief executive. If he is able to combine policy-making with detailed supervision and control, if he is able to maintain close contact with many of his subordinates, if his intentions can be communicated easily or are known from long experience, the result of all this is likely to be a high degree of centralization. On the other hand, the chief executive may prefer to delegate a large part of his responsibilities, in order to concentrate on one or two functions in which he is superior to anyone else. The guiding criterion is that of "comparative advantage," that is, those responsibilities should be exercised by the chief executive in which he has the greatest relative advantage compared to the other executives. Of course, what is best from an economic standpoint is likely to be modified by the dictates of power, status and irrationality.

The extent of delegation will also be determined by the competence of the company's executives and their attitudes toward the chief executive. They will be more likely to succeed in their delegated responsibilities if they are assured that top management has confidence in them. Management can best show this confidence by giving them the opportunity and the training necessary to make decisions themselves, and by tolerating a certain number of mistakes which are inevitable at the beginning. The degree of decentralization is thus a function of ability and trust on the part of delegant and delegee.

7. *Type of Management Function*

Finally, the degree of decentralization depends on the nature of the management function concerned. It is difficult to generalize on this point because the nature and importance of the major management functions and of their relationship to one another vary from company to company, and individual circumstances dictate the degree of centralization which is desirable. However, in the course of the AMA study, it was observed that the financial function is usually much less decentralized than most or all other management functions in a company. At the other extreme, delegation of decision-making in the field of sales management appears to be more widespread than in any other major business function. Major decisions of the personnel function, on the other hand, tend to be highly centralized in many companies because management regards its people as its greatest asset, because the ratio of labor cost to total costs is high, and/or because contractual relations with the union dictate the desirability of heavily centralizing certain types of decision-making. A number of specific case examples illustrating how decision-making has been delegated in various functions under a variety of circumstances are detailed in Appendix C.

CONCLUSION

Delegation of decision-making is more widespread today than it was 10 years ago. There is hardly any type of decision, except those involving major financial questions, which has not been delegated by the chief executive of some company covered in the AMA study. A number of companies have also gone very far in delegating decision-making down the management hierarchy, some of them with notable success.

These observations do not mean, however, that delegation of decision-making is in any way as widely practiced as this discussion of decentralization might suggest. Despite all the talk we hear about decentralization and the delegation of decision-making, an examination of the actual activities of chief executives discloses that they continue to make most or all major decisions, either directly or through a formal framework of strict rules, checks and balances, informal instructions, and through mental compulsion on the part of subordinates to act as the boss would act. Chief executives also make final decisions on matters which are relatively or absolutely unimportant. An amusing commentary on the centralization of minutiae appeared on the wall of the janitor's broom closet in a small station of one of our railroads, where a frustrated employee posted this inscription: "Before emptying trash cans, wire Omaha for approval."

Many additional examples could be cited. These may sound incredible, but they are not unrepresentative:

In several large companies the chief executive insists on approving all purchases over $2,500.

At many companies all salary changes for those earning above $4,000 or $5,000 must be approved by the president. Sometimes this is done to prevent any unjustified applications for salary increases.

In a number of small companies the chief executive insists on opening all the mail himself and signing all the replies.

In many large companies the president must pass on every public appearance, however small the audience, of every member of management and approve whatever he may say.

Frequently any grievance that is at all unusual must be presented to the top echelon; any grievance settlement costing money may have to be approved by a vice president.

General managers of sizable divisions must go to headquarters for capital expenditures above a few hundred dollars, even if these are budgeted. This may, of course, be done to prevent piling up of many small expenditures.

Company presidents must approve the transfer of all production workers in a number of fairly large companies.

Every suggestion award, no matter what size, must be approved by the company president in a number of companies.

Why is Decentralization Resisted?

Among the reasons for the resistance to decentralization the following may be mentioned:

1. *Tradition.* The business grew up under one-man direction and remained so.

2. *Necessity.* Hard times require close personal supervision.

3. *Expense.* Delegation of decisions may be costly. There is the

cost of training and making mistakes on the part of junior executives. Duplication of functions may be costly—e.g., in addition to one central personnel department, personnel men have to be set up part-time or full-time in all the branches. Their talents may not be fully utilized. Moreover, there may be friction, jealousy, lack of uniformity on the part of semi-independent and divergent divisions.

4. *Power*. Delegation seems to imply a loss of power and control, dependency on others. Centralized power, on the other hand, may seem to suggest unlimited personal capacity, with complete lack of dependency on anyone else.

5. *Prestige*. Delegation may entail a loss of status.

6. *Contact*. The competition within the company to get the president's ear, the need for contact with top people *outside* the company—both make for centralization.

7. *Ideas*. Finally, the power of vested ideas may well be stronger than the power of vested economic interests. It is hard for the one man in control to jettison all his intellectual investments.

We must concede, therefore, that even though the distribution of power and decision-making may be desirable, many obstacles lie in the path of its accomplishment.

Part II

The Mechanics of
Organization

I. Introduction

THIS section will deal with the mechanics of organization—the actual processes or methods of creating and changing the company's organization structure. The problem is essentially that of best utilizing the people and resources presently on hand, as contrasted with the building up of an organization from scratch, described in Part I.

In some cases the changes may represent just one part of a general improvement program. Such steps as the following, for example, will generally affect the organization structure:

Establishment of authority limitations

Establishment of salary ranges

Drawing up of a personnel inventory (list of executives, showing their abilities and skills, ages, experience, data on possible promotions) and establishment of an executive replacement policy

Establishment of a program of executive development

Then there are other aspects of general improvement which may affect the organization structure (though not necessarily):

Analysis, improvement and formalization of company policies (possible impact on upper organization levels)

Establishment and improvement of company procedures (possible impact on lower organization levels)

Establishment of controls (may affect basic organization structure, as at Koppers)

171

Changes in long-range plans or forecasts (may affect basic structure)

Introduction of management and organization audits (may reveal organization deficiencies)

Development of a uniform approach to improvement planning (may necessitate organization planning)

The changes and improvements in the organization structure itself may involve anything from a complete overhaul of the entire company to adjustments of only a single series of functions or a single function or position. It should be pointed out here that most organization specialists believe that organization planning is a *continuing* job; that the complete reorganization—assuming it is needed—is only the first step, since there must be continual modification and adjustment as the business grows and changes.

The actual steps in the process, however, can best be explained by describing them as they are undertaken in a complete reorganization, and for the sake of clarity this study will deal with them on that basis. The steps are much the same in all cases.

This study is intended as a guide for those who are contemplating complete and company-wide reorganization, it is true. But it is hoped also that those who are making less far-reaching changes—and those who are interested mainly in identifying and codifying their present structures—will find it helpful. "Reorganization" as it is used here is merely a convenient shorthand term for any and all changes in the company organization.

II. Deciding to Reorganize

Probably the most frequent reason for a major change of company structure is a change of top executives. Usually a *new chief executive* will survey and analyze his organization. His capacity to supervise, his working habits, his field of specialization, his relationships to the other executives may be so different from those of his predecessor as to require a complete overhaul of the structure. In any case, changes may be made sooner or later because newcomers are brought in with him or because the change at the top brings resignations. Shifts in the organization structure may result also from retirements, deaths, quits, and the hiring of new *major executives*.

Acquisition or sale of major properties, plants or companies may lead to a partial reorganization. Too often little is decided in advance about the nature of organization changes save, in some instances, the disposition of top managerial jobs. Again, changes in the *product line, technology, processes* or *human relationships* (who gets along with whom) may lead to important changes in the organization.

A shift in *economic trends* may be another cause. Companies subject to seasonal and erratic fluctuations may have elastic structures with frequent reorganizations. Executives may be shifted among jobs and incompetent men eliminated periodically. Business cycle fluctuations may lead to a tightening of the organization in times of economic decline and increased competition—

173

for example, greater centralization may be introduced in order to provide closer control over decisions and results, or the span of control increased to save manpower, and some staff posts eliminated to save money.

Also of influence are the *commonly accepted ideas on organization* and the practices of outstanding companies, both of which may change over the very long run, either in response to changed conditions or as a result of new knowledge. For example, the shift from owner-management to hired management has led to major changes in organization practices. Again, one-man control is no longer as widespread as it used to be now that the values of executive participation in top decision-making have become more widely accepted and belief in the effectiveness of decentralization is fairly widespread. The changed role of the staff specialist further illustrates how changed thinking on organization has profoundly influenced company structure. But the interval between original conception and wide adoption may be prolonged, e.g., the General Motors ideal of "decentralized operations with centralized control" took over 25 years to gain much acceptance.

Finally, a change in organization may be undertaken because it is felt that there are deficiencies in the company which may be indicative of poor organization. A list of such deficiencies might include the following (taken in part from one compiled by an AMA seminar group on organization under the leadership of Marvin Bower, Senior Partner, McKinsey & Co.):

1. Slowness in decision-making and in carrying out decisions (too many "channels," too much "paper pushing").
2. Frequent and serious errors in decision-making.
3. Delegation of various decisions to executives who lack knowledge of the phases of the business affected.
4. Inadequate communication.
5. Bottlenecks in production, finance, etc.; failure to meet delivery schedules.
6. Decision-making overly decentralized with consequent lack of uniformity in policies; or, at the other extreme, over-centralized decision-making to preserve uniformity of policies.
7. "Below-par" executives—turnover, absenteeism, high sick-

ness incidence, nervous tension, overwork, under-utilization, general dissatisfaction.

8. Inadequate long-range planning and research, lack of new ideas.
9. Interdepartmental and personality clashes.
10. Poor balancing and meshing of the different departments.
11. Staff-line conflicts.
12. Excessive span of control.
13. Poor control, lack of knowledge of results, poor compliance.
14. Inefficient committe work.
15. Lack of clear-cut objectives.

A Word of Caution

Having devoted so much space to the reasons for changing the organization, we hasten to add that in each case one should carefully consider possible reasons for avoiding it. There is a great deal of wisdom in the old proverb, "Let sleeping dogs lie." Change is always disturbing, however good its purposes may be. People fear what they no not understand fully. And sometimes their fears are justified. Changes may be made at the wrong time, in the wrong way; they may hit carefully established and smoothly working informal patterns. Let these warnings be underscored by another admonition: "Look before you leap." Too often the decision to reorganize is based merely on a hankering for "order" or "procedure," or simply on the human desire for a change.

III. Gaining Acceptance of the Decision to Reorganize

T HE *impetus* for reorganization usually comes from some one person or source. It may come through pressure from the board of directors, a top official or, more frequently, a group of top vice presidents. Or the vice president in charge of finance may insist on the need for cutting costs through reorganization. Or the production chief may complain about the undermining of his authority by staff specialists. The impetus may also come from outside— the pressure from banks and creditors, the advice of a consultant, the insistence of a governmental procurement agency, the pressure of a competitor. In some cases the idea may be planted by a chance remark to the chief executive, by a paper delivered at an association meeting or an article in a business magazine.

But unless the necessity for change is obvious, the insiders or outsiders may have to spend much time and effort to persuade the influential executives of the need for altering the existing organization. The chief executive may have to be convinced that such action would be desirable and he usually must take into account the opinions of his chief subordinates. Therefore, *it may be necessary to demonstrate the need for change.* A most effective way usually is to cite the example of another successful company in the same industry or an outstanding company in another field. Of course, what helps one company does not necessarily help another company with a different personnel setup. Nevertheless, a good example is a powerful argument—sometimes the only one.

It may also be helpful to draw up a bill of particulars, listing the major reasons for organization changes, pointing up the major deficiencies, and detailing the arguments in support of the recommended changes. Such a document should, of course, avoid references to personalities and contain no expressed or implied threats.

Sometimes it may be necessary to take a roundabout approach in order to get reorganization under way. For example, charts may be prepared to show the ages of the top executives, the number of years each is expected to remain in the company, and the possible replacements. This may reveal an urgent need for reorganization. Another indicator may be the poor health of several major executives.

Whatever the means of persuasion used, it is best to have the proposal for reorganization finally come from the important executives themselves. They will give it much better support as a consequence.

Once the support of the important executives is assured, it then may become necessary to obtain formal support from the *board of directors*. If it is a working board, members are likely to be more receptive if approached individually than if they receive the full impact of the idea all at once in a formal meeting. A nonworking board is quite likely to agree with the proposals, provided the reasoning and presentation appear to be well-founded. Usually the board will be impressed with the president's new plans. In a company which has a *management committee* or a group of top executives meeting regularly, the proposed organization change might be presented to that body in more detail than to the board, and a more extensive question and discussion period provided both for these executives and others.

Withholding Announcement

However, these detailed efforts to gain acceptance for reorganization cannot always be undertaken. Time may be short. The anticipated resistance may appear insurmountable. It may be considered undesirable to stir up questions, fear, and opposition before the changes are even started. Against this must be weighed the possibility that the news may leak out through the "grapevine" and create even more apprehension and passive resistance than if it were announced.

IV. Assigning the Job

SEVERAL considerations must be taken into account in assigning the task of reorganization. Major questions to be settled are:

a. Should an individual or a group be assigned the responsibility?

b. To what extent, if any, should the executives of the company participate in the work?

c. Should use be made of a consultant?

Individual vs. Group Responsibility

Changing the organization is a difficult job. It requires a great deal of skill and experience. The administration, analysis, and execution of a reorganization program are a continuous task, and a group of people all on the same level can perform it only with great difficulty and expenditure of time. Therefore it is advisable to assign the actual process of formulating the organization plan to one individual and provide him, if necessary, with assistants with special qualifications.

The man who heads the reorganization work should be one whose experience has been wide enough to give him an over-all knowledge of the major management functions and their interrelationships. The reorganizer must be able to differentiate between major and minor functions and put each in its proper place. In the case of some functions, he must know which outside sources, if any, can perform them. He must know the key relations to look for; for example, certain types of engineering can be combined in the automobile industry but not in the steel industry. He must be able to take account of the influence of personalities. He must be able to sell his ideas and to carry the company's executives along in such a way that they feel that the final plan is their own and accept it without reservation. Practical knowledge of organization, personal objectivity and time to do the job properly are important qualifications—more important than technical or theoretical knowledge.

In smaller companies a top official—the treasurer, the controller, the industrial relations director, or the assistant to the president—may carry most of the load. These men possess authority, have a detailed knowledge of the company, and can often handle the job on a part-time basis with only clerical assistance. The larger firm may employ a full-time specialist, perhaps as head of an organization and procedures department or a control group. Such a man and his assistants generally possess a combination of theoretical and practical knowledge of organization planning; often they know a good deal about the functioning of the company.

Many authorities believe that organization matters should be considered by the top echelon in management, preferably in the president's office. For where the organization specialist reports down the line, he may not be free to come forward with the answers he would really like to give.

However, no single department head or specialist can assume the responsibility for setting basic policies and deciding between possible alternatives. This power may be, and often should be, reserved to the chief executive; but it is in this connection that the contribution a group can make should be considered. Many companies do, in fact, use committees of higher management to obtain information and opinion basic to the improvement of the organization, or at least to communicate and coordinate decisions affecting organization. For example, at the Line Material Company, of Milwaukee, Wis. (3,500 employees), a committee on organization consisting of top executives met once a week to review progress and to make final decisions on various phases of the job as they were completed.

Several advantages are inherent in the use of such a committee. First, key department heads participate in the planning aspects of the program. Second, the committee work results in greater recognition of the value of administrative functions. And, finally, it creates "procedure consciousness" at the top organization levels. Having several sympathetic ears at the top is a factor in gaining acceptance of new administrative ideas throughout the company.

The criteria for selecting such a group may be illustrated by a description of the Administrative Engineering Planning Committee of the American Enka Corporation given to the AMA survey by J. B. Joynt, Manager, of the company's Administrative Engineering Department. This committee is responsible for the development of plans for improving administrative functions throughout the company, for establishing the order in which needed improvements will be tackled, and for determining general approaches. But it does not study or review individual procedures; that is the responsibility of the department heads concerned.

The Enka committee is composed of the heads of the following staff departments:

1. Controllership
2. Industrial relations
3. Purchasing
4. Traffic
5. Engineering
6. Industrial engineering
7. Administrative engineering (Chairman)

These particular department heads were selected because: (1) they carry heavy administrative and procedural responsibilities; (2) they exercise staff supervision over nearly all the functions in the plants where procedures are an important part of the job; (3) there is a close procedural relationship between the various departments they supervise.

Participation by Executives Generally

In addition to the question of over-all committee planning and review, there is the problem of deciding whether or not executives generally should be interviewed on some aspects of the reorganization. Much difference of opinion exists on this point.

If time appears to be of the essence, if it is felt necessary to keep the plan secret, if the very size of the problem seems to be a deterrent, then there may be no participation at all. Some executives, however, feel very strongly that, to be effective, any organization change "must have executive participation and acquiescence." If the process of changing the organization is concerned with an examination of the present organization structure, its shortcomings and possible improvements, the data will probably be more reliable and comprehensive if they are obtained through participation of executives. Even if nothing of direct value were so obtained (which is doubtful because the people on the job often know more about it than anyone else, especially about its informal relationships), the very fact that executives are informed of what is going on and are asked for their opinions may help to enlist their support for the change. This has also the advantage of leaving within the organization unit one or several members of the survey team who have been in on all the discussions and reviewed the facts leading to the final recommendations. A change in organization which is imposed on executives may remain just that. Even the most rigorous autocracy cannot impose its will on people without inspiring strong feelings of resistance.

When participation has been decided on, some companies start the process of reorganization by giving a course in the principles and methods of organization, which may take from one day to a week. If, for example, the office management function is to be re-examined, then the principles of office management organization are taught, other companies' office management departments are visited, etc. A temporary organization committee is set up. This committee in turn instructs all employees in organizational matters.[1] The actual number of executives interviewed depends on the time and money available, the importance of the problem, the approach (company or departmental reorganization), and the expected results. Because of the expense, only a representative sample, or the three top tiers of executives, may be interviewed

[1] C. Tarras Sallfors, "Principles of Organization and Management as Applied to Public Administration." A paper given before the Eighth International Management Congress, Stockholm, 1947, Vol. I, pp. 503-504.

at any length—for the rest there may be merely courtesy interviews.

Use of Outside Consultants

Outside consultants in organization work frequently have
greater and more varied experience than the inside executive.
From other organization jobs they can bring accumulated knowledge, recommend valuable procedures, point out the pitfalls to
be avoided, and introduce time-saving methods. They have more
time to devote to the organization job than do executives who
are burdened with day-to-day work. The consultant may be more
objective, better able to concentrate on one problem. He may be
in a position to furnish skilled manpower. Often, too, he can ex-
pose an idea which might be undiplomatic for an insider to mention. Criticism of shortcomings known to everyone inside the
organization may be accepted with better grace when made by an
outsider. For the same reason the outside consultant may do a
better job of selling the reorganization plan to the executives.

The consultant may merely guide the process of organization
at the start, or recommend the major steps to be taken; he may
critically analyze the finished plan; he may initiate the work himself and go through all the necessary procedures to the completion
of the plan; finally he may "sell" the plan to the executives and
aid the company during the transition period. Or he may be a
counselor and listener to the chief executive, advising on broad
and long-run organization problems.

The success of the consultant's work will depend to some extent
on the backing and time top management gives him, on the cooperation from executives generally (the one-shot proposition
enforced on an unwilling management usually ends up in a
drawer), on the amount of time which he can spend on organizational problems, the extent of free discussion, the degree of his
independence from company personalities and political influences, the prior indoctrination of executives, and especially on the
problems left for the day-to-day administration of his plan.

The consultant's success will also depend on his timing and
discretion, on his frankness and adaptability, his adherence to
what he believes to be right. Particularly important, of course, is
his "human relations" sense.

The decision to hire a consultant will depend on the funds available (companies in a high excess profits tax bracket may find a consultant less expensive than his fee might suggest). It will also depend somewhat on the size of the company. It is more likely that organizational talent will be available in the larger company —the larger the company the more likely that it will have a department of organization or methods. In the larger companies it is also possible to get some of the benefits of an outside consultant by appointing a member of the head office staff to reorganize a branch, or an organization specialist in manufacturing to aid sales reorganization—in other words, to use the so-called "outside insider." (As a guide in the selection of management consultants see Joel Dean, *The Management Counsel Profession,* Indiana University, Bloomington, Ind., 1940; *Business Consultants—Their Uses and Limitations,* prepared by A. H. Dunn, III, for the Controllership Foundation, New York, 1950.)

If it has been decided to make organization changes and to hire outside consultants, both these events might be announced simultaneously. As an example, the reorganization announcement by L. F. McCollum, President of the Continental Oil Company, to all the company's executives illustrates a possible approach:

> Our plan of organization is an important factor in the successful operation of our business. We have given this subject a great deal of attention, as you know, and we have made some changes in our organization plan during the last year or two which I am convinced represent substantial progress in this respect.
>
> Our organization is a relatively large one, however, and has many separate units operating in widely scattered areas. It is difficult for me, or for any of our executives, to devote the time and attention necessary to study all aspects of our organization in order to make certain that it is right in every detail. We feel, though, that such a study should be made. Under the circumstances, the Management Committee, after careful consideration of the problem, has decided that the most practical solution is to ask a firm of management consultants who are specialists in this field to review our organization. The firm which has been selected to do this work is the .... Company.
>
> As a first step in their work, it will be necessary for them to obtain a clear understanding of how our organization is now set

up and how it operates. The best way for them to get a good
general picture of our present organization is to ask each of you
to provide a description of your duties and responsibilities and
your understanding of your limits of authority and relationship to
other organizational units. Consequently, you are requested to
fill in the questionnaire which is attached to this letter and send
it to Mr. .... at the .... Company. Please mail
your questionnaires so that they will be received not later than
July 20.

Sometime in the course of the next few weeks a representative
of consulting firm will talk with you personally. Please give any
information requested or which you think may be helpful. I want
to urge everyone to be completely frank and outspoken in his discussion with our consultants. Only by working with them on this
basis can they do their job most efficiently and be of maximum
assistance to us in this matter.

V. Timing the Organization Change

Reorganization may be a one-time change, a change over a short period of time, or a long-run gradual, continuing change.

The "Earthquake Approach"

The AMA survey found the one-time change, sometimes dubbed the "earthquake approach," to be the most frequent in organizational work. It is usually undertaken by a group of a few men; it often entails radical alterations; and it is announced and put into effect almost simultaneously.

Frequently, though not necessarily, of course, it coincides with the arrival of a new chief executive or the appointment of an inside or outside organization counsel or expert. The new president may find that the organization "suit" of his predecessor does not fit him at all. For example, there may be too many people reporting to him, too much centralization, too many old-fashioned practices. The new inside organization expert may feel he must justify his appointment by finding a great many shortcomings and making radical changes. Similarly, the outside consultant may feel he must earn his fee by making a display of fireworks. Since he is hired for a brief period, he may feel he has to crowd all his work into a "quickie" proposal and show immediate results. Under such circumstances, only those who belong to the "inner circle" may have an opportunity to work their way up on the executive ladder in the frequent redrawing of the organization chart.

As an example of the "earthquake approach" we may cite the announcement of organization changes sent to all subsidiaries by the president of one large company. He took them completely by surprise, saying that the changes would be effective the next day at 10 a.m.—except for those who wished a one-way ticket to New York to complain to him. No one took the offer, but the changes were never effective because of the silent sabotage of his executives.

This one-time reorganization may turn out to be destructive of harmonious, sensitive relationships, built up laboriously over the years. Such a reorganization may result in loss of security for many able executives, loss of men who can move elsewhere, restraint of free expression, damage to prestige, and a widespread break in morale. It is a radical operation, performed without an anesthetic.

Short-Run Plan

The short-run approach spreads the organization changes over a period of time, roughly from six months to three years. Usually changes in the organization are substantial and are introduced all at one time. However, the advance study of the organization structure tends to be quite thorough, and executives are consulted about their organizational relationships and their suggestions for improvement. The changes are introduced and carefully explained in meetings, through guide books and films. Opportunity for discussion and amendment is provided.

Sometimes this short-period approach leads to a short-run plan which embodies only those changes which are absolutely necessary, frequently because of personality problems. At the same time, a long-run plan may be drawn up to guide the company over the years toward an ideal organization.

Long-Run Plan

The long-run plan is made for a period of more than three years. It is frequently drawn up on the basis of executive consultation, though it may be revealed only gradually if some of top management's plans are not to be disclosed. The ideal plan may be broken down into several subsidiary ones, providing for various stages of growth or sizes and differing cyclical and financial conditions. Under this "gradualist" approach changes are introduced slowly, as deaths and retirements occur. In addition, the plan and the changes are reviewed constantly to improve, to refine, to modify, to clear indistinct areas, to eliminate overlapping, and to explain matters which may be misunderstood. Under this system, organizational change is a never-ending process as conditions change, but it is designed to create as few upsets as possible and to lead to as high a degree of cooperation as possible.

The basic steps in making organization changes are the same, however, in any case. The first part of the job is to examine the present organization—define company objectives, relate the basic characteristics of the business to organization, describe the existing structure and the existing relationships in detail. The second part is the construction of the ideal organization.

VI. Defining the Present Organization

T HE first step in reorganization work—and one that has a marked influence on all the others—is to define company objectives. (The nature of these objectives has been indicated in Part I, Stage I.) Suppose, for example, that a policy of product diversification has been decided on. Organizationally this will mean that the product division may be the primary division of work, or at least the prevalent division in production and sales activities. Another organizational consequence is that staff functions may be held to a minimum and centralization emphasized as long as the high extra costs of adding new lines are not covered by additional revenue. Similarly, the span of control may have to be reduced as the attention required by diversification increases. The organizational consequences of other basic company objectives may be traced in a similar fashion.

At Sylvania Electric Products, Inc., for example, the basic company objective of decentralization has led to the establishment of separate small organizations in rural areas. The English Rolls-Royce Company continued to decide all policy problems of the American Rolls-Royce Company. For example, it limited the size of the American production organization in order to maintain quality standards.

Basic Characteristics of the Business

The type of man who heads the business always exercises a profound influence on the organization structure. Thus the organi-

188

zation is likely to be highly centralized where the chief executive is highly energetic, where he is distrustful, where there is a high degree of formality, where initiative is not encouraged. The background and experience of the leading personalities will in part determine the functions on which they concentrate and those which they will delegate. A second characteristic is basic technology. Where production and sales are local, as in the cement and building products industries, organization may be geographical. Where products are sold through entirely different channels, organization may be product-oriented. Where traffic or legal considerations are of major importance, these functions may have large staffs, importantly placed in the organization. In oil companies, for example, sales offices are frequently separated from the rather inaccessible sources of supplies in depopulated areas. The number and content of management functions determines the nature and degree of delegation and the span of control. When there is a multiplicity of functions and much technical knowledge required to exercise them, delegation and independence down the line will almost always be required.

Third, the economies of the scale of production determine the degree of concentration of activities in one location and the length of the chain of command.

Fourth, a favorable financial position with large surplus funds and little competition may permit a rather loose, informal organization structure or a much more elaborate organization structure than might otherwise be justifiable.

Describing the Existing Organization Structure

A description of the current organization may already exist in the form of an organization chart and organization manual. Or it may be possible to construct the picture from existing records, announcements of the chief executive, orders from various management representatives, written procedures, and job descriptions. Any or all of the information may be obtained by questionnaire or by interview. The questionnaire method is much less expensive and less time-consuming. If it is used, it is preferable that the information requested be brief and factual. On the other hand, the interview method may yield a good deal more information, may bring out the "feel" of the situation and uncover vital information about the informal organization and the human relations factors involved. The cost of the interview may be considerably reduced by concentrating on representative cases only. In analyzing results, it should be borne in mind that with both the questionnaire and the interview there may be language difficulties, misunderstandings and lack of free disclosure, and that these dangers are greater in the case of a questionnaire.

The following is an example of a questionnaire that has been used to obtain information for the purposes of reorganization, resulting in fairly detailed disclosure. (It was accompanied by the announcement of organization changes. This explanation should be passed on from one level of management to another, preferably orally if that is company practice.)

ABC COMPANY

ORGANIZATION QUESTIONNAIRE TO EXECUTIVES*

1. Your name
2. Your department
3. Your division
4. Title or name of your position
5. Your location
6. To whom do you report?
7. Title or name of the position of the immediate supervisor
8. Give the names and titles (or names of positions) of those who report to you.

 In (6) and (8) a distinction might be made of the types of actions which must be reported: (a) actions reported before they take place; (b) after they take place; and (c) those which need not be reported at all.

9. Describe fully the responsibilities of your position as you understand them to be at present. (As part of this description you should also include your existing responsibilities and relationships with other units within your division and with other divisions of the Company, with affiliates and with any outside service agencies.)

10. What is the extent of your authority
 (a) For establishing policy?
 (b) For incurring expense?
 (c) For personnel changes including selection, promotion, termination and compensation?

* Sufficient white space is left for detailed answers in the original document.

11. Indicate any committees in the Company or trade groups of which you are a member. If you are chairman, include a description of the purpose, scope of activities and accomplishments of your committee.
12. List by name or title the regular reports which (a) you receive and (b) you prepare, and indicate whether daily, weekly, monthly, etc.
13. List the basic records you are responsible for keeping.
14. Mention anything else of interest in understanding your responsibilities and activities, including any special problems needing attention, any suggestions for improvements or general comments on the over-all Company organizational structure.

At the American Enka Corporation two major approaches to organizational analysis are undertaken. First there is an inquiry to all departmental managers from the top down, covering identification of the major work processes and activities, and their breakdown into specific responsibilities, as well as the proper relationships between major organizational units. The second approach is from the bottom up, through a procedure study of the daily flow of documents between organization units. Alternately the lowest units in the hierarchy may be studied first and then the subsequent relationships further up, so as to build from the "grass roots" rather than incur the dangers of imposing the top management pattern. But this may be a wasteful method because objectives at this low level may be quite out of accord with those of top management. It is therefore a supplementary approach.

A much more elaborate method of describing executive jobs has been developed by Professor Sune Carlson of the University of Stockholm in Sweden.[2] It was evolved over a period of years in conjunction with twelve chief executives of non-competing Swedish firms. Each was "analyzed" over a period of weeks by a kind of "time study" of executive activities whereby every action of the chief executive was regularly recorded on a standardized questionnaire blank. This record was supplemented by interviews with and notes by the private secretary, the telephone ex-

[2] *Executive Behavior; A Study of the Work Load and the Working Methods of Managing Directors*, C. A. Stromberg Aktiebolag, Publisher, Stockholm, Sweden, 1951.

change operator and interviews with the chief executive himself.

In the analysis, Carlson classified executive activities under five major types of specialization, following Chester I. Barnard.[3] The nature of the executives' working habits may be summarized as follows:

1. *The place where the executive's work is done.* The executive's total working time during the investigation period (24 days) average:

	PERCENTAGE OF TOTAL TIME
Own office	35
Head office	12
Home plant	3
Somewhere inside the firm	6
Outside the firm on company business	36
At home	8
	100

2. *Contacts with persons and institutions.* A representative case showed the following distribution of activities in percentage of total working time during the investigation period:

	PERCENTAGE OF TOTAL TIME
Inside the firm	
Conferences	27
Working alone	10
Plant	9
Lunches	5
Visiting subordinates	5*
Outside the firm	
Conferences and visits	33
Traveling	3
Work at home	8
	100

[3] *The Functions of the Executive,* Harvard University Press, Cambridge, Mass., 1938, pp. 127-132.
* This low percentage suggests that a corresponding study made in America might produce widely different results.

It should be noted that the chief executive officer spent only one-tenth of his working time alone (the range was from 10 to 35 per cent). The median figure of average daily working time in the study was around 9¾ hours, and the individual figures varied between 8½ and 11½ hours.

Administrative deficiencies found by Professor Carlson in analyzing the distribution of the chief executive's working time included: excessive time spent on outside activities; lack of time for inspecting and visiting works and offices; lack of time for reading and contemplation; excessive nature of the total working load. Other subjects covered in Professor Carlson's study of top management's work habits included communication and executive decision-making and action.

Defining Existing Relationships

The fourth step in reorganization should consist of a reconstruction of existing organization relationships. This should be done principally on the basis of the information obtained through interviews, questionnaires and study of organization material. Missing links may have to be supplied by those in charge of the reorganization process. This aspect of the work may be limited merely to the drawing up of an organization chart. However, it might be supplemented by a written breakdown of job content, job relationships, comments and observations by executives. Those in charge of reorganization should at this point have a clear picture of the status quo. They should be aware of the major organization problems, such as duplication of activities, poor communication, lack of cooperation and other organization deficiencies discussed earlier.

VII. Construction of the Ideal Organization

Perhaps the most important step in the reorganization process is the construction of the "ideal" organization (the term "ideal" is not used here to mean "perfect" but the most desirable as contrasted with the existing organization). Construction of the ideal organization should embody the best thinking of those who have written on the subject and the best practices found in industry. Drawing on these sources, on their own personal background and experience, and on the comments of those participating in the survey, the reorganizers will seek to eliminate the shortcomings inherent in the existing organization structure.

Criteria of Sound Organization

The concept of the ideal organization is closely tied up with the "principles" of organization which have been developed over the last hundred years by many eminent thinkers and practitioners of management. Their purpose has been to guide others in reorganization as well as to develop sound organization practices. Few would question the desirability of using such guideposts, which are the result of the labors of many able men, rather than leaving reorganization to intuition, to the forces of the moment, and to the necessarily limited experience of the individuals who happen to be concerned with any particular situation and whose direct personal knowledge is necessarily limited.

The principles of organization have been attacked as "obvious," "unscientific," "dogmatic," as falsely representing "the one best way," as overestimating the rationality of people, as forcing executives into a straightjacket. Sometimes the critics are attacking strawmen, taking isolated statements out of context and imputing to them meanings that no responsible thinker ever intended. Rarely does the critic substitute anything better. Nor is there much proof that in the absence of principles one can rely solely on one's own experience and intuition. On this point history seems to have taught that "an irresolute general who acts without principles and without plan, even though he may lead an army numerically superior to that of the enemy, almost always finds himself inferior to the latter on the field of battle. Fumblings and the middle course lose all in war.[4]

Some of the criticism is justified. For, despite acknowledged authority of writers on organization, it is not maintained that the principles which they have evolved are necessarily applicable to every situation, or are "scientific" in the sense that they can be subjected to repeated proof; in human situations such repeated proof is seldom possible. Nor, it should be noted, has the problem of the interrelationship of the principles been solved. But the critics often fail to realize that those who formulated the principles of organization did not intend them to be as unchangeable as the laws of Moses. This was pointed out long ago by the great French thinker and successful industrialist, Henri Fayol, when he wrote that the soundness of a business "depends on a certain number of conditions termed indiscriminately principles, laws, rules. For preference I shall adopt the term 'principles' whilst disassociating it from any suggestion of rigidity, for there is nothing rigid or absolute in management affairs; it is all a question of proportion. Seldom do we have to apply the same principle twice in identical conditions; allowance must be made for different changing circumstances, for men just as different and changing, and for many other variable elements. Therefore principles are flexible and capable of adaption to every need; it is a matter of knowing how to make use of them, which is a difficult art requiring intelligence, experience, decision and proportion."[5]

4 Major Thomas R. Phillips, *Roots of Strategy,* The Military Service Publishing Company, Harrisburg, Pa., 1940, p. 434.
5 Henri Fayol, *General and Industrial Management,* Sir Isaac Pitman & Sons, Ltd., London, 1949, p. 19.

Note that Fayol emphasizes "principles" in the sense of "conditions" which are "flexible" and must be adapted to every need. The most important kind of knowledge about organization principles is the knowledge of how to apply them. The principles of organization are somewhat like common sense based on experience, which *may* help its possessor to arrive at a successful solution of his problems. Principles applied without common sense are as likely to fail in this field of endeavor as in any other. From our survey of reorganization it may be asserted that if used in Fayol's sense and with discretion, principles of organization may be helpful in designing the "ideal" organization structure. It should be noted, too, that most of the principles have been evolved by men with a good deal of practical organization experience.

There appears to be a high degree of unanimity among the leading writers of organization on the nature of the major principles of organization. This was brought out clearly in the brilliant synthesis of organization principles by Lt. Colonel L. Urwick in his article on "Principles of Management," in the *British Management Review.*[6] (A list of other books and papers dealing with the subject is included in the references at the end of this book.)

The term, "principles," as used in the foregoing discussion, refers to the criteria which the organization is designed to meet.

The AMA survey indicates that there are nine criteria which have been most frequently used in the process of reorganization. These will be discussed below, and an attempt will be made to indicate methods of testing them.

1. Effectiveness[7]

The criterion of effectiveness refers to the accomplishment of the purpose of the enterprise; it is therefore of a social and nonpersonal nature. It is designed to serve as a broad yardstick of the economic performance of the enterprise. It is concerned with the question of how well the organization meets the test of supplying goods and services. The primary standard is, of course, "fair" profit or net income, as a percentage of sales (current perform-

---

[6] Volume VII, No. 3, 1948, pp. 15-48.

[7] The following discussion of the criteria of "Effectiveness" and "Efficiency" has been adapted from Chester I. Barnard, *op. cit.,* p. 60.

ance) or capital invested (long-run performance) and, in some of the larger companies, percentage share of the market. Subsidiary criteria of the effectiveness of the organization include similar net income measures applied on a comparative basis to various sub-groups, such as plants, divisions, products, or managerial functions. To obviate over-reliance on a single measurement, multiple rations may be used, selected on the basis of consistency and magnitude of contribution.

The effectiveness of an individual function may be measured by computing the dollar expenditure per employee or the number of company employees per employee in that function. For instance, the personnel function in a number of large companies showed a personnel expenditure of $50 per employee and approximately one industrial relations employee for every 100 company employees.[8] These ratios may, however, be quite unreliable as guides.

Following the economist A. C. Pigou,[9] the product contribution of the organization to the community might be measured in terms of "social revenue" and "social costs"—i.e., by the income yield and expense to the community. For example, an organization change might, of itself, have adverse effects on employment in a local community. Recognizing this, management might substitute a new local activity, such as a research department, to compensate for the removal of its headquarters elsewhere. Management might also decide to pay the expenses of employees who will move to the new location, including any losses on the sale of their old homes and the purchase of new ones. These would be organizational contributions by the company to the community's social revenue. On the other hand, the abrupt abandonment of an industrial site might saddle the community with the costs of unemployment, unutilized buildings and other social burdens.

The effectiveness of an industrial function should be measured by comparing its contributions to company revenue against its costs. Thus a manufacturing division's costs (wages, salaries, share of overheads) would be compared to the value of product added.

[8] Ernest Dale, "Payroll Costs in Industrial Relations," MANAGEMENT NEWS, (AMA) October 31, 1949, p. 3.

[9] The Economics of Welfare, MacMillan and Co., Ltd., London, 1938, pp. 127-212.

The effectiveness of an organization department can be measured only partially in terms of its contributions to net company revenues—such as better decisions and cost reductions through conservation of manpower and reduction of errors. Its contributions in terms of morale and cooperation are hardly measurable. Measurements in terms of profitability are also likely to vary over time; for example, the immediate cost savings of the organization department might be lost in the long run through subsequent deterioration of teamwork and morale.

2. Efficiency

The criterion of efficiency requires the fulfillment of the personal and individual objectives of those who are connected with the enterprise. This definition, it should be noted, departs somewhat from general business usage. "Efficiency," used in this sense, rests on the premise that the company has met the criterion of effectiveness and can fulfill its financial obligations. Survival may also require that the business fulfill obligations of a broader nature.

Standards for measuring the efficiency of the organization, as defined here, have not yet been developed to a point where they can be accurately applied. However, some of the major considerations have been formulated. One of the best statements in this connection is that of J. M. Clark.[10]

Clearly, proper attention to the organization structure is essential to the fulfillment of the personal and individual objectives of all who are connected with the enterprise. In the case of executives, for example, a proper organization structure means clearcut lines of authority and responsibility, participation in policymaking, the right to be heard, the opportunity to develop to the full measure of their potentialities, and other conditions which contribute directly to their personal satisfaction as well as their individual effectiveness.

"Efficiency" is seen to be a rather vague criterion which differs as different personalities interpret it. For example, the chief of the enterprise may favor values which are not accepted by his subordinates. He may prefer autocracy for the sake of speedy and disciplined action, while subordinates may prefer greater partici-

[10] *Social Control of Business,* McGraw-Hill Book Company, New York, 1939, p. 220.

pation and a slower tempo. Different personalities also set different goals of effectiveness. One president may aim at maximizing the profits of his organization, another at "fair shares" for all parties connected with the enterprise, another at survival leading to maximum expansion or maximum employee satisfaction.

3. Division of Work

"The primary step in organization is to determine and to establish as separate entities, the smallest number of dissimilar functions into which the work of an institution may be divided."[11] The nature and number of the basic functions is determined by their relative importance in contributing directly to the purpose of the enterprise. Two basic functions in manufacturing business frequently are production and sales. In a retail business buying is a basic function, taking the place of production in an industrial concern. To these, finance, personnel and/or procurement are sometimes added. The importance of the other functions varies tremendously. Thus, advertising is a major function in the soap business, contributing very directly to the major purpose of the enterprise, namely sales. In some parts of agriculture advertising is a minor function since it has no perceptible influence on sales of products, such as wheat.

Auxiliary functions should be evolved in accordance with the factors considered in Stage I, "Formulation of Objectives—The Division of Work." Such auxiliary activities contribute to and/or facilitate the performance of the basic functions, but do not contribute directly to the purpose of the enterprise.

4. Functional Definition with Authority and Responsibility

The functions or job contents necessary to reach objectives must be defined. This step is governed by two precepts: (1) "Define duties clearly."[12] (2) "The work of each man in the management should be confined to the performance of a single leading function."[13]

Functional or job definition is elaborated as follows by Henri Fayol:

11 H. A. Hopf, *Organization, Executive Capacity and Progress,* Hopf Institute Of Management, Inc., Ossining, N. Y., 1945, p. 4.
12 Henri Fayol, *op. cit.,* p. 54.
13 Frederick W. Taylor, *Shop Management,* Harper & Bros., New York, 1911, p. 99.

Authority is the right to give orders and the power to exact obedience. Distinction must be made between a manager's official authority deriving from office and personal authority, compounded of intelligence, experience, moral worth, ability to lead, past services, etc. In the make-up of a good head, personal authority is the indispensable complement of official authority. Authority is not to be conceived of apart from responsibility, that is apart from sanction—[or "accountability for the performance of duties," as Mary Parker Follett expresses it] . . . Responsibility is a corollary of authority, it is its natural consequence and essential counterpart and wheresoever authority is exercised responsibility arises.

The best safeguard against abuse of authority and against weakness on the part of a higher manager is personal integrity and particularly high moral character of such a manager, and this integrity, it is well known, is conferred neither by election nor ownership.[14]

5. The Chain of Command

The chain of command, as described so well by Fayol "is the chain of superiors ranging from the ultimate authority to the lowest ranks. The line of authority is the route followed—via every link in the chain—by all communications which start from or go to the ultimate authority. This path is dictated both by the need for some transmission and by the principle of unity of command, but it is not always the swiftest. It is even at times disastrously lengthy in large concerns, notably in governmental ones. Now, there are many activities whose success turns on speedy execution, hence respect for the line of authority must be reconciled with the need for swift action.

"Let us imagine that section F has to be put into contact with section P in a business whose scalar chain is represented by the double ladder G-A-Q.

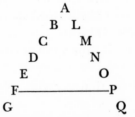

---

[14] Henri Fayol, *op. cit.*, pp. 34-35. See also James D. Mooney and Alan C. Reiley, *The Principles of Organization*, Harper & Brothers, New York, 1939, pp. 14-24, and the earlier edition, *Onward Industry!*, Harper & Brothers, New York, 1931, a pioneer study of organization.

"By following the line of authority the ladder must be climbed from F to A and then descended from A to P, stopping at each rung, then ascended again from P to A, and descended once more from A to F, in order to get back to the starting point."

6. Channels of Contact

Fayol continues, "It is much simpler and quicker to go directly from F to P by making use of FP as a 'gang plank" and that is what is most often done. The chain of command will be safeguarded if managers E and O have authorized their respective subordinates F and P to treat directly, and the position will be fully regularized if F and P inform their respective superiors forthwith of what they have agreed upon. So long as F and P remain in agreement, and so long as their actions are approved by their immediate superiors, direct contact may be maintained."[15]

The nature and need for channels of contact are well described in the organization manual of the Jones & Laughlin Steel Corporation:

a. The plan of organization should permit and require the exercise of common sense and good judgment, at all levels, in determining the best channels of contact to expedite the work. These channels of contact are not described or limited by the lines of responsibility and authority of the organization structure as shown on the organization chart.

b. Contacts between all units of the organization should be carried out in the most direct way consistent with good sense. In making contacts beyond the lines of responsibility and authority on the chart, it should be the duty of each member of the organization to keep his senior informed on:

(1) Any matters on which his senior may be held accountable by those senior to him.

(2) Any matters in disagreement or likely to cause controversy within or between any units of the organization.

(3) Matters requiring advice by the senior, or his coordination with other organization units.

(4) Any matters involving recommendations for changes in, or variance from, established policies.

[15] *Ibid.* p. 35.

c. Staff instructions to units under supervision of others should be channeled through that supervisor if the instructions are of direct concern to and require personal attention of that supervisor. Such channeling can be minimized by the routing of copies to the supervisor with the action papers going direct.[16]

7. Balance

"A special task of continuous reorganization is to see that the units of the organization are kept in balance—that there is a reasonable relative apportionment of strength among its departments.[17] " 'Balance' on the battlefield implies the disposal of available forces in such a way that it is never necessary to react to the enemy's thrusts and moves; a balanced army proceeds relentlessly with its plans."[18]

Balance requires (a) the proper proportions between centralization and decentralization and (b) flexibility:

Centralization—"Responsibility, authority, and accountability should be centralized at key points to provide leadership, direction, and control. This will also aid in establishing major objectives and policies and maintaining consistency of action. It will also facilitate dealing with emergencies and exceptions from plans, standards, and routine. These are the matters requiring top executive attention."

Decentralization—"There should be a decentralization of responsibility, authority, and accountability to place the ability to decide and act within the scope of approved plans and policies as closely as practicable to the point where need for decision or action originates."[19]

Flexibility—"The vitality of an enterprise is measured by its power of spontaneous reaction to changes in conditions, and of internal modification and rearrangement to meet such changes."[20] . . . "To

16 Jones & Laughlin Steel Corporation, *Organization Manual*, Pittsburgh, Pa., June, 1950, pp. 4-5. This principle was originally formulated by General Brehon B. Somervell and others in the *U. S. Staff Manual*.

17 Henry S. Dennison, *Organization Engineering*, McGraw-Hill Book Company, Inc., New York, 1931, p. 185.

18 Montgomery of Alamein, quoted in Urwick's *"Principles of Management,"* op. cit., p. 47.

19 Jones & Laughlin Steel Corporation, *Organization Manual*, op. cit., p. 4.

20 Lt. Colonel L. Urwick, "The Principles of Direction and Control," in *Dictionary of Industrial Administration*, Sir Isaac Pitman & Sons, Ltd., London, 1928, p. 178, and *Cost and Production Handbook*, The Ronald Press Company, New York, 1934, p. 1345.

wring the maximum possible advantage from standardization and simplification, and at the same time to retain always the full measure of flexibility postulated by the circumstances."[21]

8. Control

The principle of control involves:

(a) *Comparison*—"All figures and reports used for purposes of control should be related to standards of performance required and, if comparable, to past performance."[22]

(b) *Information*—"All information used for purposes of control should be strictly objective both in source and presentation. Any statement concerning persons implying criticism should be accompanied by the comments of those affected. Rules of evidence should govern the acceptance of any statement."[23]

(c) *Integrity of Command*—"Control is a valuable auxiliary of command. Properly exercised, it can give the leader necessary information which the hierarchy of supervision would sometimes be incapable of supplying." But for control "to become confused with the command and operation of the various services is an encroachment involving duality of direction in its most serious form. . . . The tendency of control to encroach is widespread, particularly in large organizations."[24]

(d) *Uniformity*—"All information used for purposes of control should be in terms which correspond with responsibility, e.g., main heads of account should be identical with the organization structure. No individual's effort should be expressed in figures which he is not in a position to influence."[25]

(e) *The Exception Principle* — "The manager should receive only condensed, summarized and *invariably* comparative reports covering, however, all of the elements entering into the management. (They) should have all the exceptions to the past averages

21 Lt. Colonel L. Urwick, *The Elements of Administration,* Sir Isaac Pitman & Sons, London, 1943, p. 31.

22 Lt. Colonel L. Urwick, "Principles of Direction and Control," *op. cit.,* p. 179 and *Cost and Production Handbook, op. cit.,* p. 1345.

23 Adapted from Lt. Colonel L. Urwick, "Principles of Direction and Control," *op. cit.,* p. 179, and E. F. L. Breech, *Management, Its Nature and Significance,* Sir Isaac Pitman & Sons, Ltd., London, 1948.

24 Henri Fayol, *Administration Industrielle et Generale,* Dunod Frères, Paris, 1925, p. 157 translated and adapted by L. Urwick).

25 Lt. Colonel L. Urwick, "Principles of Direction and Control," *op. cit.,* p. 179 (adapted) and *Cost and Production Handbook, op. cit.,* p. 1345.

or to the standards pointed out . . . thus giving him in a few minutes a full view of progress which is being made or the reverse."[26]

(f) *Utility*—"Figures and reports used for purposes of control vary in value directly in proportion to the period separating them from the events which they reflect. They should be designed with the objects of assisting decision in the present and avoiding waste in the future, and not as a record."[27]

(g) *Avoidance of "Red Tape"*—"Avoid red tape—to combat the abuses of over-regulation, bureaucratic formalism and paper-mongering."[28] "That is what bureaucracy essentially means—a reliance upon procedures and precedents and a distrust of the exercise of personal power of true leadership caliber."[29]

9. Perpetuation

"The plan of organization should provide a 'ladder' of positions of increasing scope of responsibility, authority, and accountability so related to each other that at all times there are replacements in training for each higher position. One of the most important responsibilities of top management is the successful perpetuation of the Corporation through making available qualified personnel for future management needs. These needs must be filled by executives with a breadth of experience gained from a variety of management responsibilities as well as depth of training in a specialized management area."[30]

[26] Frederick W. Taylor, *Shop Management, op. cit.,* p. 126.
[27] Lt. Colonel L. Urwick, "Principles of Direction and Control," *op. cit.,* p. 179 and *Cost and Production Handbook, op. cit.,* p. 1345.
[28] Henri Fayol, *Administration Industrielle et Generale, op. cit.,* p. 179.
[29] Ordway Tead, *The Art of Leadership, op. cit.,* p. 51.
[30] Jones & Laughlin Steel Corporation, *Organization Manual, op. cit.,* p. 7.

VIII. Putting the Organization Plan into Effect

Wₑ ʜᴀᴠᴇ ᴅɪꜱᴄᴜꜱꜱᴇᴅ at great length the nature of the ideal organization. These considerations do not mean, however, that an attempt should be made immediately to force the existing organization to conform to the ideal. It cannot be over-stressed that the real value of the ideal structure is essentially as a guide to the long-range plans of the company. As such, it should be re-examined whenever there arises an immediate necessity or opportunity for a change in organization through retirement, transfers, etc. Then, and perhaps only then, should major steps be taken to make the existing structure move toward the ideal.

However, it should be noted that when a company gets into a reorganization process it will frequently adopt an organization plan of an intermediate character which is somewhere between what exists and what ideally should be. This will usually include the correction of the worst organizational deficiencies, which have been described on pp. 174-175.

Setting Up the Basic Functions

To start the actual reorganization, the major functions and positions of the ideal organization need to be "brought down to earth." Where the necessary positions do not at present exist, the cost of creating and filling them must be determined. This may be prohibitive in some cases—e.g., a top industrial engineer is likely to earn more as a consultant than most corporations can afford to pay. Or the chief executive may object to the creation of a certain job. Or the pay structure may be thus upset. As a result, a function may have to be split into several minor ones. For example, instead of a $50,000 a year controller, three accountants may be hired at $12,000 each. Basic changes are further restricted by the limitations of present personnel. However profitable the organization changes might be, they frequently cannot and will not be carried out until the personnel situation changes.

Once the basic functions have been set up and agreed upon, each job should be written up as it should be performed within the framework of the organization structure adopted. Job descriptions should be started at the top level and then worked downward. In describing the content of each job, the incumbent's agreement should be obtained and then that of his superior. Final approval may have to be given by other executives. Any points at which no agreement can be obtained should be resolved at a higher stage, ultimately by the president, if necessary. Only if there is genuine acceptance all around should the final job draft be signed and issued.

Matching Incumbents Against Job Requirements

The next logical step is to match the incumbents of existing positions against the job requirements—which may have been increased or reduced on the ideal organization. Some consultants and reorganization specialists are reluctant to engage in such a procedure because they feel that they are not sufficiently familiar with the work of the executives concerned to render such a judgment. Others make a very rough appraisal of the man and his job, usually in committee so as to reduce errors of judgment. An approximate rating scale may be employed (occasionally a detailed percentage evaluation) such as (1) "outstanding," (2) "good," (3) "average," (4) "poor," (5) "incompetent." (1) and (2) are considered to be promotional material, (5) may be slated for a job with reduced responsibilties or separation.

Occasionally a detailed matching process is employed to fit man and job. One such example is reported by L. Rene Gaiénnie, Director of Personnel of Fairbanks, Morse and Co. To save time and avoid undue variations, the same rating elements are used in the evaluation of the average performance required on the job and the rating of the job incumbent, for example: (1) job knowledge, (2) intelligence, (3) skill in handling people, and (4) versatility. If the resulting ratio is equal, the incumbent just fills his job requirements. If it is unequal, it indicates whether, and to what degree the job is heavier than the man, or vice versa.

Reorganization of Committees

In addition to the reorganizing of various functions and individual jobs, it may be necessary to reorganize the company's committee system. The first step in committee reorganization should be an examination of the existing committee in terms of its advantages as a group decision-making body and with a view to the desirability of amalgamating it with another committee or of abolishing it in order to assign its functions to individuals. This process has been discussed in detail in Stage VI of Part I. "Coordination of Management Functions: Group Decision-Making," and in the Appendix on Committees. The value of such a review of committee functions is illustrated by the experience of companies which have been able to reduce the number of their committees substantially.

Improving Business Procedures

The process of reorganization will give rise to a number of opportunities for the evaluation and improvement of business procedures. In some cases it will necessitate a review and realignment of existing procedures.

Procedures are concerned with clerical operations in which several employees and one or more departments are involved. The objective in improving procedures usually is to reduce costs of handling paperwork and to improve uniformity. Procedures specify, in writing or by informal tradition, what clerical work should be performed, in what order it should be performed and who should perform it. For example, in a billing department it is necessary to analyze the details of the bill's contents; determine the various steps of the work involved and their sequence; decide how the operations are to be performed (alphabetically by customer, territory, product, etc.); and assign the people to perform the work.

Procedures research and analysis is such a complex subject that it requires a volume of its own to describe it. One such book is Richard F. Neuschel's *Streamlining Business Procedures.*[31] This book is particularly valuable for its treatment of specific procedures analysis, improvement and techniques. It describes the initiation of a procedures project, methods for gathering and analyzing the facts; developing, presenting and selling recommendations; installing the approved procedures; and developing and maintaining procedure instructions manuals. Some valuable illustrative case material is included. Another book which treats some aspects of procedures is Norman N. Barish's *Systems Analysis for Effective Administration,*[32] especially the chapter on "Analyzing the Functional Allocations and System Flows." Still another volume, dealing with the study of administrative procedure and clerical work, is *A Manual for Administrative Analysis,* by John M. Pfiffner and S. Owen Lane.[33]

[31] McGraw-Hill Book Company, Inc., New York, 1950, pp. 105-284.
[32] Funk & Wagnalls Company, New York, in connection with *Modern Industry* magazine, New York, 1951.
[33] Wm. C. Brown & Company, Dubuque, Iowa, 1951.

IX. The Organization Chart

Organization charts are merely recordings of decisions already reached. The chart is, therefore, primarily a technique of presentation. Use of the organization chart affords a number of distinct advantages. Its construction forces its authors to clarify their ideas. If properly developed, it provides a bird's-eye view of the general structure of work and work relationships in the company much as a topical map shows the major features and contours of the countryside. It shows who supervises whom. In indicates some of the major pecularities of a company's structure—its strength and weaknesses. It may serve as a historical record of changes, a training device, a means of informing the public about the company's work relationships. It may serve as a guide in planning for expansion, in considering proposed changes in reorganization, in making short- and long-run plans, in formulating the ideal plan.

But in using the chart major *shortcomings* of the device must not be overlooked. An organization chart shows merely formal relationships. It indicates what relationships are supposed to exist, and not necessarily the actual relationships. It does not show the host of informal relationships which exist among executives. These may well be numerous and are often more important than the formal relationships. (The informal relationships may be such, for example, that a man has more than one superior, or that supervision is not exercised by the immediate superior, but rather by the staff department.) Moreover, organization charts may impose an unnecessary rigidity; they are static, whereas the organizations they represent are ever-changing, and for this reason they may be quickly outdated unless they are regularly and frequently reviewed.

A number of important *cautions* need to be kept in mind in making charts. Many executives forget that a position on the organization chart merely indicates relationships, not status. For example, the head of a sizable plant in a large company used to be shown up high on the organization chart holding the title "President" and "General Manager." After a change of organization he found himself two tiers below staff vice presidents, with the title "General Manager," and was much grieved that he, as a line executive, should be less important than a staff man. This feeling of injustice might have been avoided to some extent if the plant manager had received the title of Vice President-General Manager and an explanation about organization charts. To draw an analogy from the military, no field commander objected to having staff officers with the rank of lieutenant general working on Eisenhower's headquarters as long as they, too, carried the title of lieutenant general and also reported to the Supreme Commander. Such an arrangement is of importance since line executives are frequently shown on organization charts in a position below staff men. It should also be borne in mind that the existence of good organization *on paper* does not in and of itself overcome organization difficulties or problems of relationships.

The actual *construction of the chart* should be preceded by a study of the existing division of work, of major subdivisions, relationships and titles. The working chart can be drawn more easily with the aid of separate blocks of paper, one for each sub-division, which can be moved around as arrangements change. In preparing the chart, each separate responsibility should be assigned a separate box. The box should contain merely the title of the incumbent, his particular responsibility, operations or activity, possibly the title of the department or division, etc., and his code number in the organization, if he has one. "Assistants to" or secretaries are shown in the same box as the executive whom they are assisting. Assistant managers have a separate box. However, some authorities feel that such a practice may give a false appearance of supervisory responsibility. Some therefore suggest that "the assistant to" be shown in a separate box, with a line connecting to the position which he assists. The downward line from one box to another shows delegation of responsibilities; the upward line, obligation.

In many instances there is added in the box the name of the person exercising the responsibility, with a statement of his major responsibilities or job content. Some companies also include a statement of salary, age of incumbent, photograph of incumbent, name of potential replacement, budget allocated. Others believe that these details personalize what should be essentially an impersonal record, and therefore they omit them.

Where a company organization is complex, it may be well to draw a master chart, indicating for each major activity the page number of the chart book or manual on which further delegation of responsibilities is elaborated.

The chart should also record:

> *Titles or summary statement of the activities shown* (This usually includes the name of the company as well as the particular activity shown—e.g., the Ford Motor Company Engineering Staff)
> *Name of the executive* who has prepared the chart
> *Date* of preparation
> *Approval* (of company president, executive vice president and/or organization counsel)
> *Legend*—explanation of special lines or features

Of course, the chart should be manageable in size and readable. It should be revised as major changes affecting it take place, with approval procedures as explained above.

Different management functions may be shown in different colors or the distinction between line and staff departments may be so indicated.

The various types of organization charts which have been used successfully are shown throughout Part I of this report.

Aids in Chart-Making

The physical preparation and maintenance of organization charts may be facilitated by the use of inexpensive prefabricated self-adhering rectangles and tapes which are commercially available.

(The rectangles and outlines for the organization charts appearing in this study were prepared by Chart-Pak, Inc., Stamford, Conn., a supplier of materials for simplified chart-making.) Names and position titles are typed on rectangles and lines of authority are shown on printed adhesive tape. These are mounted on a plastic board and may be easily removed for revision. Another such aid consists of a slotted board into which are inserted transparent plastic windows which hold typewritten cards. (One supplier is Management Control Charts Company, Chicago.)

X. Preparing the Organization Manual

An organization manual is an authoritative guide to the company's organization. It can be a useful instrument of management which more than justifies the considerable amount of work involved in its compilation. Where a good organization manual is in use, each person can determine what the responsibilities of his job are and its proper relationship to others in the organization. Jurisdictional conflicts and overlapping can be avoided. The sources of approval and the degree of authority at various levels are also made clear.

The information on functions and jobs may serve as a basis of job evaluation and as a check on individual development. Moreover, the manual may preserve a rich fund of managerial experience of older executives and serve as an aid in training younger ones. It may be a helpful volume of reference for absentee management and, as such, provide a tool of control. Further, it helps the individual executive to understand the long-term objectives of management and the complex relationships of the business. Above all, it will force all who participate in its compilation to present the organization plan in a workable and intelligible fashion.

However, some of the drawbacks of manuals should be noted. Many companies feel they are too small to need a manual to describe matters known to everyone (an annual sales volume of $5 million is mentioned as the minimum company size at which a

213

manual is justified). Some find it too expensive, too confining and time-consuming to prepare a manual and to keep it up to date. Others reason that it may put on the record relationships which no one would like to see exposed. There is also fear that it may lead to regimentation and stratification. As Lt. Colonel Urwick puts the objections: "In a great number of undertakings of all kinds, written instructions are neither uniform, clearly expressed, self-consistent, readily amendable, logically arranged, nor up-to-date. Either little or no attention is given to the question of publication of information or too much attention is given to it by too many people. There is no central control, and subordinate officers become enmeshed in a chaos of regulations which defy interpretation while providing a thousand avenues for circumlocution."[34] These disadvantageous aspects of the organization manual can probably be eliminated in medium-sized and large companies by intensive training of executives in utilizing its contents, with emphasis on the informal aspects of organization. However, organization manuals sometimes remain locked up in the desk of the chief executive because it is feared that they are potentially explosive, and they remain nothing more than monuments to the one-time enthusiasm of the chief.

Some of the criticism against rigidity or undue formality in organization planning may be offset by injecting some flexibility into organization manuals so that each organization unit may have, and retain, a character of its own. This requires, however, that the basic principles, format, and the arrangement of the organization manual be adhered to. The Standard Oil Company of California, for example, dropped the name "organization manual" and substituted the name "Management Guide" to lend a permissive rather than an mandatory tone to its plan. This, it is felt, encourages members of management to develop and apply their own ideas about improvements.

Contents

Organization manuals may cover the organization of the company as a whole, individual plants or departments, or major management functions. Contents may include creed, objectives,

[34] L. Urwick, *The Elements of Administration, op. cit.,* p. 79.

definition of terms, organization principles, organization problems, job descriptions.

1. Job Descriptions

All manuals contain job descriptions (for illustrations see Appendices to this volume). The type of jobs included will depend upon the size of the audience for which the manual is intended—i.e., the lower down the hiearchy the manual is to be distributed, the larger the number of job descriptions. In some manuals, job descriptions are limited to positions paying above $5,000 or $7,000 a year; in others, only important and stable jobs are included. The job description should include, as a minimum:[35]

(a) *Descriptions of responsibilities* (routine responsibilities can be omitted, because the description must be reasonably brief in order to be readable and useful).

(b) *Description of authority.* Here common sense and good judgment are needed. Any exaggeration may result in overlapping with another description. For example, a forms and equipment control supervisor may be authorized to disapprove all requisitions for the purchase of new equipment which in his opinion is not needed or is unsuitable. On the other hand, the office manager may approve the purchase of equipment within certain dollar limits. Friction can be avoided if the authority of the forms and equipment supervisor is described as "recommend the disapproval of a requisition" rather than "may disapprove."

(c) *Organizational relationships.* Finally, there should be a record of the job title of the superior who has delegated responsibility and the job titles of subordinates supervised.

The job description may also cover:

(d) *The basic function of the job* (broad objectives, purpose and action of the job.)

(e) *Provision for coordination.*

(f) *Accountability* (to ensure compliance).

(g) *Duties common to all executive positions* may include the

[35] Adapted from James Hendrick, General Foods Corporation, Address to the Systems and Procedure Association, New York, December 7, 1948 (mimeographed), p. 6.

following (adapted from the organization manual of the A. C. Gilbert Company):

(1) To understand, support loyally, and explain thoroughly objectives, creeds and policies to subordinates so that they in turn understand and support them.

(2) To delegate authority and responsibility in accordance with the Organization Charts and Manual.

(3) To recommend changes in the Charts and Manual that would improve efficiency, clarify organization and obviate disputes.

(4) To control hiring and release of subordinates according to policies and procedures, to coordinate and discipline them, and periodically to rate them.

(5) To apply and follow all written procedures (Procedures Manual).

(6) To train understudies and designate lines of succession.

(7) To coordinate the activities of one's unit with those of other units and render assistance willingly to others (teamwork).

(8) To strive constantly toward simplification and consolidation of all activities and to eliminate those that are non-essential (cost-consciousness).

(9) To keep informed and up-to-date on all matters which might contribute to efficiency and progress.

(10) To practice good housekeeping and to keep neat, complete, and easily accessible records; to destroy them when they become obsolete.

(11) In spite of personal feelings, to support and willingly enforce decisions rendered by superiors.

(12) In following channels of contact, to keep the superior informed of any matters for which that superior is held responsible.

(13) To program and plan the work systematically, see that subordinates do likewise, and then require adequate reports to control their execution.

(14) To perform any additional duties the superior may require (although not written in the Organization Manual),

Job descriptions should be separate from the candidate's specifications. The former are designed to describe objectively the elements which make up a position, while the latter specify the human qualities necessary for the adequate performance of the job.

(h) *Procedures for preparing, using and revising "candidate specifications"* (adapted from the organization manual of the A. C. Gilbert Company):[36]

(1) Introduction: Candidate specifications are useful for selecting qualified executives for employment, promotion, and transfer. They enable us to look at the man point-by-point and thereby avoid over-all snap-judgments. They are most useful in explaining to a candidate in a constructive, objective manner, wherein he is weak or strong and why he may not have been selected for a better job. He will then know his specific failings and can go about correcting them. Specifications should be kept current to match changes in job requirements.

(2) Preparation: The personal qualities and traits required to fulfill best the duties and fully meet the need for teamwork and compatibility within the company, including the acceptable age range, should be thought out and listed. Last, the knowledge requirements, including experience, background, education, and special abilities essential to carry out the job duties should be listed.

Then the actual specification should be written, with the items summarized under the following headings:

A. Age Range and Preferred Age
B. What He Should Be
C. What He Should Know
D. What He Should Do.

i. *What He Should Be:*
The personal qualities important in most executive positions might be listed under such headings, as the following:
Character
Intelligence
Personality
Physical Condition
Outside Interests
Ambition
Requirements set down under these headings should be keyed to the particular job as closely as possible. They should represent the qualities a candidate should have to

---

36 The A. C. Gilbert Company retained Booz, Allen & Hamilton, Management Consultants, to assist in original formulation of objectives and preparation of the organization manual, candidate specifications, and appraisal techniques.

carry out the prescribed duties under the circumstances and conditions attendant upon the job.

ii. *What He Should Know:*
Executive knowledge requirements may be separated into three categories:
Experience and Background
Managerial Abilities
Education

iii. *Making Appraisals:*
In making appraisals against the specifications, the following rating scale may be used:

	Rating points
Extremely Unsatisfactory	1
Noticeably Unsatisfactory	2
Satisfactory	3
Noticeably Satisfactory	4
Extremely Satisfactory	5

An over-all, or summary, rating based on any arithmetic averaging of the rating scale should not, as a rule, be attempted. Such an average would be erroneous and misleading, since obviously it would not take stock of the weight of each item. A low rating on just one key item may be sufficient to reject the candidate— e.g., lack of a language qualification. Common-sense review of the ratings, with an evaluation of the strengths versus the weaknesses, should make it possible to judge the candidate and formulate a recommendation.

2. Organization Creed

Another subject of the manual is a brief statement of the *organization creed,* emphasizing management's philosophy with regard to such subjects as teamwork, cooperation, service, good fellowship, price and quality of the company's products. As an example of an organization creed, the objective of the Standard Oil Company of New Jersey may be quoted from its organization manual: "To maintain a business climate favorable to reasonable profit-making, its management must impose upon itself a proper concern with many social responsibilities. No business exists in economic isolation. It is part of the economic and social environment of its time. Its policies and actions affect many segments of that environment—and in turn are affected by them." A foreword often takes the place of the creed and sets forth the objectives of the manual.

3. Objectives

Objectives may deal with long-term and general objectives in various management functions, such as:

> Engineering
> Sales
> Financial
> Manufacturing
> Sales Objectives

For a detailed discussion of objectives, see Part I, Stage 1.

4. Names and Titles

Significant terms used in the organization manual should be defined. Unfortunately, the literature of organization suffers from the "tyranny of words." There is little agreement on the meaning of commonly used words in this field, and for this reason many differences of opinion arise unnecessarily. To make matters worse, new writers in the field frequently confuse the issues by creating their own terminology, paying little or no attention to the labors of their predecessors or to current practices. In this connection, it is noteworthy that the Management Research and Development Division of the Society for the Advancement of Management (under the leadership of Harold F. Smiddy, Vice President, Management Consultation, Service Division, General Electric Company) is attempting to standardize the terminology.

The names most frequently given to groups performing similar or related tasks within an organization, in the order of their importance, may be cited from the Hoover Commission's studies and suggestions: department, service, bureau, division, branch, section, unit. If we omit "service" and "bureau" and place "division" ahead of "department" (following Alvin Brown's suggestion), we achieve the order of importance which most commonly exists in industry, according to the AMA's study. Thus the major or basic responsibilities might be delegated by the chief executives to "divisions." If these basic responsibilities are not substantial in volume of business or activity required, they might be called "General"—e.g., General Auditor or General Counsel. Second in importance is the "department"—a term long in general usage. In business the word "department" is often connected with a major delegation of a basic responsibility. "Branch" might denote third-level responsibility, i.e., the delegation of certain positions of the departmental responsibility. However, since the term is largely connected with government, business firms might prefer to use such terms as "region," "district" or "zone." Fourth level responsibility may be denoted by "section," and parts of sectional responsibility may be called "units." Additional categories may be obtained by use of the prefix, "sub."

Titles of those who exercise responsibilities also show great variations. Here, again, greater uniformity would be desirable. But this will be difficult to accomplish as long as titles are used to impart prestige rather than to indicate clearly the responsibilities exercised.

The chief executive usually carries the title, "president," unless there is an active chairman of the board. Operating responsibilities may be delegated to an executive vice president. Those who have major or primary responsibilities often carry the title of vice president. But in instances where this title is suggestive of the role of an assistant, the independence of the responsibility may be signified by the title, "Director." However, the prestige of the title, "vice president," and its general connotation of independence (it may be compared to that of "Governor" of a state) are likely to strengthen its usage. One of several of the more important vice presidents may get the prefix "senior," while others may carry the prefix "assistant" or "first" or "second vice president"— in large organizations or as commercial or territorial representatives. Here, as well as on lower levels, the name of the responsibility may be added to the title—e.g., Vice President—Marketing. Below this level there is not much evidence of widespread practice.

The third level in the management hierarchy may be called (roughly in order of importance and status) "director," "manager," "supervisor." These titles represent a definite stage of delegation and are not usually handed out freely. They are limited to executives with real responsibility and supervision. Alternately, as pointed out by Alvin Brown, the heads of functions at this level, like the engineer, accountant, inspector, etc., might receive the added qualification of "chief," "general," "principal," "supervising." But there is no need for such adjectives unless there are several executives of a kind. An example of allocation of names and titles to executives in staff and line operations at a large company (Ford) appears in the Appendix, pp. 306-309.

5. Organization Principles

Many manuals include a summary of major organization principles (See Part II, pp. 194-204). Some of them carry "The Ten Commandments of Good Organization," issued by the American Management Association (which is often distributed with the manual as a wall chart.) This frequently-quoted statement of major principles is as follows:

1. Definite and clear-cut responsibilities should be assigned to each executive.
2. Responsibility should always be coupled with corresponding authority.
3. No change should be made in the scope or responsibilities of a position without a definite understanding to that effect on the part of all persons concerned.
4. No executive or employee, occupying a single position in the organization, should be subject to definite orders from more than one source. (This should not interfere with functional direction exercised by staff specialist departments, such as accounting, personnel, purchasing.)
5. Orders should never be given to subordinates over the head of a responsible executive.
6. Criticisms of subordinates should, whenever possible, be made privately, and in no case should a subordinate be criticized in the presence of executives or employees of equal or lower rank.
7. No dispute or difference between executives or employees as to authority or responsibilities should be considered too trivial for prompt and careful adjudication.
8. Promotions, wage changes, and disciplinary action should al-

ways be approved by the executive immediately superior to
the one directly responsible.

9. No executive or employee should ever be required, or expected,
   to be at the same time an assistant to, and critic of, another.
10. Any executive whose work is subject to regular inspection,
    should, whenever practicable, be given the assistance and facil-
    ities necessary to enable him to maintain an independent
    check of the quality of his work.

6. Discussion of Major Organization Problems

Occasionally major organization problems are discussed in the
manual. An outstanding example is that of the Johns-Manville
Corporation, which treats in detail such problems as: responsibilities and their performance; decisions; the relationship between
operating men and administrative specialists; the proper role of
the assistant; and the nature of supervision.

The best known and most widely read organization manual in
the country is *The Management Guide* of the Standard Oil Company of California.[37] More than 15,000 copies have been distributed throughout the United States and in 25 foreign countries.
The man responsible for much of the basic thinking on organization in the Standard Oil Company of California is L. L. Purkey,
head of its Organization Department for almost 20 years. *The
Management Guide* refers to a hypothetical company, but its defi-
nitions of functions, responsibilities, authorities and principal
relationships are used at the Standard Oil Company of California.
Of particular interest are the three dimensional relationships
maintained by the various positions covered in the *Guide*—that
is, relationships with superiors, with subordinates, and with co-
ordinates. A brief summary of the contents of *The Management
Guide* may be found in the Appendix, p. 305-306.

As an example of a detailed and thorough organization manual that of the Koppers Company may also be cited. It was compiled under the direction of one of the country's outstanding
organization authorities, General Brehon B. Somervell, President

[37] By George L. Hall, Department on Organization, Standard Oil Company of
California, San Francisco, California, 1948. Single copies are free. Additional
copies can be obtained for $1.00 each to cover costs of printing and distribution.
Requests should be addressed to L. L. Purkey, Manager, Department on Organization, Standard Oil Company of California, Standard Oil Building, San Francisco
20, California.

of the Company. The company's organization is divided into five levels—ownership (stockholders); trusteeship (board of directors and board committees); general management (president and the major staff departments); division management (operating divisions); and the general management committees. At each level each position is described in detail as to (1) basic function; (2) scope; (3) duties and responsibilities; (4) method of measuring successful performance; (5) organization relationships; and (6) limits of authority.

A smaller and less detailed organization and policy manual is that of the Line Material Company of Milwaukee, Wisconsin. This was compiled by J. Frank Soles, Jr., Assistant to the President and Plant Manager, under the direction of the Company's president, W. D. Kyle, Jr., and a committee of executives. In the foreword to the manual the president emphasizes the objectives of the manual—better utilization of abilities, teamwork and greater profits—which are to be accomplished by "clear-cut ground rules" and broadened delegation of responsibility. This is followed by a general analysis and plan of organization in chart form and definition of terms. Subsequently each job is headed by the date issued, the function (job title), relationship, and code number. This is followed in each case by a statement of purpose (of the function), field of action (area of jurisdiction), authorization (range of authority), organization (major functions and responsibilities supervised), functions (necessary to achieve purpose), collaboration (functional responsibilities to other departments).

Steps in Preparing the Manual

One individual should be made responsible for the preparation of the manual. He may be the assistant to the president, head of the organization department, director of personnel, or some other qualified executive. He may be advised by a committee of top executives who may also review and pass on his work. Initially, topics for the manual may be suggested by the executives of the company. The manual may start as a series of bulletins which are ultimately welded together. After deciding on the topics, a work schedule should be prepared, showing the order in which topics will be treated and the time to be spent on each. Sources of information may include executive questionnaire and interview material, company by-laws, board statements, chief executive and management bulletins, job descriptions, statements of authority, and any existing company manuals or literature which may be related to organization. The work should proceed on an "as is" basis and a cut-off date set to assure completion of the job within a reasonable time. All material to be published should be examined and approved by the higher management committee, where this is operating.

The extent of the work will be limited by the time and money available, for organization manuals are expensive in both respects. For practical purposes it might be well to confine it to the more important and stable functions, and even here brevity and condensation are necessary. A basic minimum would cover (1) major responsibilities; (2) relationships; (3) principal authority limitations ; (4) organiaztion charts.

The manual may be arranged according to subject matter, functions, or departments. Or functions might be numbered according to a decimal system, such as the following (the digit indicates the stage of delegation):

1 Board of Directors
2 Chairman of the Board
3 President
31 Vice President for Research and Development
33 Vice President for Production
34 Vice President for Sales
36 Vice President for Finance
361 Fiscal Department—Treasurer
3616 Credit Service—General Credit Manager
36169 Credit Units—Credit Managers

As a rule, the manual also contains a table of contents and an index.

The manual should be as brief and as readable as possible, not too ambitious or expensive—but it should be well printed and indexed. It should lie flat for easy reading and notation; it should be in loose-leaf form so that revisions can be readily made. The manual may be distributed to all executives or only to the top men, with relevant sections going to those concerned.

Revision of the Manual

The manual may be revised annually, quarterly, monthly, or upon major changes of the organization. Or revisions may be undertaken as a result of widespread personnel changes or physical decentralization. Revisions may take the form of regular bulletins or replacement sheets. It is most important to set up a procedure of maintenance, but revisions whose importance does not justify their expense should not, of course, be undertaken.

Costs

It is difficult to generalize or to cite figures about the expense of making organization surveys. To quote one example (which is not necessarily representative) in a capital goods company of 3,500 employees, the organization manual was completed in four and a half months by the assistant to the president and a secretary. Total cost, including the time of an executive committee which met once a week, was $12,000, or $3.50 per employee. In another company of 1,500 employees with five plants and great complexity of organization relationships, the organization survey cost $30,000, or $20 per employee. The cost of a similar survey by an outside organization was about $25,000. In an organization with 30,000 employees the cost of an organization analysis, recommendations and preparation of chart was $80,000. In companies with more than 50,000 employees the internal costs of such a survey are usually well above $100,000.

Fees of consultants vary from $100 to $200 per man-day plus out-of-pocket expenses (some of the top men receive $250 a day plus expenses). In practice the cost of an outside organization survey depends on the size and nature of the business, objectives of the survey, location of plants, number of executives to be interviewed, and the degree of their responsiveness.

The cost of maintaining an organization structure varies greatly. In a company with 100,000 employees and many branch plants, the services of two full-time organization experts and four secretaries cost about $25,000 a year, or 25 cents per employee. A company of 8,000 employs one executive full-time and a secretary at a cost of $10,000 a year or $1.25 per employee. But another similar company, with the same number of employees is known to have over a score of organization experts!

XI. Gaining Acceptance of the Plan

A PRIME ELEMENT in gaining acceptance is knowledge and understanding of the organization plan. If the nature of the change is communicated to those affected by it in an abrupt or haphazard manner, the reaction to it may be negative. A plan can be forced on people, but they may obstruct it in many different ways which are difficult to detect and still harder to overcome.

Methods of Persuasion

The first problem is that of persuading those concerned to go along with the changes of organization. Methods of persuasion which the chief executive or the superior may wish to consider include the following:

1. *Demonstrating the advantages of the organization change.* Unless the change is advantageous, it will be wasteful to introduce it. Therefore, it is often desirable to show those affected by the change how they themselves will benefit from it. For example, in a decentralization program, it is often easy to demonstrate the advantages of reducing heavy burdens of work and overtime, and eliminating poor or unnecessarily delayed decisions. Knowledge of such a change may literally free subordinates from hypertension and stomach ulcers. It will give them a chance to devote themselves to more important problems which may increase their own earning capacity as well as that of the company.

2. *The example of others* is often persuasive. Citing the example of a successful, similar change affecting another executive or department of the company, a competitor in the industry, or an outstanding firm is usually convincing. Or executives who have benefited from past changes can be brought in to meet with those who are to be affected by a change. If this is not feasible, published material about successful changes in other organizations can be distributed.

3. *Indirect approach.* One may utilize an indirect approach to persuade others of the need for a change. For example, a new method of selecting executives, a study of executive morale, a salary evaluation program may show the need for organization changes. An executive inventory may be drawn up to show the number of years before retirement of major executives and the lack of trained successors for their jobs. This may move some executives to delegate certain responsibilities so as to give younger men a chance to prepare for these positions.

4. *Asking advice.* Explaining the nature of one's problem often helps men to see things differently, for it enables them to understand why others require a change and how the gains would outweigh the losses. They may be asked how they would handle the problems. For example, in one medium-sized company a new president found that his immediate subordinate had the title of Vice President and General Manager, but was in effect only in charge of Marketing. When this Vice President was consulted about the problem of assigning to the new President the duties of general manager, he volunteered to have his title changed to Vice President in Charge of Sales.

5. *Compensation.* Executives may be compensated in some form for any real or imagined loss suffered through the organizational change. They may receive a promotion in position, higher salary or stock option, a more important title, access to higher executives in the company, a new post created entirely for them, or perhaps a larger office or an extra secretary.

6. *A retirement plan.* Sometimes, when all else fails, hope for change lies only in retirement. A retirement plan, requiring that all executives leave the company at a certain age, with provision

for continuing income, may be used as a last resort to force out men who would resist "until their dying day."

7. *Deficiencies.* A more painful approach consists of pointing out the deficiencies in a tactful way and asking for suggestions to overcome them.

8. *Participation in the development of reorganization.* The means of encouraging and maintaining such participation have been discussed earlier.

Meetings on Organizational Changes

The organization plan is more likely to be accepted and carried out, if it is carefully explained, if executives have a chance to participate in its development, if employees have a chance to express their opinion about it and ask questions, and if something is done to remedy defects which became apparent at the meetings. For this reason many companies arrange a series of "step-down" conferences, starting with top management, to present and explain the plan.

For purposes of these meetings the final organizational plan may be summarized and written up in brief and understandable language. It may be presented in written form in an organization manual, in summary form in an organization guide, on large charts or slides, or on a film (e.g., the excellent film presentation of the Continental Oil Company's decentralization program). This basic material is usually prepared by the company's organization department or organization expert, the personnel or public relations department, possibly an outside organization counsel, and perhaps a communications expert.

At the first organization meeting the company's president may present the organization story to the Board of Directors (if Board approval is needed) or to the top management group. Each head of a major management function and the chief departmental managers present the plan in turn to their chief subordinates, and so on until the foreman group as been reached. Each of those who present the story should be specially coached to carry out this important task.

To illustrate the content of such an organization meeting, it may be helpful to summarize the contents of a *Leaders' Basic*

Guide for the Plan of Organization, presented by the president of the Continental Oil Company to his top management group. The major purpose of the new plan was to introduce decentralization in order to increase the authority of the various operating regions. The outline of topics covered, and the approaches used in discussing them at the Continental meetings, were as follows:

I. OBJECTIVE OF MEETING

1. Effective Date of Plan
2. Studies Made in Connection with Plan
3. Procedure for Meeting, announced as follows:
   "In a few minutes we shall see a film that presents the 'why' of the plan. It will also give you a rather brief historical sketch of the company, which may be nothing new to a number of you, but I should like to suggest that particular attention be paid to the growth Continental has undergone in the past 75 years."
4. Changes Caused by Growth, accompanied by the following comments: "Rapid growth usually calls for changes in organization, and I think you will be able to see in the film why it is now necessary for us to decentralize our operations. Small companies can afford to be centralized, but in companies the size of Continental, centralization can have a strangling, paralyzing effect."
5. Review of important points of film, questions after the film, and suggestions during the film.

II. PROBLEMS OF GROWTH

1. Summary of Defects of Centralization
2. Objectives of Continental Plan:
   "First, we want to make it possible for each person in the Continental Oil Company to do a better job by delegating enough authority to him to get the job done. The number two objective is to get better results for Continental Oil Company."
3. Retention of Responsibility by Top Officers:
   "When any organization decentralizes, a certain amount of responsibility for results must be retained in the home office. The policies themselves have to be laid down, generally from the board to the president and from the president to the officers. Control must be exercised by

headquarters. Procedures must be established; and the general administration, in the sense of policies, plans, programs, and control, is something which logically is the function of the headquarters staff."

    4. Summary of the Advantages of Decentralization

    5. General Summary

III. NEW ORGANIZATION CHART

    1. Headquarters Staff

    Turn to organization chart and explain boxes in following order: 1. Stockholders; 2. Board of Directors and Chairman of Board; 3. Board Committees and Secretary; 4. President; 5. Executive Vice President; 6. Assistant to President; 7. Men reporting to President; 8. Men reporting to Executive Vice President. Follow with discussion of physical moves.

    2. Relationship of Regional Men and Headquarters

    3. Regional Organization

IV. RESTRICTIONS OF AUTHORITY (through organization and policy guides):

"We have prepared what we call organization guides in which we have organization charts, maps, and job descriptions. In these guides we also define functions, responsibilities, and authorities.

"In addition to that, we have a Policy Guide. At the end of each job description is a statement which reveals that each person has the power to act and has authority to act in carrying out the responsibilities of the job which is assigned to him with certain limitations.

"If we tried to write out that your authorities are 1, 2, 3, 4, 5, we'd have to get down to the most minute detail. Rather than do that, we want to see that you are empowered with authority to act within certain limitations; and those limitations become far fewer in number than the general authorities which you have. So in the back of the organization guide will be an outline of authority limitations."

V. CLOSING REMARKS (stress on the need for re-delegation):

"Each executive should see that the individuals, in turn, not only have the authority but the training and the

advice necessary to reassign and redelegate these responsibilities and authorities."

A Leaders' Guide was used by the President during the first
day of the Continental Oil meeting to explain the new organization plan, emphasizing the major changes. The second day was
given over to a question-and-answer period. The meeting ended
with a discussion on how to inform the other members of management of the organizational changes. Stress was laid in the meetings
on the particular problems of the department members present,
the persons who owed responsibility to them and to whom they
owed responsibility.

In addition to its concern about the reaction of employees to
reorganization, the company was also very solicitous about the
impact of the change on the local community. At the time of the
announcement to department heads, the executive committee of
the local Chamber of Commerce was informed. Later a dinner
was given at the Chamber for the local businessmen to whom the
changes were explained by the Executive Vice President. Assur-
ances were given that any loss of employment would be made up.
Simultaneously, the organiaztion changes were explained in the
local newspapers.

The problem of gaining acceptance of the reorganization plan
is probably the most difficult aspect of the change itself. Here the
human problems greatly outweigh the engineering problems. It
is therefore necessary to explore and utilize all the possible psy-
chological aids, to draw upon past experience, and at all costs, to
be patient. Ample time for adjustment to change is perhaps the
most important factor in gaining acceptance.

Since successful installation is the most difficult part of organization, each part of the program should be assigned to an individual who is responsible for carrying it out to completion by
some definite date. Finally, it will be necessary to follow-up on
the effectiveness of the program, the expenses entailed, results
achieved, and the over-all effects on morale.

Conclusion

Conclusion

Notable changes have occurred in what has traditionally been called "organization engineering," since F. W. Taylor and H. Fayol devoted systematic study to it. These changes have included:

The increasing complexity of managerial functions and their interrelationships.

The increasingly public role of the corporation in terms of its responsibilities to the parties connected with the enterprise, such as the public, consumers, labor, suppliers, bankers.

The increasing importance of labor unions and government in the affairs of the organization.

The impact of an expanding economy which has made possible vigorous experimentation and has also caused some looseness in organizational structuring.

The rise of bureaucratic tendencies in some enterprises, leading to increased administrative overheads and break-even points requiring a relatively high volume of production.

The emphasis on organization as a special management skill.

The development of criteria of good organization and the collection of much organizational experience.

A greater recognition of the impact of human relationships on the organization and its structure.

An understanding of these changes, which are merely the reflections of broader-scale changes taking place in our industrial society, is essential to our knowledge of company organization. In this study we have attempted to reconcile the traditional concepts of organization to the important changes which directly affect their application. Some of the major findings will be summarized in the following pages.

Summary

1. *Organization must be studied as a process of growth.*

Since companies' size and their problems are continuously changing, we must learn how to adapt the organization to these changes. This may be done by analyzing the organization problems that arise at various stages of company growth—problems having to do with the formulation of basic objectives, the delegation of responsibility, the span of control, the role of the staff assistant and specialist, committee work and coordination, decentralization and reorganization.

2. *Basic company objectives determine the basic company functions as well at the division of work.*

There are a number of important new methods of dividing work among executives, including various factors related to time, the lines of management communications to different groups connected with the enterprise, and the interrelationships of the basic functions. In this study three major types of criteria—economic, non-economic and size—have been developed so that the appropriate division of the company's work may be determined, with a view toward accomplishing its objectives.

3. *Organization structuring should take greater account of the personality factor.*

Much of the past work in the field of organization has failed adequately to recognize the influence of executive personality on the company's organization structure. This may be one reason why the need for reorganization has arisen so frequently.

It would, of course, be wrong not to pay close attention to the engineering aspects of organization. But, on the other hand, account must be taken of the people whose feelings and attitudes directly affect, and are affected by, the organization. Such an attempt has been made in this study.

In so far as it is possible to "type" the chief executive we may be able to analyze and predict his probable behavior with regard to the organization. There are a number of characteristics about the chief executive which may have a vital influence on the organization structure. They include the basic beliefs of the chief executive, his administrative philosophy, his own training and management background, his history with the company, the circumstances governing his rise to the presidency, his age, the influence of formal organizational pressures and of informal pressures, the decision-making type which he represents.

4. *The span of control is an important determinant of executive effectiveness.*

The most satisfactory "span of control" (the number of executives supervised as distinguished from having access to a superior) is one which avoids an over-long complicated chain of command and which does not over-tax the executive's mental and physical capacities. Rather than hold rigidly to a predetermined span of control of from three to six men (we found that executives at the presidential level have a span of control nearer eight or nine), it is advisable to weigh the advantages of increasing delegation to a greater number of subordinates against its disadvantages and increase or decrease the span of control until the two are in balance.

5. *The "Staff Assistant"*

The AMA survey shows that the staff assistant or "assistant to" is one of the most useful and yet most misunderstood functions in the organization structure. An extremely widespread complaint on the part of top executives participating in the AMA survey had to do with the tremendous pressure of affairs on them. They are working long hours—from eight to 12 a day—staying till midnight in the office in some cases, taking work home at night and over the weekend, and limiting themselves to short and inadequate vacations. Almost all the time of top executives is spent with other people, and an increasing proportion with others than company executives—such as government officials, representatives of trade associations, local community contacts, non-working directors. The result is lack of time on the part of the top executive for adequate contact with his associates and subordinates, lack of time for rest and recreation, for reading—particularly of a non-business nature—and most serious of all, lack of time for reflection, for developing long-range plans, for thinking up new ideas.

This grave situation could be eased in part by resort to the staff assistant. It is a device largely used, for similar reasons, by the military. In our interviews with General Eisenhower he stressed the opinion that business men made too little use of the staff assistant. Many companies, however, fear that the use of the staff assistant may be merely an excuse for executives to refuse to delegate important responsibilities.

6. *Staff excutives are assuming more command powers, resulting in divided authority and conflicts with line executives.*

In an increasing number of companies, top executives complained about the lack of clear-cut jurisdiction between their staff and line men.

The reconciliation of staff and line operations is one of the most difficult problems of organization. Approaches for integrating the activities of staff and line executives include the following:

a. A continuing program of education to familiarize staff executives with line operations and problems, and vice versa.

b. Use of an informal approach by the staff executive.

c. Use of persuasion rather than command.

d. Better communication between staff and line on all matters of mutual concern.

7. *Committees are a widespread form of management, but the benefits of committee management for specific types of activities, as compared to alternative methods of management, have been little explored.*

It was found that committee action is probably superior in the handling of matters which may give rise to jurisdictional problems within the company; individual action is superior in organization planning, execution, and decision-making. Committee action is slightly superior in handling problems of communication, slightly inferior in planning, formulating objectives and administration. Committee action is about equal to individual action in control, innovation and advisory activities.

Major requirements for successful committee operation may be summarized as follows:

a. Diverse opinions should be integrated.

b. The principles of group effectiveness should be more widely applied.

c. Committee mechanics should be perfected to the point where they serve, rather than impede the work of the committees.

d. Only subjects which can be handled more effectively by groups than by individuals should be selected for committee discussion; the selection of subjects to be assigned to committees requires careful study.

8. *Decentralization*

In and of itself, decentralization is neither desirable nor undesirable; it depends on the type of decentralization we are talking about and its applicability to a company's individual needs. In the physical sense, decentralization refers to the limitation of the size of plants and the establishment of branch units. In its broader sense, it refers to the delegation of responsibilities from higher management to subordinates down the line. In evaluating the degree of managerial decentralization within a company, the important questions to ask are: How many decisions are made lower down the management hierarchy? How important are these decisions? How far down the line can they be made? To what degree are they checked? How effectively are different decisions made at various levels of management? Applying these tests to a limited sample of larger companies, it was found that the traditional "one-man control" is still very strong in the majority of firms studied. This is especially true of finance, personnel, purchasing and legal functions, to a lesser extent of production and sales. Even minor decisions may have to be passed on by the chief executive. This may ensure that only well-considered proposals are brought up for consideration, but the delays in decision-making and the costs entailed may far outweigh the advantages of such close control.

In order to determine whether or not delegation of authority should be undertaken in any given situation, a detailed analysis must be made of such criteria as the following: size of the company, nature of the company's business, economic trends, political trends, management philosophy, personality factors, and the nature of the management functions for which decentralization is contemplated.

9. *Changing the company organization is a gradual process.*

Successful organization changes require such conditions as the following:

  (a) Active participation of all concerned at all stages of change.
  (b) Utilization of talent competent in the various engineering and human relations aspects of organization planning.
  (c) Thorough analysis of the functions and relationships of significant jobs.
  (d) Study of the existing organization structure.
  (e) Construction of the ideal organization on the basis of specific organization criteria.
  (f) Modification of the ideal structure in the light of personality influences, existing structural needs and individual economic circumstances.
  (g) Setting up the basic functions and matching of incumbents against job requirements.
  (h) Winning acceptance of the plan.
  (i) Constant review and modification to make the organization structure more closely conform to the ideal plan.

In sum, good organization is like good wine: It takes loving care and much patience before it becomes mature and mellow.

Some Unresolved Problems

It is clear that important advances in organization have been accomplished over the last two or three decades. Our body of knowledge on the subject has increased considerably, but its application is still uneven. The greatest lacks probably are a reliable indicator to tell us how we are progressing and a good steering mechanism to put us back quickly and smoothly on the right course.

What is most needed, therefore, is a General Theory of Organization which would enable us to arrive at approximately correct solutions of our basic organization problems. We need a model so that we can isolate three or four basic variables and on the basis of these, construct the "optimum" organization.

Failing this we might try to solve a number of unresolved organizational problems and in the process arrive at the General Theory. These unresolved problems include the following:

1. *Measuring the effectiveness of the organization.* This will require a fairly adequate separation of the variables influencing the organization and a fairly accurate method of measuring their influence. We need to be able to judge the quality of results provided by different types of organization, making allowance for the different types of problems to be met by the individual company and the different kinds of people directing it. In this field, organization specialists might avail themselves of some of the tools of economics and accounting, such as marginal analysis, the theory of location, the economies and diseconomies of scale, the analysis of administrative overhead in relation to production costs, the break-even point.

2. *The impact of personality on organization and of organization on personality.* To some extent this will require the development of a more adequate typology of executive personality and much wider application of the tools of the social sciences.

3. *The process of executive decision-making.* Much still remains to be learned about the major forces influencing different types of business decisions and the relative importance of short- and long-run influences.

4. *Adapting the organization structure to changes in the business cycle.* Our extremely volatile economy requires speedy structural adaption of the organization to changing business conditions. More remains to be learned about adapting the organization to economic change quickly, with a minimum loss of efficiency.

5. *The "optimum" in organization.* Further analysis of the "optimum" in organization is needed, especially with regard to subsidiary problems such as the division of work, the span of control, the use of the staff assistant, the extent of committee management desirable for different types of activities.

6. *Clarification of line and staff relationships.* This widespread problem has been largely solved "on paper," but not in the plant. It requires rethinking, both on a theoretical and practical level.

7. *The meaning of social responsibility for managerial action.* If management is accountable only to the owners of the business, the proper criterion for its behavior is the best possible utilization of their property or maximization of profits. But what guideposts should be substituted, if management is also held responsible to labor, government and the local community? Or do we need to think out anew the role of management as an arbiter—in terms of the "reasonable expectations" of the parties to the business enterprise, or in terms of "fair" wages, "fair" profits and "fair" prices? How should we adapt the division of work to these changes in management's objectives?

8. *The integration of expert advice.* The role of the technician and the expert has greatly increased in importance. But how shall we guard against the dangers of over-specialization, over-extension and departmentalization in business? How can we successfully integrate different types of expert advice?

9. *Methods of organization study and organization nomenclature.* Can we spend less time quarreling over concepts and terminology and work constructively with the body of organization knowledge handed down to us by our predecessors? Should not we be better acquainted with the writings on organization by the pioneers and build on their foundations rather than create our own?

10. *Teaching and interpreting available knowledge of organization.* Finally, should not we make the results of our research more widely known and more understandable and teach more effectively what we already know? More widespread acquaintance in management with basic organization knowledge is clearly needed. Allied to this is the need for a better understanding of what organization can and cannot do.

A Look at the Future

Today many of us are wrapped up in a net of organization theories which inhibit our freedom and initiative. In our attempts to achieve order, by trying to do what we think the tin gods of organization will approve, we are merely becoming more involved. The tyranny of organization theory spoils good practice; undue organization analysis results in paralysis, and one is left with an utter sense of futility in the midst of organizational over-head and waste.

We put this problem to the young president of one of our largest companies who is very ably and sincerely trying to solve it. He answered without hesitation: "The greatest contribution to the effective organization would be the reduction of our plants to a maximum size of 2,500 men." The ideal organization which he had in mind was one in which the plant managers would know all their men by sight or name and in which each individual would have a chance to utilize his abilities to a maximum.

Let us conclude by a brief attempt at forecasting the future: The ideal organization in, say, 25 years will be one in which there will be the fullest measure of effectiveness and efficiency. The organizational plan and all its details will be determined by the dictates of economy. The size of the plant will be determined by a highly rational calculation of the economies of scale. The optimum may be 2,500 employees or more, or less—it will depend on which is the most economical. The organization will also be measured by the non-economic criteria, by analysis of the personal and irrational factors and their meshing with the economic factors.

For example, the present emphasis on uniformity of company practice may well give way to "rational irrationality." For we find increasingly that uniformity is a chimera. We enforce centralized control and we are careful to pay the same salary for the same work of executives in different plant locations. But is the work of two executives ever the same? Do we pay merely for the same hours worked or the same output? Are the conditions of supply and demand and the cost of living the same in different locations? How do we get relative uniformity for different jobs? And even if we get uncontestable uniformity through iron-clad job evaluation, would it be worth the loss of freedom in personnel action which is so important to an executive in a branch plant? The price we are paying for "administrative convenience" is becoming too great.

By 1975 we may well have a firmer belief in the superiority of decentralized action than we have today. Our large companies will continue, but their headquarters may become management companies aiding groups of manufacturers and distributors with advice in their final decision-making. Just as the efficient small company will have a battery of outside consultants to help it, so the large corporation may function as a consultant at head office, as some already do. In this way the economic advantages of size may be combined with those of independent existence.

Appendices

TOP MANAGEMENT DESCRIPTIONS

This Appendix describes the jobs of a company president, executive vice president, and chairman of the board in a large corporation. It is based on an analysis of these three jobs in a number of large companies. Each job is described in terms of:

> Basic functions
> Organizational relationships
> Specific responsibilities
> > Management, corporate, organizational, personnel, financial, committee, and public responsibilities
> Authority
> Accountability

To the foregoing, a statement of authority limitations should be added. Several alternative analyses of the position of chairman of the board are included.

PRESIDENT

A. *Basic Functions*

In accordance with Article . . . , Section . . . of the By-Laws of the . . . Company, "The President shall be the Chief Executive Officer of the Corporation. In the absence of the Chairman of the Board, he shall preside at all meetings of Stockholders and Directors. He shall be *ex officio* a member of all committees, and shall have general and

245

active management of the business of the corporation, and shall see that all orders and resolutions of the Board are carried into effect."

B. *Organizational Relationships*

   1. *Framework of Operation*
      The president is responsible to the board of directors
   2. *Individuals Reporting to the President:*
      (For possible lists, see Stage III on The Span of Control)

C. *Specific Responsibilities*

   1. *Management Responsibilities*

      a. To plan, develop, and approve specific policies, programs, and methods, designed to implement the general policies established by the board of directors and to direct their administration and execution.

      b. To see that subordinates are delegated adequate authority to carry out their responsibilities and objectives but that appropriate limitations of their authority are defined in writing and clearly understood with respect to policy, contractual commitments, expenditures, and action affecting personnel.

      c. To engage in long-range planning and innovation and to see that full advantage is taken of the long-range potentialities of the business.

   2. *Corporate Responsibilites*

      a. To keep the board of directors fully informed on the condition of the business and on all important factors influencing it.

      b. In accordance with Article . . . , Section . . . of the By-Laws, "to execute certificates of stock, bonds, mortgages, and other contracts requiring a seal under the seal of the corporation, unless required by law to be otherwise signed and executed and unless the signing and execution thereof shall be expressly delegated by the Board to some other officer or agent of the Corporation."

      c. To nominate officers of the company for election by the board of directors.

      d. To consult with the executive committee in intervals between meetings of the board of directors on matters regarding authority of the board or of special interest to it.

3. *Organizational Responsibilities*

To develop, maintain, and administer a sound plan of organization; initiate improvements and enforce the organization plan of the company; initiate, control, and approve the addition, elimination, or alteration of any major position in the company.

4. *Personnel Responsibilities*
   a. To establish a basic personnel policy.
   b. To initiate and control policies of selection, promotion, demotion, and removal of any member of management.
   c. To set up a personnel inventory, an executive development program, evaluation and succession policies.
   d. To approve appointment and retirement of officers and major members of management.
   e. To initiate and control a program of national wage and salary administration.
   f. To approve basic employee policies and relationships with organized labor.
   g. To approve managerial and employee benefit and vacation plans.

5. *Financial Responsibilities*
   a. To supervise the annual and quarterly budgets.
   b. To control the profitability of operations.
   c. To maintain proper inventories.
   d. To guard the long-run solvency and capital structure of the company.

6. *Committee Responsibilities*

To serve specifically on the following committees: (list)

7. *Public Responsibilities*

To direct and participate in such outside activities as are deemed advantageous toward enhancing the prestige of the corporation; broadening the scope of the corporation's operation, and fulfilling the public obligations of the corporation as a member of industry and the community.

D. *Authority*

The president is authorized to take any reasonable action necessary to carry out the responsibilities delegated to him so long as such action does not deviate from established policies and practices as defined by the board of directors or conflict with sound business judgment, except for specific limitations placed upon his authority by the board of directors or the by-laws of the company.

E. *Accountability*

 Criteria for Exercise of Responsibilities

 1. To obtain the optimum profit and return on the investment of the company over the long run.

 2. To obtain and maintain the optimum percentage of the potential market sales for major products of the company.

 3. To maintain at all times the optimum class, type, design, and quality of products, approve new products, and assure the optimum service of all products of the company.

 4. To obtain the optimum utilization of expenditures.

 5. To assure fulfillment of operating budgets and foster economy.

 6. To assure efficient management throughout the company.

EXECUTIVE VICE PRESIDENT

A. *Basic Functions*

In accordance with Article . . . , Section . . . , of the By-Laws, "The executive vice president shall perform such duties and exercise such powers as . . ."

The executive vice president is primarily responsible for the actual operation of the business in contrast to the president's basic responsibilities for company policies; he has authority over all organization levels below the rank of president pertaining to his particular operation group. He is responsible for coordinating all major activities of his operating group and its operating divisions and for obtaining results in keeping with company policies and objectives. He directs the activities of the operating group and those of the vice presidents and general managers of the operating divisions.

B. *Organizational Relationships*

 1. *Framework of Operation*

  The executive vice president reports to the chief executive officer.

 2. The following individuals report to the executive vice president: (list)

C. *Specific Responsibilities*

   1. *Management Responsibilities*

      a. To direct the operating group and through it the divisions in accordance with established policies and objectives.

      b. To assist the chief executive officer in developing company objectives and in formulating policies for achieving them.

      c. To recommend desirable changes in company policies for approval of the chief executive officer.

      d. To analyze and appraise regularly and systematically the effectiveness of all operations of the company under his control, to see that company policies are observed, and to take prompt corrective action as needed.

      e. To see that executives under his direction are delegated adequate authority to carry out their responsibilities and objectives, but that appropriate limitations of their authority are defined in writing and clearly understood with respect to such matters as policy, contractual commitments, expenditures, and action affecting personnel.

   2. *Organization Responsibilities*

      a. To see that the approved basic plan of organization is established and observed.

      b. To establish a sound organization structure in the divisions.

      c. To see that policy and procedure guides covering the activities of the company are developed and maintained for operations under his control.

   3. *Accounting and Financial Responsibilities*

    (with the advice and assistance of the Accounting Service Group)

      a. To establish sound accounting and financial administration.

      b. To review budgets for operations under his control and to render such modifications and recommendations as he deems appropriate before their submission to the president.

      c. To establish a budget of operations for approval of the Appropriations Committee and the president.

      d. To obtain and evaluate information on general and specific business conditions as a guide for the company's operations and to keep the president advised.

    e. To see that policy and price changes are carried out in accordance with basic pricing policy.

    f. To analyze and report to the president the results of the company's operations.

4. *Legal and Corporate Responsibilities*
   (with the advice and assistance of the Law Department)
    To see that all agreements are in accordance with company policies.

5. *Engineering and Research Responsibilities*
   (with the advice and assistance of the Engineering Department)

    a. To establish basic engineering policies, training, development, and advancement.

    b. To provide facilities for basic and applied research.

6. *Manufacturing Responsibilities*
   (with the advice and assistance of the Manufacturing Department)

    To provide for manufacturing activities, including provision for manufacturing plant, operation, and servicing.

7. *Human Relations Responsibilities*
   (with the advice and assistance of the Human Relations Service Group)

    a. To lay down administrative directives for carrying out the company's personnel policy.

    b. To lay down administrative procedures for the selection, promotion, demotion, and removal of members of management under his direct control.

    c. To recommend, for the approval of the chief executive officer, competent executives for the operation of all major company activities under his control, to see that they are properly trained and fully informed, and to coordinate the efforts of all executive personnel reporting to him.

    d. To set up administrative procedures for rational wage and salary administration and the retirement and succession of members of management.

    e. To participate in the formulation of managerial and employee benefit and vacation plans.

    f. To participate in the formulation of relationships with organized labor.

8. *Marketing Responsibilities*
(with the advice and assistance of the Marketing Department)
> To provide for all marketing and sales activities, with special reference to policy formulation on product development, trade relations, market research.

9. *Committee Responsibilities*
> To serve specifically on the following committees:
> (list)

10. *Public Responsibilities*
1. To maintain close personal relationship with officers of important customers, prospective customers, and vendors.
2. To promote satisfactory relations with government agencies, industry and trade groups, press, and public.

D. *Authority*

The executive vice president is authorized to take any reasonable action necessary to carry out the responsibilities assigned to him so long as such action does not deviate from established company policies and is consistent with sound business judgment except for specific limitations placed upon his authority by the president, the By-Laws of the company, or the Policy Guide.

E. *Accountability*
a. To set and meet profit objectives for the operations group.
b. To seek constantly for improvements and cost reductions.
c. To establish effective accounting controls in all parts of the operating divisions.
d. To review staff and operating division managers' reports of progress, problems, and solutions of problems within their respective areas of responsibility.
e. To build morale in the organization.
f. To develop unit, coordination, cooperation, and understanding among staff and operating division managers and other personnel.

CHAIRMAN OF THE BOARD

The job content of the chairman of a company's board of directors varies greatly.

Most frequently he holds the position of an "elder statesman," a former president or the most respected of the board members. His nominal function is to preside at the meetings of the board and perhaps aid in the preparation of agenda. His real function is likely to be that of advisor on major and difficult problems, occasionally functioning as a final court of appeal.

This counseling function may be of major importance in one or two fields, such as finance (the board chairman may be simultaneously chairman of the executive and/or finance committee), research, law, public or governmental relations. The following description of the board chairman's job at the Continental Oil Company is representative of the functions of the elder statesman type.

Chairman of the Board

Basic Functions

In accordance with Article IX of the By-Laws of the company. "The Chairman of the Board shall preside at all meetings of stockholders and directors and shall advise and counsel with the President and with other officers of the Corporation, and shall do and perform such other duties as may from time to time be assigned to him by the President and the board of directors."

Organizational Relationships

The chairman of the board is responsible to the president and to the board of directors.

The secretary reports to the chairman of the board.

Specific Responsibilities and Objectives

1. To preside at meetings of stockholders and directors.
2. To advise and counsel with the president and other officers of the company.
3. To establish and maintain good relationships with Federal Government units concerned with the petroleum industry and with Continental Oil Company in particular.
4. To establish and maintain friendly relationships with major stockholders and supply them with such information as may be properly requested from time to time.
5. To handle special requests for information from directors of the company.
6. To carry out special assignments as may be requested by the president or board of directors.

Authority

The chairman of the board is authorized to take any reasonable action necessary to carry out the responsibilities assigned to him so long as such action does not deviate from established company policies and practices and is consistent with sound business judgment except for specific limitations placed on his authority by the president, the board of directors, or the by-laws of the company.

A second type of board chairman is one who is the company's chief executive. He participates in most major decisions and the president is subordinate to him. However, the chief executive as chairman is likely to be less involved in problems of execution and operation than he would be as president. One large company describes this difference in function between basic policy formulation by the chief executive as chairman of the board and his second-in-command, the president, as follows:

> For example, the decision to manufacture a new kind of product, or to undertake research relating to a new kind of product, or to cease the manufacture of a product line, or to sell direct to consumers instead of to dealers, or to employ an important new medium of advertising, or to change basic rates of pay, or to adopt a new form of sales incentive compensation, or to increase or decrease any operating budget out of normal proportion to sales volume, or to make a major change in the assignment of responsibilities to the principal officers or divisions of the Company, or an important change in the salary administration plan or standards, would be a decision on basic policy.
>
> On the other hand, in order to relieve the chairman, the president will assume responsibility and make decisions on such matters as, for example, to change the quality or type or sizes of a product, or to undertake research for the improvement of an existing product, or to discontinue certain types or sizes only of a product, or to sell or not to sell to specific dealers or types of dealers, or to continue an existing medium of advertising, or to increase or decrease operating budgets in reasonable proportion to sales volume, or to change the rates of pay for particular jobs (less than $12,000 yearly,) or to change the rate of sales incentive compensation on a particular product, or to transfer territory from one sales district to another. All such decisions concerning the regular operations of the business would not be decisions on basic policy.

His job description is as follows:

Chairman of the Board

The board of directors has created the office of chairman of the board as the chief executive officer of the Company. The chairman has sole responsibility to the board of directors for the administration of the Company.

The board of directors authorizes the chairman of the board to:

1. Determine basic policy other than that reserved to the board itself.
2. Redelegate administrative responsibility.
3. Exercise specific responsibility for:

    (a) Acquisition and new business development. This refers to the development of new lines of product, whether by the acquisition of other companies or by development through the Company's own activities.

    The president will provide for such assistance and cooperation as the chairman may need from within the Company in order to carry out this responsibility.

    (b) Public relations and stockholder relations. This refers to formulation of practices and plans for the maintenance and improvement of relations with the public and stockholders and to provide advice and assistance, where required by the president, to divisions and departments under his supervision.

    (c) Corporate and legal affairs. The chairman will provide for legal advice as required by the president and the divisions and departments under his supervision.

    (d) Financial policy and general financial reports. Without limiting the president in specifying methods and procedure as an aid to the performance of his duties, the chairman reserves the power to prescribe additional financial activities, and the form and content of reports prepared for the board of directors, the chairman, the stockholders and the public.

    (e) Capital expenditure budget and capital expenditures exceeding $25,000.

    (f) Appointments, promotions, compensation, and termination of employment of persons receiving salaries of $12,000 or more per annum.

In some companies there is not one chief executive but there are two with co-equal powers. Theoretically the chairman of the board and the president may divide their responsibilities on a "policy-making" and "operations" basis, but in practice the difficulty of distinguishing between these two functions may make for disputes over their respective authority. This conflict may result in the ouster of one or the other.

Sometimes the board chairman is responsible for the operations of some subsidiary companies, especially in the foreign field. In this case he may be on the same level as an executive vice president or other vice presidents, subordinate to the president.

APPENDIX B

COMMITTEES

This appendix describes major types of management committees. The following types are examined:

> Advisory Committee
> Accounting and Financial Committee
> Manufacturing Committee
> Marketing Committee
> Legal and Corporate Committee
> Relations Committee
> Engineering and Research Committee
> Retirement Board
> Comptroller's Coordinating Committee
> General Coordination Committee

The analysis, based on the activities of committees operating in a number of large firms, includes a statement of basic functions, scope, responsibilities, composition of membership and authority for each type of committee. Finally, there are presented a checklist for committee procedures, a schedule of committee meetings in a large company, and a method of evaluating committees.

THE MANAGEMENT ADVISORY COMMITTEE

Basic Functions

The basic function of the Management Advisory Committee is to act in a consulting capacity to the president on major questions of company policy, procedures, and control.

Scope

The duties and responsibilities of this Committee embrace the directive and integrating functions with respect to over-all company problems.

Responsibilities

To consider any major policy-making or coordinating problem brought to its attention through any member of the committee, such as:

Major capital expenditures	Disposal of major company
Major research projects	property
Expansion	Major organization changes
Establishment of profit	New major objectives and
objectives	programs
Determination of operating	New or modified policies or
budgets	procedures
	Improvement in the presentation
	of operating and control data

Membership of the Committee

President

All executives reporting directly to the president

(Other executives such as heads of staff departments and general managers of operating divisions might serve on a rotating basis or be co-opted.)

Authority of the Committee

This committee will counsel the president to help him reach decisions on policy and operating matters. To ensure the continuing effectiveness of the Committee, a follow-up is to be exercised on the results of its recommendations.

ACCOUNTING AND FINANCIAL COMMITTEE

Basic Functions

The basic functions of the Accounting and Financial Committee are improvement of existing accounting systems, evaluation of major economic analyses as a guide for policy making, review of operating results, and development of policies and procedures pertaining to capital and operating expenditures.

Scope

The Accounting and Financial Committee is to concern itself with a study of major accounting and financial policies and their administration as they concern the company as a whole or operating groups and divisions, especially in terms of their impact on other management functions.

Responsibilities

The Accounting and Financial Committee shall:

1. Undertake progressive modification of basic accounting and auditing procedures to keep them in line with the changing requirements of the company and governmental regulations and make possible more effective cost and financial control of parts as well as the whole of the company.
2. Undertake the use of major economic studies concerning short- and long-term problems of the company, as a whole and its individual components, the industry, and the national and world economy. Determine the validity of economic recommendations for purpose of policy decisions.
3. Interpret to the president systematically, promptly, and in usable form the results obtained by the different operating groups and operating divisions with respect to operating expense, capital expenditures, and budget performance, so that the president may evaluate performance.
4. Interpret to the president the major financial proposals and changing economic events affecting the business.
5. Correlate credit policy with the over-all economic outlook and the competitive situation, in consultation with representatives of the sales departments. (Note: Specific operational problems on credit and collection should be taken up with the treasurer. Over-all operational problems should be discussed with the treasurer by an advisory committee.)

Membership of the Committee

Treasurer
Comptroller
Company's chief economist or economic advisor
Major accounting and financial representatives from the operating departments
(Note: Others may be included—if recommendations of the Com-

mittee are to be carried out through them and/or as a means of education of those responsible for financial performance.)

Authority

The Committee is to report to the president and interpret to him the results of its deliberations, with or without recommendations. In so far as the recommendations are approved, and are applicable to operations, they shall be passed on to the executive vice president and as far down the line as applicable.

MANUFACTURING COMMITTEE

Basic Functions

Review, analysis, and coordination of basic manufacturing policies, procedures and methods of all operating groups and operating divisions to promote the greatest possible interchange of information and cooperation.

Scope

The duties and responsibilities of this Committee cover the production policies and operations of all operating groups and divisions.

Responsibilities

1. To develop basic policies, procedures and administrative techniques in regard to manufacturing, purchasing, packaging, and shipping.
2. To integrate manufacturing policy with that of other departments of the Company, especially sales.
3. To develop policies aimed at the maximum utilization of capital equipment and its intra-company availability, of managerial talent and of labor (incentives, safety, etc.) and the continuous consideration of labor-saving through the introduction of mechanical equipment.
4. To set up procedures and constantly review new and outstanding manufacturing developments and product cost reduction for materials control, handling and utilization.

Committee Members

Vice Presidents in Charge of Manufacturing, Engineering, Marketing

The six most competent executives from the operating divisions.

Authority

This Committee shall serve as a counseling and advisory group to the president. Recommendations resulting from Committee action shall be presented to the president for his consent where matters of general policy or extra budgeting expense are concerned.

MARKETING COMMITTEE

Basic Functions

To review and coordinate marketing activities of the various operating and selling units of the company and coordinate them with other management functions, especially manufacturing. To develop plans for more effective analysis and control of distribution costs, pricing, inventory control, market analysis and forecasts, product service, basic advertising, trade mark policies, and market forecasting in so far as they affect the company as a whole.

Scope

The duties and responsibilities of this Committee cover all matters concerned with the sale of products by any operating division. The Committee shall not concern itself with the normal marketing activities of any individual operating or selling unit of the company unless such activities appear to require consideration from an overall company policy viewpoint.

Responsibilities

1. Approval must be obtained from this Committee before any commitment may be made in connection with the following specific matters:

   a. Projects which may result in the development of a new product or a new business;

   b. Projects which involve:

      i. the purchase for resale under the company's name or trade mark of any product made by an outside person or firm;

      ii. the sale of any company product for resale under the name or trade mark of an outside person or firm;

      iii. the purchase for resale under the manufacturer's name or trade mark, of any product of a competitor.

   c. Transfers between company units of responsibility for the marketing of any product or line of products.

    d. Dropping the marketing of any product or line of products.

    e. Changes in either the form or authorized use of the company's signature and monogram (except as otherwise provided).

    f. Changes in the present provisions for sales to employees and in the basis or method of operation of employee stores.

    g. Proposed major changes in product appearance affecting more than one department or involving a matter of general policy. After review by the Manufacturing Committee they should be referred to the Marketing Committee for approval before being put into effect.

2. Approval must be obtained from the Committee before making any commitment which involves a (major) departure from established marketing practice or which should receive consideration from the viewpoint of its possible effect on the over-all marketing policy of the company. Examples of such matters are:

    a. Changes in selling prices which involve all or a substantial number of the items in a product line and concerning which an announcement is to be made to the public or the trade.

    b. Changes in types or methods of distribution and in assignments of distributors' activities which affect the boundaries previously established by this Committee for domestic trading associations.

    c. Utilization of existing, and issuance of proposed new, product guarantees or warranties.

3. The Committee shall determine and control basic plans, procedures, and policies such as the following:

> principles of pricing products
> methods of analyzing distribution costs
> control of inventory
> customer and product service
> sales training
> market research
> marketing budgets.

4. The Committee shall determine basic advertising policy. Duties include those of:

    a. Reviewing and evaluating advertising campaigns and material developed by the Advertising Division and advertising agency and recommending action to be taken in respect to such matters;

    b. Advising the president with respect to advertising policy;

    c. Reviewing and making recommendations with respect to proposed advertising budgets.

Members of the Committee

Vice President in Charge of Marketing Policy,
   Public Relations and Advertising
Vice President and Director, Research Laboratory
Vice President in Charge of Manufacturing Policy
Experts on Pricing, Distribution Costs, Inventory Policy, Trade-
   Marks

Authority

This Committee will serve as a counseling and advisory group to the president. Recommendations resulting from committee action will be presented to the president for his consent when they are of company-wide or major application or involve budget action or changes.

LEGAL AND CORPORATE COMMITTEE

Basic Functions

To provide counsel and recommendation on major matters or those without precedent involving the legal rights of the company or the maintenance of operations within the limits prescribed by the law.

Scope

The duties and responsibilities of this Committee cover major matters of a legal nature involving functions performed on behalf of the company by an employee, director, officer, or organizational unit of the company or involving major matters arising between the company and any customer, supplier, agent of the company or outside party.

Responsibilities

1. To furnish legal counsel and legal review of major company policies on which joint judgment is requested.

2. To develop and establish policies, practices, and procedures for the handling by the Legal Division of such transactions as the following:

   a. Acquisition or disposal of interest in real property
   b. Patents and new processes and products
   c. Pricing policies
   d. Governmental bodies and officials
   e. Patent, trade-mark, and copyright protection
   f. Taxes

3. To analyze and appraise from time to time the work and activities of the Legal Department and its effectiveness.

Committee Representation

Members to be included on the Committee are as follows:

Vice President and General Counsel
Comptroller
Treasurer
Secretary

Authority

The Committee should confine itself to major legal problems and policies and make recommendations regarding these to the president.

RELATIONS COMMITTEE

Basic Functions

Consideration of policies, procedures, and problems relating to human relationships within the company as well as with those outside the company, who deal with or are affected by the company; promotion of maximum efficiency in personnel utilization. Development of plans for effective exchange and coordination of ideas relating to all aspects of human relations, with special reference to labor relations, personnel administration, a rational wage structure, education of all levels of personnel, and suggestions.

Scope

The duties and responsibilities of this Committee embrace human relations problems and activities of any unit of the company.

Responsibilities

1. To formulate human relations policies. This will require review of basic personnel policies suggested by the staff service group in such areas as selection and training, incentives, rationalization of the wage and salary structure, personnel inventory and executive development, employee savings and stock bonus, union relationships.

2. To review and recommend programs to obtain the good will of stockholders, customers, prospective customers and the general public.

3. To recommend basic policies and budgets regarding:

   a. Suggestion systems (to stimulate continuing interest in the systems)
   b. Educational work
   c. Contacts with educational institutions, including college-recruiting, determining initial rates of pay for recruits, and providing services such as equipment, films, publications, scholarships and loans
   d. Training of new employees and upgrading
   e. Safety

4. To recommend an annual program of donations, dues, subscriptions, and use of business and advisory services, as suggested by the various groups and divisions of the company.

Committee Membership

Vice President in Charge of Employee Relations Policy
Vice President in Charge of Public Relations and Advertising
Vice President in Charge of Manufacturing
Vice President and General Counsel
Treasurer
Major Division Managers in Charge of Employee and Community Relations

Authority

This Committee will serve as a counseling and service group to the president. Recommendations resulting from committee action will be presented to the president for his consent and action.

ENGINEERING AND RESEARCH COMMITTEE

Basic Functions

1. To analyze, review, and submit recommendations on matters related to engineering development and research that require the approval of the president or have been especially assigned to the Committee by the vice presidents.
2. To provide channels whereby the Vice President in Charge of Engineering and Research may develop and maintain a clear understanding of divisional, group, and over-all problems related to engineering and research.
3. To assist the Vice President in Charge of Engineering and Research to develop broad policies and programs for his department.

Committee Members

Vice President in Charge of Engineering
Vice President in Charge of Research
Vice President in Charge of Manufacturing
The most competent managers of engineering and research from the operating division.

Authority

This Committee will serve as a counseling and advisory group to the president. The conclusions and recommendations made will be presented to the president for his concurrence and action.

RETIREMENT BOARD

Appointment

The general administration of the retirement plan of the . . . Company and the responsibility for carrying out the provisions of the plan are placed in a Retirement Board of not less than six persons appointed by the board of directors of the . . . Company.

Responsibilities

Subject to limitation of the rules and regulations of the plan, the Retirement Board shall:

1. Establish rules for the administration of the plan and the transaction of its business.
2. Accept, from time to time, service and mortality tables for use in required actuarial calculations.

3. Establish the company's rates of contribution to the plan.
4. Establish, from time to time, the rate of regular interest to be used in mathematical calculations.
5. Maintain accounts showing the fiscal transactions of the plan and such data as may be necessary for actuarial valuations.
6. Prepare annually for submission to the board of directors a report showing the assets and liabilities of the plan and a brief summary of the operation of the plan.

Membership

Treasurer (Chairman)
Chairman of the Board
Vice President in Charge of Manufacturing
Vice President in Charge of Employee Relations
Comptroller
Chief Company Insurance Expert (Secretary)

COMPTROLLER'S COORDINATION COMMITTEE
(Standard Oil Company of California)

Membership

Comptroller, Chairman
Assistant Comptroller
Assistant Comptroller
General Auditor
Chief Accountant
Manager—General Accounting Service Division
Manager—Organization & Methods Division
Assistant to the Comptroller, Secretary

Purpose

1. To develop, coordinate and arrange for application of the best collective judgment and experience of the Comptroller's Department on important accounting, auditing policies and procedures.
2. To provide counsel to the various units of the Comptroller's Department in connection with major problems and developments.
3. To keep the members informed regarding the company's general administrative and operating policies to the end that the related accounting and auditing activities will receive appropriate consideration.

4. To coordinate the general activities of the various divisions and sections of the Comptroller's Department, and to serve as a forum for discussion of matters of general interest.

5. To serve as a clearing house for information obtained by members through contacts with other departments and with sources outside the company.

6. To provide for forward planning in connection with over-all accounting, auditing and related activities.

7. To conduct special or confidential studies in important accounting, auditing and related matters, and to coordinate the activities of the various sections of the department devoting effort to such studies.

8. To coordinate within the department the administration of the job evaluation and salary administration program to the end that uniform and equitable salary treatment may be accorded to all such employees in the department.

Procedure

1. Meetings held weekly on Wednesdays at 2:00 P.M.
2. The chairman will take action for the committee in consultation with its members.
3. The secretary will prepare for meetings, record and follow up actions, and prepare brief minutes.

COORDINATING COMMITTEE
(Carrier Corporation)

The Coordinating Committee of Carrier Corporation is responsible for coordinating the activities of the major divisions of Carrier Corporation to insure proper meshing of those activities. Although the Coordinating Committee is not an operating committee, it is empowered to make decisions and take action within established policy. The committee also may be given specific special assignments and powers by the president.

Members of the Coordinating Committee include:

Executive Vice-President—Chairman
Vice President and Assistant to the President—Vice Chairman
Comptroller
Vice President in Charge of Engineering
Vice President in Charge of Manufacturing
Vice President in Charge of Allied Products Division

Vice President in Charge of Financial Division
Vice President in Charge of the Personnel Division (on call)

Since the activities of the Coordinating Committee are related to the working relationships between divisions, these working relationships must be classified so as to indicate the type and degree of committee attention required. The following classification may be used:

1. *The type of inter-divisional working relationship involved in specific programs.* These relationships should receive particular attention from the Coordinating Committee to make sure that they are "on the right track." Briefly, the Committee's function in these cases is one of constantly reviewing and coordinating the efforts of the various divisions in carrying out a particularly important program. An example might be the initial planning and follow-through on the development, production, and shipment of new products, which involves continuous coordination of the efforts of the engineering, manufacturing, sales, and financial divisions. Such "special attention" programs may be brought before the committee by any of its members, by the chairman, or by the president (in some other companies, any member of management may bring problems and questions to the committee).

2. *Inter-divisional working relationships that are part of the normal, every-day routine.* Each member of the committee advises its secretary of any apparent deficiencies in existing procedures. These matters are investigated and either corrected by the procedures section or, if necessary, brought before the committee.

3. *Emergencies—individual problems that normally would be covered by routine procedures or policy but that require immediate action because of time limitations.* They may be brought to the Coordinating Committee for solution on a request initiated by any member of the organization. Preferably, such requests are made through the proper organization channels, but acute problems may be presented to the Chairman or Secretary directly.

4. *Unclassified problems*—for example, cases in which doubt exists regarding the divisional responsibility or authority to handle a particular problem.

Coordination in the proper sense of the word refers to "the contributions of the respective participants and the arrangements for maintaining cooperation among them, in the light of a course of action already determined." Coordination through a formal committee at either the administrative or the policy level is probably less common in smaller companies, where coordination is more likely to be accomplished through informal channels at the top (president and department heads "clearing" with one another) and through reports. In very large companies members of the board of directors or of the chief committee may become "contacts" for the major divisions and subsidiary companies. Some of the "contact" directors may have small staffs to aid them in the task of coordination. Large companies may also have small coordinating committees to deal with specialized subjects. The need for a committee arises when men working in the same or related fields are not in close enough contact to be acquainted with one another's work and problems. Even though no individual may be formally charged with the burden of coordination, disagreements among members of a coordinating committee often must be referred to an individual, usually the president, for resolution.

COMBINING COMMITTEES—ESTABLISHING NEW COMMITTEES

In combining the work of existing committees or setting up new committees, it may be advisable to apply a checklist of procedures such as the following, developed by one large company:

1. Membership List—permanent; members to be co-opted.
2. Schedule of meetings—dates and place. (Sessions should be bunched together to save the time of the participants and to leave free periods without committee meetings.)
3. Length of meeting, starting and finishing time.
4. Chairman and secretary (their duties).
5. Preparation of agenda. How and by whom it is prepared—items of agenda to be forwarded to and received by committee chairman and secretary. Final date for submission of items of agenda.
6. Procedure whereby secretary distributes agenda and reports (should be read before the meeting to save time).
7. Procedure for recording of committee minutes and reports.
8. Types of committee action—functions, procedures, and limits of authority .
9. Provision for check on recommendations and on action taken.

EVALUATING COMMITTEES

The following memorandum and Committee Data Sheet were used by Standard Oil Company of California to evaluate the work of existing committees with a view to consolidating or dissolving committees whose current accomplishments did not justify their continuation. The data sheets, with the covering memorandum, were sent to committee chairmen for completion.

Memo to: ....

A survey is being made of the justification for continuing each committee currently listed as active in the roster of Company committees. This roster indicates that you are Chairman of the .... Committee.

As a means of gathering factual data regarding the need for continuing each committee, the time demands on members of management involved in its meetings and on the Secretary and his staff in carrying on its activities, and also the effect on Company operations if it were discontinued, the attached questionnaire has been prepared. Will you please arrange to have the Secretary of the .... Committee fill out this questionnaire, which will be reviewed by the Committee and yourself before its release and then will be forwarded to the Manager, Department on Organization, who is coordinating data assembled on this subject.

....

President

COMMITTEE DATA SHEET

1. Name of Committee: ....

2. Present Membership: ....
Recommendation to disband this
committee approved:

   .... (Signature)

   .... (Title)

3. Meeting Schedule: ....
   (Indicate regular schedule if any; otherwise indicate "On
   call when matters require Committee's attention," or other
   appropriate statement.)

4. Number of meetings held in past year:

5. Approximate man-hours per year involved in—

	Past 12 Mos.	Est. for Ensuing 12 Mos.*
(a) Attendance at meetings of Committee	....	....
(b) Secretary and his organization, in planning meetings, distributing agenda, writing minutes and recommendations, etc.	....	....

6. Brief statement of Committee's accomplishments during
   past year: *(Use separate sheet if more space required for
   answers to items 6, 7, 8)*

7. If Committee were disbanded, how would functions assigned
   to it be carried on?

8. Comments and recommendations:

Data compiled by........................... Date.........

---

   * Based on anticipated and/or scheduled activities of this
   Committee for ensuing 12 mos. Explain under "Comments
   and Recommendations" any significant difference between
   actual man-hours shown in 1st column and estimates in
   2nd column.

DECENTRALIZATION

This Appendix details the findings of an AMA survey of the extent of decentralization in major management functions. The functions examined include production, personnel, finance, accounting and statistics, marketing, purchasing, traffic, and specialized functions, principally in large companies.

It should be noted that the survey results apply only to a small sample and are not necessarily representative or generally applicable. We merely touched on those areas on which information was readily available. However, they indicate the type of analysis that might be undertaken in assigning these functions. It should be noted that the degree of decentralization in one function may well be dependent on that of another. For example, if there is a tight central control of the finance function, there may not be much possibility of freedom of personal action with regard to expenditures in other departments.

In the following analysis, centralization has been used to mean concentration of major decisions of the particular management activity at the head office; decentralization, to mean delegation of some major decisions of the activity at the branches. Sometimes it may be said that centralization refers to decision-making by top management, decentralization to decision-making lower down the management hierarchy; to that extent the results apply to companies without branches.

THE PRODUCTION FUNCTION

It is difficult to generalize about decision-making in the production field, for a number of complex factors are involved—the nature of the product, the production process, materials, markets, labor supply, availability of technical skills, transportation facilities, the economical scale of production, the balancing of different types of investment. Usually the production function is the first to be delegated by the chief executive and the degree of delegation increases as the scale of production broadens.

Small and medium-sized companies tend to delegate the production function in job order work. Many of the larger companies have a high degree of delegation of the production process, dividing their operations into product divisions. (The limit to decentralization is usually the point at which major machinery, materials handling equipment, etc., is no longer adequately utilized.) Central coordination is usually maintained through the production or operating budget, through controls over production results, and through the activities of a vice president in charge of manufacturing and/or committee management. This is frequently accompanied by centralization of specialized services, such as technical research, engineering, product development, etc.

The du Pont Company may be cited as an example of delegated operating relationships. Production and sales—and, to a considerable extent, research activities—are carried on by 10 manufacturing departments. Each of these operates very much like an independent company, but is responsible to the president and Executive Committee, from whom its major policies are drawn. Each manufactures and sells groups of products, allied either from the standpoint of manufacture, sale, or both. The product division among these departments is such that, with few exceptions, all the operations within a department have a chemical relationship to each other.

These manufacturing departments function as independent entities within the company. They buy and sell among themselves, generally on the same terms quoted to outside concerns; being a member of the company family does not result in any particular preference. Occasionally their products compete with each other in the same market.

Each industrial department is headed up by a general manager, appointed by the Executive Committee. In turn each general manager appoints an assistant general manager, subject to the approval of the Executive Committee. Beyond that point the general manager assumes responsibility for the organization of the department and its operating results.

The general manager is invariably a man who has worked successfully in the company for many years, and as a rule has worked his way up through the department he heads. In almost all cases he is technically trained. The assistant general manager conforms to the same general pattern, and is qualified to act in the absence of his superior, or to take his superior's place, temporarily or permanently, as circumstances require. The du Pont Company attaches considerable importance to its program for replacement and succession and believes in having trained personnel ready at all times, and at all levels, to step into higher positions.

The effectiveness of this program was demonstrated during World War II, when literally hundreds of key men were taken from their jobs and assigned to work on war projects. In the case of some of its commercial plants, the entire upper management group was displaced. Yet production at those locations went on without interruption or serious difficulty as the men down the line were promoted to the jobs they had been trained to fill.

The general manager is fully responsible for the activities of his department and for the company's investment in plants, laboratories, processes and other facilities under his jurisdiction. He has virtually complete authority over all the factors which enter into his costs and over selling prices. Thus his power is commensurate with his responsibility, in accordance with the basic policy of the du Pont organization.

The general managers look to the Executive Committee, however, for guidance on broad company policy and for a certain degree of coordination between departments. Major decisions affecting plans for construction, capital expenditures, expansion and development, etc., are also referred first to the Executive Committee, and then to the Finance Committee, where necessary.

THE PERSONNEL FUNCTION

Some major decisions of the personnel function tend to be highly centralized, for reasons which will be made clear in the following discussion. They include:

1. *Selection and placement for important executive jobs,* because of the far-reaching effects on managerial efficiency and the high payroll expenditures involved.
2. *Executive development and promotion*—again, to insure managerial efficiency and to prepare executives to fill higher jobs as needed.
3. *Salary changes, bonus, pension and stock-purchase arrangements* are closely linked to profits, incentives, and work satisfaction and therefore are usually determined by top management.
4. *Wage rate changes* for certain groups of employees have an important impact on the labor supply, labor morale, company finances—especially when other employee groups may be affected and/or where the ratio of labor cost to total costs is high.
5. *Labor contract changes* frequently involve important areas of management rights and/or major payroll costs. Therefore such decisions are highly centralized.
6. Contract administration involving *grievance decisions* which may be precedent-making.

It should be noted, however, that even in highly decentralized companies, relatively minor personnel decisions may be carried high up in the organization. At some large companies, for example, divisional personnel managers may go to head office personnel for minor grievance decisions rather than face the possibility of reversal. In a number of large companies all grievances must be referred to the vice president in charge of personnel—and sometimes these cost far more to process than they are worth. It is not unusual to find major inconsistencies in the delegation of decision-making, with local managers granted wide latitude on hiring and firing, for example, with no authority to make transfers or grant salary increases.

THE FINANCE FUNCTION

The finance function is usually less decentralized than any other management function in a company. This tends to be so even where a general policy of decentralization exists. When there are geographically scattered branches or plants, the local financial executive is often under the direct supervision of the finance chief at the head office. It should be noted also that finance may remain under the direct control of the board of directors or its finance committee.

The reasons for the relative lack of decentralized control are obvious. Because the fundamental objective of almost every company is financial a single decision at the financial policy-making level can spell the difference between survival and failure. For this reason, and because top management regularly uses various types of financial reports to check on the effectiveness of its operations, the finance function is accorded a high place within the company, and only rarely are any but the routine aspects of the function decentralized. In view of the high degree of centralization of the finance function, even in companies which are otherwise widely decentralized, the question arises as to how much leeway is afforded local managers in making capital expenditures. In many companies, capital expenditure schedules are laid down in central policy statements, specifying the sums which different members of the management hierarchy are permitted to spend without requesting special permission. These capital expenditures vary to some extent in different companies, but in general they are limited to relatively small amounts. This generalization appears to be confirmed by the data in the accompanying table, which, though based on a small sample, summarizes the practices of a number of companies noted for their decentralized policies.

LIMITS ON CAPITAL EXPENDITURES AT VARIOUS LEVELS OF MANAGEMENT

Type of Company	Board of Dir.	Pres.	Exec. Vice Pres.	Div. or Dept. Vice Pres.	Div. Mgrs. (Several plants)	Plant Mgrs.
Large Chemical Company (1)	Over $1,000	Up to $1,000	Up to $1,000	Up to $1,000	Up to $1,000	
Large Chemical Company (2)	Over $10,000	Up to $10,000				
Large Food Company (1)	Over $25,000			Up to $5,000	Up to $1,000	Up to $500
Large Food Company (2)	Over $250,000	$10,00 to $250,000		$4,000 to $10,000	$500 to $4,000	Up to $500
Large Oil Company	Over $300,000	$100,000 to $300,000	$25,000 to $100,000	$5,000 to $25,000	Up to $5,000	Up to $5,000
Large Materials Company	Over $50,000	$25,000 to $50,000	$10,000 to $25,000	$5,000 to $10,000	$1,000 to $5,000	Up to $1,000
Large Light and Power Company		Over $10,000		$1,000 to $10,000	Up to $1,000	
Medium-Size Heavy Capital Goods Company	Over $10,000	Up to $10,000		Up to $10,000		
Medium-Size Textile Company	Over $50,000	$5,000 to $50,000		Up to $5,000		

Budgeting, as might be expected, is almost always centrally controlled. The various divisions make up budgets at regular intervals, for review and approval by top management. Often the detailed items of expenditure will have to be approved individually once more by the top officials.

Decisions regarding the raising of capital and sources of funds as well as the payment of dividends are usually made by the Board of Directors or the Executive or Finance Committee.

ACCOUNTING AND STATISTICS

The preparation of accounting and statistical reports and their auditing are usually centralized (with the preliminary data assembled locally) so that top management controls can be made effective and comparable results be obtained through standardized methods of reporting. Some companies employ traveling auditors for dispersed branches; others have auditors attached to the individual departments and divisions, reporting directly to top management. The over-all analysis and presentation of accounting and statistical data are usually performed most economically through a central department, though complaints are sometimes raised about slowness of reporting and inadequate circulation of results.

THE MARKETING FUNCTION

A. *Selling*

In a study of decentralization in sales management by J. A. Murphy, in the magazine, *Sales Management* (November 10, 1946), it was concluded that the delegation of decision-making in this field is more widespread than in any other business function. There may be a high degree of centralization in all other departments of a company, but sales is very frequently the exception.

The reason is, of course, that selling, unlike production, must usually be done away from headquarters, and customers are often scattered. Rarely, if ever, can a salesman's approach be rigidly prescribed by the head office. Instead, he must adjust himself and his selling techniques to constantly changing circumstances, and have some freedom of action, if he is to be in fact a salesman and not merely an order-taker.

Selling authority must usually be delegated when a company's distribution extends well beyond the headquarters area and it becomes desirable to set up branch sales offices. Or the introduction of major lines may lead to decentralization. Thus the Ford Motor Company delegated to newly established divisions the responsibility for sales of major products like Ford, Lincoln, etc., which had formerly been under the supervision of the head office sales manager. At that time one group handled the sales of several models. But now the specialists, handling a limited product line, are making larger sales over a wider area and, despite higher total selling costs, profits are better. John A. Roebling's Sons Company made a similar successful transition.

Another major reason for decentralization of sales is customer convenience, particularly in the field of retailing. Decentralization is common here—e.g., the large grocery chains, mail-order houses with retail outlets and, more recently, the opening of suburban branches of department stores. Because of the dangers, on these operations, of

lack of adequate selection of merchandise, overstocking or over-aging
of inventories, some degree of central coordination is usually maintained through a vice president in charge of sales and through committees which hold regular conferences. General policies are formulated centrally—e.g., those affecting the use of the company's name
or the coordination of divisions to avoid competitive selling practices
between member units (e.g., the recent reorganization of Remington-
Rand for the latter reason).

It must be noted, however, that much "decentralization" of marketing (and of other functions) exists in name only. The units are
separated by physical distance, it is true, but strict control is maintained from the head office. Without express permission from the
main sales office little or no variation is permitted (usually for co-
gent reasons) in the prices and discounts quoted or in merchandise
specifications; there are strict limits on the amount of credit granted;
the expenditures for travel and entertainment, number of calls to be
made, the sales quotas—all may be prescribed in considerable detail,
and regularly checked upon by the home office. Even the sales talk
may be worked out as a standard procedure. The amount of the sale
may be the only variable. The reason for centralization in these
situations is management's conviction that strict control must be
maintained over the utilization of expensive time and talent. Centralization of sales offices is usual when the scale of sales is small
and sales costs constitute a small proportion of total price.

B. *Market Research*

The locus of decision-making for this function depends a good
deal on how the selling itself is handled. But even if selling is decentralized, it may still be economical to have a central department to
plan the market research and coordinate the results.

Often a central market research department can, of course, hire
more specialized and expert researchers than the branches can afford.
The actual collection of data may become decentralized, the forecast
of sales centralized and the determination of sales policies localized
within the framework of general sales policy.

C. *Advertising*

In advertising the general trend is largely toward centralization of
decision-making. Advertising is usually centralized when one or a
combination of the following conditions exist:

1. When advertising is a major factor in the profit or loss of

the company, (e.g., the personal control over advertising exercised by the late G. W. Hill at the American Tobacco Company).

2. When the status and prestige of the company as a whole is closely associated with its advertising.

3. When better rates and service can be obtained from agencies by placing large accounts. This advantage can be retained, however, if the central office places the contracts, against which the branches charge their advertising.

4. When the centralized market research and advertising department has a more experienced and competent staff.

5. When advertising is national rather than local, and contacts must be made at national headquarters.

D. *Export*

Export activities are usually centralized at head office, because they are highly complex. One major exception is the establishment of independent manufacturing plants or selling branches in foreign countries.

PURCHASING

The point of purchase may be determined to some extent by a classification according to the type of purchase. Purchase of capital equipment must usually be decided by top management because of the size of the investment. Again, basic materials used in the manufacture which constitute a substantial proportion of total costs are purchased centrally. Even where purchasing is decentralized in the branch plants, materials which are used at all or most of the branches are often purchased centrally. Thus, for example, the Ford Motor Company, which recently decentralized purchasing into its six divisions, continues to buy steel, glass and tires centrally. On the other hand, when the materials represent a minor part of total costs, and especially if they involve small outlay as to repair and maintenance, the authority to buy may be broadly delegated. The tendency toward decentralized purchasing is greater:

1. In plants with different purchase problems, such as:
   a. widely separated plants, especially where communication is difficult;
   b. plants with different product lines and purchase requirements;
   c. plants in which local purchases are important or supplies perishable;

     d. plants which are semi-independent and on a competitive basis; for example, in some companies the record of each division is judged on its profit-and-loss statement and, for this reason, the General Manager has been endowed with authority to purchase as he wishes if it will enable him to meet his responsibility for profit maximization.

2. At times when purchase price declines are expected, so that hand-to-mouth buying becomes important.

3. For those materials which are purchased in small quantities or where central purchasing does not result in appreciable savings.

Decentralization of purchases does not appear to be frequent within single-plant companies or even where several plants of the same company are in the same locality, because of the duplication of effort. The results of one survey of the extent of decentralized purchasing were reported as follows:

> In about 30 per cent of the companies having separate or branch plants, the great bulk of the purchasing is done at the central office, with a minimum of buying authority granted to the branches. In about 15 per cent, buying for each plant is largely an independent operation, coordinated in some cases by having the various purchasing officers meet in conference at quarterly or more frequent intervals, at which time experiences can be interchanged and generally uniform policies developed. In somewhat more than half the cases, centralization of authority is accepted in principle but adapted to the circumstances by delegating a considerable degree of independence in action to the branch purchasing officers, while retaining central control through organization channels, standardized procedures, and systematic accountability to the headquarters purchasing office.*

The present trend is strongly toward such a middle course.

It should be noted that even where there is decentralization of purchases there is usually a centralized staff function of purchasing. The director of purchasing at the head office is responsible for the

---

* Stuart F. Heinritz, *Purchasing*, (Copyright 1947, 1951 by Prentice-Hall, Inc., New York). Second Edition, 1951, p. 71. Reprinted by permission of the publishers.

establishment of basic policies and procedures. Even if the central purchasing department makes the general contract for materials, the plants may be left free to place their orders directly against the contract. There is usually a regular interchange of information among the various directors of purchasing, possibly also a central coordination committee.

Some large companies have established a Buyers' Guide, prepared and released by the general purchasing agent's office to members of local line management. It is used for the procurement of materials and supplies needed for local operations. The Guide is maintained and controlled by a central purchasing organization. "Deputy buyers" are set up in the regular line organization to handle a large proportion of local buying. In one large company 87 per cent of the purchases are made by decentralized personnel. This delegation conserves the time of the central purchasing staff for the performance of functions associated with negotiation, contract purchasing, and maintenance of the Buyers' Guide. Foremen, staff aides to line executives, and field management draw their purchase orders by reference to the Buyers' Guide, which tells how to purchase, what to pay, and how to allocate business among different vendors.

The objectives of the Buyers' Guide are to decentralize and simplify routine ordering functions, to the end that the user may order directly from sources of supply established by the purchasing department through purchasing contracts or special price agreements.

Control is maintained on these decentralized purchases in two ways: (1) by audit in the central purchasing offices of vendors' invoices; and (2) by audit of field ordering points. In addition to Buyers' Guide sheets, there has been established a procedure whereby field points may place standing orders with local suppliers to take care of small, repetitive purchases. Under this arrangement only one billing is received per month, and much paper work is eliminated.

To illustrate, the following typical excerpt from the Buyers' Guide of a large company covers the purchase of caustic soda—an item contracted for on a yearly basis. The information set forth in the Guide permits the user to order direct from the source established. Thus the actual order placement is delegated to the user, but the procedure is uniform and the merchandise is obtained from established sources.

Buyers' Guide

Date   5-16-51   *Sheet No.*   S-57-A

Commodity	*Soda, Caustic—Liquid, Solid and Flake*

Ordering Description

Liquid: Specify quantity in gallons—furnished in 750 or 2000 gal. tank trucks and 8000 gal. tank cars.

Solid: Specify quantity of 720 lb. (non-returnable) steel drums.

Flake: Specify quantity of 400 lb. (non-returnable) steel drums.

To meet Spec. #2050 of 2-2-34—solid or flake.

To meet Spec. #2132—liquid.

Stamp: "For Resale—X-1400 etc." or "Not for Resale."

Southern Division:	*Source:*	*Phone Number*
Carloads	"A" Electrochemical Co. Box 876, Los Angeles, Calif.	Le-5-6000
Solid & Flake only Small requirements in drums only	"B" Chemical Co. 2026 Santa Fe Ave., L. A.	St-5-7000
Liquid, in drums Small requirements	"C" Chemical Co. 100 So. Spring St., L. A.	Tu-5-8000

Price	(1) Per contract. (2) As Agreed.
F.O.B.	(1) Shipper's cars or trucks. (2) Shipper's warehouse.
Ship Via.	Follow General Routing Instructions
Note: (a)	(1)—Buyer Co. must furnish shipping instructions on or before the 10th of each month for quantities required during next succeeding month.
Note: (b)	Allow 7 to 14 days lead time—*liquid.*
Note: (c)	Allow 30 days lead time—*solid or flake.* Liquid caustic soda drums are returnable for credit of $20.00 each.

TRAFFIC

When shipping is direct from supplier to branch plant and from the branch plant to customer, it is usually left under local control. Many companies centralize the setting of basic policies, studies of transportation rates, and negotiation with carriers. Centralization also exists in the case of vertical integration where the steady flow of work depends on an efficient and unified routing system among the various units of production.

SPECIALIZED FUNCTIONS

Each of such specialized functions as legal, patent, insurance, real estate and scientific and economic research are frequently centralized in one department because of their highly specialized personnel requirements, and because of the fact that they most frequently serve management at the policy-making level. In the case of research, the nature of the work itself may make some degree of decentralization desirable, but because of the expense involved, duplication of facilities should be avoided wherever possible. In any event, the results of research are more likely to be used to best advantage if the research director reports directly to top management.

CONTENT OF MAJOR MANAGEMENT FUNCTIONS
(With specific job contents for large and medium-sized firms)

A list of major management functions and their contents may be helpful in reorganization and in preparation of job descriptions, organization manuals, and charts. The major management functions, analyzed in this Appendix on the basis of a number of manuals, job descriptions, and interviews, are as follows:

Production	Organization
Sales	Traffic
Research and Engineering	Office Management
Finance	Purchasing
Law	Plant Management
Personnel	Coordination Requirements for
Public Relations	the Production and Sales Departments
Secretary	

Most of these functions are described in condensed form for a number of companies in general, as well as specifically for a large and a medium-sized firm. The large company is engaged in manufacturing. It has more than 20,000 employees and operates 20 plants with an annual sales volume of over $200 million. The medium-sized firm is the Line Material Company of Milwaukee, Wisconsin. At the time of analysis it had about 3,000 employees and nine manufacturing plants.

In drawing up management functions it is most important to obtain the proper coordination and collaboration between them. One such example is given for the production function and one for the sales function.

In using this information, the following cautions should be borne in mind:

1. The listed functions are not always present as identified functions or activities in all organizations. An attempt has been made to be comprehensive so that companies can select and check against an extensive list. But the lists are not necessarily typical.
2. In a given company the particular activities listed *may* or *may not* be placed under the function to which they are assigned here.
3. Some of these functions may be administered in part by one department and in part by another department.
4. They may be grouped in many varying combinations.
5. This list is not meant to suggest an order of importance or relationship.
6. Some responsibilities are found in common under all functions, such as the need for policy formation and planning, for study of the practices of other companies, for carrying out special assignments of the president, for coordinating with other functions.

THE PRODUCTION FUNCTION

General Content:

1. Design and construction of plants
2. Planning and justifying plant capital expenditures
3. Supervision of production orders received
4. Promise of delivery, schedule of manpower equipment and materials flow, coordination with sales

5. Planning of the production flow and assignment of orders
6. Supervision of production
7. Development of production controls, such as:
    (a) Coordination with marketing and engineering
    (b) Quality control
    (c) Control of over-all production, machine, and manpower performance

Other functions which may be exercised by the Production Department include purchasing, design of plant and product, plant maintenance, inventory, industrial relations, research, traffic, safety, engineering and industrial engineering.

THE PRODUCTION FUNCTION IN THE LARGE COMPANY

I. *Objectives*

Planning and coordinating production activities throughout the company to aid in developing, maintaining, and operating efficient production facilities to compete and to obtain adequate return on capital investment

II. *Functions*

1. Design and construction of large projects
2. Assistance in coordinating the development of production methods for new and changed products
3. Establishing policies to govern manufacturing methods and standards
4. Providing assistance, advice, and services to all branches of the company on such functions as the following:
    Engineering
    Quality Control
    Purchasing
    Traffic
    Housing for Employees
5. Advice on capital expenditure
6. Review of production performance

III. *Relationships*

The Vice President for Production reports to the President

THE PRODUCTION FUNCTION IN THE MEDIUM-SIZE COMPANY

1. Development of a Manufacturing Control Group in order to:
    a. Coordinate sales and engineering for planning production and developing production schedules

    b. Assign production to plants

    c. Maintain over-all control of plant inventory

    d. Coordinate product development

    e. Order and schedule requests for manufacturing

2. Provision of a Centralized Manufacturing Engineering Group in order to:

    a. Standardize

    b. Plan and estimate new products

    c. Obtain best utilization of machines, manpower, and materials handling through Industrial Engineering

    d. Establish quality control

3. Providing plant managers with adequate authority and personnel

4. Review of plant budgets

5. Supervision of plant managers and establishment of weekly reports

THE SALES FUNCTION

General Content:

1. Planning, administering, and controlling the general sales program

2. Market research (actual and potential shares, profitably, consumer habits, and acceptance)

3. Product development (new and modified products, uses, defects, style, color, number of items, reduction of variety, obsolescence, packaging)

4. Determination of prices, discounts, credits, adjustments, allowances, services

5. Distribution channels (number, size, and location, profitability, dealer agreement, training, territorial changes)

6. Sales territories, accounts, and quotas

7. Selection, training, compensation, turnover, incentives of sales personnel

8. Sales Control (budgets, expenses, performance)

9. Advertising (budget media, campaigns, trademarks, brands)

10. Promotion (trade shows, exhibits, displays, campaigns, contests, lists, samples and manuals, house organs, dealer aids, bulletins, motion pictures, radio, television, premiums, testimonials)

THE SALES FUNCTIONS IN THE LARGE COMPANY

I. *Objectives*

Planning, promotion, and coordination of sales and merchandising policies to insure the progress of the company and all its divisions; focusing attention on the greatest opportunities and special weaknesses

II. *Functions*

1. Provision of the following services
   a. Selling in common markets
   b. Market surveys and territorial analyses
   c. Advertising and sales promotion
   d. Government relationships
2. Development of selling and merchandising policies
3. Coordination of sales and production
4. Aiding the divisions in developing incentive compensation plans

III. *Relationships*

The Vice President for Sales reports to the President

THE SALES FUNCTION IN THE MEDIUM-SIZE COMPANY

1. Specific services provided:
   a. Sales administration
   b. Sales negotiations
   c. Field sales
   d. Foreign sales
   e. Government sales
   f. Marketing
   g. Sales promotion
   h. Advertising
   i. Product sales
2. Coordination of sales and manufacturing (with periodic master schedules specified)
3. Product distribution

THE RESEARCH AND ENGINEERING FUNCTION

General Content:

1. Design and construction of plant facilities and machinery
2. Maintenance, repair, and replacement of plant and machinery
3. Engineering methods

4. Setting engineering standards
5. Control of engineering performance
6. Research and design of new products; test and proof of their practicability
7. Adapting new products to plant production
8. Establishment and operation of test laboratories
9. Plant product engineering

GENERAL ENGINEERING IN THE LARGE COMPANY

I. *Objectives*

Execution of mechanical development, design, and construction, when estimated cost exceeds $100,000, and review of all other projects. Execution of any project which entails deviation or new standard equipment or requires the services of a packaging or materials handling specialist.

II. *Functions*

1. Equipment design, development, and construction
2. Design and construction of plant facilities
3. Maintenance, repair, and replacement of machinery
4. Engineering methods
5. Setting of engineering standards
6. Audit and report on the application of engineering processes
7. Interchange of engineering reports

III. *Relationships*

The Director of the General Engineering Department reports to the Vice President for Production

RESEARCH AND ENGINEERING IN THE MEDIUM-SIZE COMPANY

1. Research and development: new products
   a. Conceiving, developing and designing new products
   b. Testing and proving practicability and uses of new and improved products, materials, and processes
   c. Improvement of product quality
   d. Technical services for other divisions
   e. Studying customer's requirements and assisting customer to determine uses of new products
2. Plant Product Engineering: re-design of all regular line products for improvement and cost reductions
3. Establishment of test laboratories

4. Plant Product Engineering
   a. Product group engineering
   b. Product development
   c. Product engineering
   d. Drafting and blueprinting

FUNCTIONS OF THE TREASURER

General Content:

1. Financial Planning
   a. Reporting financial results to the officers of the company
   b. Planning the company investment program
   c. Planning borrowing requirements
   d. Forecast of cash receipts and disbursements
   e. Advice on dividend payments
2. Cash Management
   a. Opening accounts and deposit of funds in banks
   b. Management of petty cash and bank balances
   c. Payment of company obligations through proper disbursement procedures
   d. Maintaining records of cash transactions
3. Credit Management
   a. Determination of customers' credit risks
   b. Orderly handling of collections
   c. Handling cash discounts and terms of sale for prompt payment
   d. Collections
4. Security Flotations
   a. Recommendation of type of security most desirable for company's borrowing requirements and correlating these with company's long-term ability to pay
   b. Negotiation with investment bankers
   c. Provision for trustee, registration of transfer agent, compliance
   d. Compliance with governmental regulations
   e. Retirement of bonds and stock
   f. Stockholder relationships, disbursement of dividends, etc.
5. Signing of checks, contracts, leases, notes, bonds, and stock certificates, mortgages, deeds, and other corporate documents, endorsement for deposits, collection of checks
6. Custody of funds and securities

FUNCTIONS OF THE VICE PRESIDENT FOR FINANCE
IN THE LARGE COMPANY

Objectives

The Vice President for Finance is responsible for the supply of financial services and the control of expenditures and results

Functions

1. Appraisal of the financial results of the operations of each division and the benefits received from the expenditures
2. Supply of financial services and assistance
3. Appraisal of proposed expenditures
4. Setting up of systems for computing product costs in the several operating divisions
5. Comparison of expenditures with budget
6. Setting up the principles and methods of keeping accounts and accounting control
7. Setting up procedures for the receipt, banking, custody, and disbursement of money
8. Forecasting the financial results of the company
9. Directing the internal audit
10. Conduct of external financial relationships, including the determination of tax liabilities, the authorization of credit, collection of money due, disposition of surplus assests, and relations with fiduciary agents
11. Provision of insurance
12. Preparation of accounting and statistical reports

Relationships

The Vice President for Finance reports to the Chairman of the Board, who is the Chief Executive.

FUNCTIONS OF THE CONTROLLER

General Content:

1. Providing basic information for managerial control through formulation of accounting and costing policies, standards and procedures, preparation of financial statements and maintenance of books of account; direction of internal auditing and cost controls
2. Budgeting and control of operations and results

3. Specific control activities:
   a. General accounts—primary and subsidiary accounts; devising checks on the company's finances and safeguarding its assets; checking invoices, accounts receivable and payable; controlling cash payments and receipts, payroll accounts, fringe benefits, plant and equipment records; cost accounting activities of the various management functions
   b. Preparation and interpretation of regular financial reports and statements
   c. Inventory control
   d. Statistics
   e. Taxes
4. Internal audits
5. Interpretation of control data

Functions of the Controller in the Large Company

Objectives

The Controller (or Comptroller) of Accounts is responsible for the effective financial and cost controls of the company's activities

Functions

1. Prescription of principles and methods to govern accounting controls throughout the enterprise
2. Provision of adequate protection against loss of the company's money and property
3. Prescription of principles of accounting determining cost of product, and normal volume of production in order to compute costs and install appropriate systems
4. Verification of the propriety of expenditures
5. Providing comparison of capital expenditures with appropriations
6. Preparation of the accounts of the corporation
7. Determination of income and expenditure allocation among plants and departments
8. Proposals regarding the nature of the corporation's financial statements
9. Preparation of the financial statements
10. Preparation of analyses assisting others to improve the earnings of the enterprise
11. Observation of the manner of performing accounting responsibilities

Relationships

The Controller of Accounts reports to the Vice President for Finance.

FUNCTIONS OF THE TREASURER AND CONTROLLER IN THE MEDIUM-SIZE COMPANY

1. Accountability for the safekeeping and custody of corporate funds, securities owned by the company, and the corporate seal
2. Establishment of a General Accounting Department with the following duties:
   a. Post-audit of plant transactions
   b. Installation and maintenance of primary books of account
   c. Setting up policies, procedures, and standards of accounting and cost records and reports
   d. Setting up methods of cash disbursement, accounts receivable, plant and equipment records
   e. Cash management
   f. Preparation of financial statements and reports
   g. Credit approval
3. Establishment of a cost accounting department with a view to:
   a. Prescribing and administering factory timekeeping and payroll procedure
   b. Maintaining inventory controls
   c. Supervision of timekeeping methods
   d. Setting up a cost system in each plant
4. Establishing a budget department to present standards of performance to management with a view to:
   a. Showing the results of operations
   b. Establishing standards of performance
   c. Preparing a budget forecast
   d. Informing executives of variations from the budget
   e. Continuous revision of the budget

FUNCTIONS OF GENERAL COUNSEL

1. Provision of legal advice to the enterprise and its departments
2. Anticipating and guarding against legal risks
3. Conduct of litigation
4. Appointment of legal counsel

5. Study of proposed and existing legislation; informing the persons concerned
6. Study of patents and proper protection of the enterprise
7. Participation in actions of a major character, such as the following:
   a. Financing, charter amendments, changes in the corporate structure
   b. Acquisition and disposal of important segments of the enterprise or real estate
   c. Determination of action in order to comply with legislation
8. Preparation or approval of contracts involving leases, licenses, options, labor contracts, guarantees, releases, purchase contracts of real estate and continuous raw materials contracts, employment and insurance contracts; contracts involving engineering, advertising and other services, distributors and dealers, easements or rights of way, bonds
9. Approval of sales and advertising copy as well as public statements
10. Protection of the company's products, devices, processes, and trademarks by patents, copyrights, and registration

THE PERSONNEL FUNCTION

General Contents:

The subjects of personnel administration include the following 11 major areas:

1. Employment
   a. Selection and placement
   b. Testing
   c. Induction
   d. Changes in status
   e. Exit interview
   f. Guidance and counseling
2. Salary and Wage Administration
   a. Job analysis and job evaluation
   b. Salary and wage adjustments
   c. Employee rating
   d. Hours, vacations, holidays
3. Medical
   a. Development and administration of a program of industrial medicine

    b. Pre-employment examinations
    c. Maintenance of hygienic working conditions
    d. Advice on non-industrial disability cases
    e. Medical care of industrial injury and occupational illness cases
    f. Selection and supervision of the company's medical staff

4. Safety
    a. Safety standards
    b. Safety inspections
    c. Accident reports
    d. Safety education

5. Training
    a. Job instruction and orientation
    b. Supervisory training
    c. Executive training programs
    d. Preparation of training materials
    e. General information media, library, company publications

6. Benefits and Services
    a. Group insurance
    b. Hospitalization plan
    c. Retirement plan
    d. Social and athletic programs, recreational facilities
    e. Credit union
    f. Miscellaneous services
    g. Suggestion systems

7. Working Conditions
    a. Plant housekeeping
    b. Cafeteria
    c. Sanitary facilities
    d. Ventilation and lighting
    e. Rest periods
    f. Plant protection

8. Research
    a. Development of standard practices and procedures
    b. Research on all phases of personnel and industrial relations
    c. Preparation of manuals and forms
    d. Recording and reporting cost of living, company personnel statistics, comparisons of policies and salary plans of other companies

e. Cooperation with all divisions and departments on research and statistical activities

f. Keeping up with industrial relations research outside the company; establishing and maintaining professional contacts

9. Records
   a. Personnel files of all employees
   b. Company history of each employee, promotions, transfers, etc.
   c. Absence reports
   d. Turnover reports
   e. Accident records
   f. Employee attitudes

10. Labor Relations
    a. Study of best labor relations practices throughout industry
    b. Study and development of sound labor relations policies
    c. Following labor legislation, state and federal
    d. Counsel and participation in union negotiations
    e. Counsel on union contract administration
    f. Handling of arbitration cases
    g. Relations with governmental labor agencies
    h. N.L.R.B. cases, union elections, certifications
    i. Handling of matters pertaining to labor unions other than those representing company's employees

11. Payroll
    a. Preparation of payrolls and distribution of salary and wages
    b. Coordinate timekeeping functions for the company
    c. Maintain tax deductions, social security deductions, etc., information

In addition, there may be special sections for Communications and Community Relationships.

PERSONNEL FUNCTIONS IN A LARGE COMPANY

I. *Basic Objectives:*

1. Creation of a feeling of understanding between the company and the men and women in the organization and development of plans and practices toward these ends
2. Consistency of all personnel practices

II. *Functions*
   1. Contract negotiation assistance
   2. Assistance in selection and development of plant industrial relations personnel
   3. Compensation—Salary Administration
   4. Safety and Health
   5. Employee benefits
   6. Training
   7. Employment
   8. Employee communications

III. *Relationships*

The Vice President for Relationships reports to the President.

PERSONNEL FUNCTIONS IN THE MEDIUM-SIZE COMPANY

1. Union Relations
2. Personnel Relations
   a. Employment
   b. Training
   c. Wage and salary administration
   d. Communications and public relations
   e. Records

PUBLIC RELATIONS

Principal Types of Participation:
   1. Participation in stockholder relations
      a. Aid in preparation of periodic reports
      b. Stockholder letters and meetings
      c. Stockholder surveys
   2. Participation in customer relations
   3. Participation in governmental relations
   4. Participation in relations with employees and labor unions
   5. Community relations
   6. Relations with industry
   7. Conduct of or participation in relations with the press and other news media

PUBLIC RELATIONS IN A LARGE COMPANY

Objectives

Development of the most effective practices and plans for the maintenance and improvement of the company's acceptance by various segments of the public (excluding product and service acceptance among customers)

Functions

1. Studies and surveys of the degree and nature of the company's acceptance
2. Establishment and maintenance of proper relations with news media
3. Provision and maintenance of channels of information to employees
4. Assembly, preparation, and distribution of facts to stockholders
5. Preparation and release of company information about its activities
6. Review of public addresses and articles prepared by company representatives to insure conformity to the policies and practices of the firm
7. Assistance and advice to all segments of the company on the creation, release, and distribution of information to the public
8. Preparation and advice in the formulation and accomplishment of goodwill programs and better understanding in communities in which the company operates

Relationships

The Director of Public Relations reports to the Vice President and Assistant to the Chairman

FUNCTIONS OF THE SECRETARY

1. Preparation and transmittal to stockholders of notices of all annual and special meetings and proxies, and passing on their validity and quorum requirements
2. Service as secretary at stockholder meetings, keeping minutes, and preparing certificates
3. Preparation and transmission of notices of Board meetings and their agenda, attending the meetings as secretary, and keeping minutes
4. Similar service as secretary of the Retirement Committee
5. Custody of the seal of the corporation, its charter, and certificate of incorporation
6. Preparation and filing of all reports of general corporate activity (excluding tax returns)

DIRECTOR OF ORGANIZATION PLANNING

I. *Objectives*

The purpose of the function of organization planning and control is to set up and maintain a rational division of work and to check its effectiveness (through a program of integrated studies)

II. *Functions*

A Company-wide program of organization analysis and improvement is to be carried out, roughly in the following order of priority:

1. Analysis and evaluation of the company's organization structure
2. Development of a uniform approach to program and project planning and progress reporting
3. Analysis, improvement, and formalization of the Company's policies and procedures. This is to be accomplished partly by a process of recording in manuals the policies necessary to exercise competently the different management functions
4. Management organization and policy audits
5. A personnel inventory of existing members of management
6. A replacement and executive development policy
7. A policy of salary controls and adjustments
8. Application of work simplification and work measurement to administrative and clerical functions
9. A policy of executive selection
10. A policy of executive merit rating
11. Organization, executive and labor force controls to assure satisfactory structure and optimum size force

III. *The Director's Program Responsibility*

In the development of a program the responsibilities of the director of organization planning and control are in the main as follows:

1. A description of the program, including its objectives and scope
2. A general plan of action for its accomplishment
3. A statement estimating probable costs
4. A statement estimating probable benefits
5. A schedule for its completion
6. A system for controlling results and reporting progress
7. Approval through the appropriate executive officer

IV. *Relationships*

The Director of Organization Planning reports to the President.

FUNCTION OF TRAFFIC MANAGEMENT

*General Content:**

1. Purchase of transportation, collecting information on the availability, speed, safety, and costs of different types of transportation
2. Receipt of materials and supplies, issue of shipping and delivery instructions, check of incoming goods, arrangements for warehousing
3. Shipping products out of the plant, proper packing for transportation, division of proper quantities (carload lots), proper marking of point of origin and destination, preparation of "shipping papers," loading rules and regulations, utilization of transit services, participation in the intra-plant movement of raw materials
4. Auditing transportation accounts
5. Adjustment and settlement of claims
6. Knowledge of shippers' rights and privileges as well as their duties and obligations toward the carriers

The exact nature of the traffic department varies largely with the size of the enterprise and the nature of the work. Some aspects of the traffic functions are usually emphasized much more than others. A division of duties found in many traffic departments includes rates, claims, billing, shipping, accounts, and records.

TRAFFIC MANAGEMENT IN A LARGE COMPANY

Objectives

Provision of speedy, safe, and economical transportation

Functions

1. Coordination
   a. Planning for the utilization of the most efficient transportation agencies
   b. Seeking the most efficient means of plant traffic operation, in collaboration with the plant traffic managers
   c. Interpretation of federal traffic regulations
   d. Review of traffic performance

* This material has been summarized from a chapter of a forthcoming book on *Industrial Traffic Management in Domestic Commerce* by Professor T. W. van Metre.

2. Rates and classifications
   a. Obtaining lower transportation costs from transportation agencies and establishing classification categories
   b. Opposing rate applications injurious to the business
   c. Uniform preparation of shipping documents
3. Claims
   a. Placement of claims for loss, damage, or overcharge
   b. Audit of freight bills
4. Sales services
   a. Providing the divisions with data concerning different means of transportation for use in competitive selling
   b. Advice regarding apportionment of tonnage on the basis of traffic data
5. Cost studies and reports
6. Other services
   a. Importation from abroad
   b. Provision of passenger transportation for the company's employees
   c. Shipment of employees' household effects
   d. Operation of company airplanes

Relationships

The Director of Traffic reports to the Vice President in Charge of Production.

OFFICE MANAGEMENT FUNCTION

General Content:

1. Provision of office equipment
   a. Operation and maintenance of the office equipment
   b. Provision of adequate physical surroundings, such as proper heat, light, ventilation
   c. Proper application and standardization of office equipment
2. Planning office methods and operations, such as standardization of office forms and the rationalization of office methods
3. Office personnel policies, such as the recruitment, selection, training, and day-to-day supervision of office personnel
4. Collection and control of office costs

OFFICE MANAGEMENT IN THE LARGE COMPANY

Objectives

Prescription of uniform methods for the performance of the company's work whenever such uniformity will significantly increase the effectiveness or decrease the cost of such work

Functions

1. Supervision, through unit heads, of office work and services
2. Prescription of economical methods of office work (and their description in clear form) wherever this is not the responsibility of someone else
3. Study and information of effective types of office equipment
4. Standardization of office forms, equipment

Relationships

The Office Methods Specialist reports to the Vice President for Finance

THE PURCHASING FUNCTION

General Content:

1. Study of markets, suppliers, prices, and government regulations
2. Forecast of optimum balances and aid in inventory control
3. Determination of proper balance between centralization and decentralization
4. Preparation of standard purchase specifications
5. Negotiation of contracts and of purchases
6. Review of the activities of purchasing agents
7. Disposal of scrap

The purchasing function may also include traffic control, supervision of deliveries, inspection and testing, storekeeping.

THE PURCHASING FUNCTION IN THE LARGE COMPANY

I. *Objectives*

Planning and reviewing to insure the uniform and effective performance of purchasing

II. *Functions*

1. Preparation and assistance to the operating divisions in writing standard purchase specifications
2. Negotiation of large purchase contracts

3. Study of price trends and recommendations for advance commitments under favorable market conditions

4. Analysis of purchase data of vendors for possible use by the company's divisions selling to such vendors

III. *Relationships*

The Director of Purchasing reports to the Vice President for Production.

THE PURCHASING FUNCTION IN THE MEDIUM-SIZE COMPANY

1. Organization and direction of central purchase office
2. Approval of all purchases over $500 and referral to president for counter-approval
3. Determination of products and quantities to be purchased centrally and locally
4. Development of optimum purchasing specifications
5. Study of market trends
6. Representation of company in all contracts with vendors
7. Follow-up on deliveries to see that company's schedules are met without interruption
8. Development of policies and procedures for sale and disposition of scrap
9. Periodic review of the purchasing activities of the plants

THE PLANT MANAGER'S FUNCTION

General Content:

1. Production in accordance with policy and administrative standards
2. Product engineering
3. Quality control
4. Inventory control
5. Cost control
6. Recruitment and training of supervisory personnel and employees
7. Initiation and recommendation of capital expenditures and maximum utilization of equipment
8. Coordination with purchasing and sales

THE FUNCTIONS OF THE PLANT MANAGER IN THE LARGE COMPANY

I. *Objectives*

Maintenance and operation of plant economically and effectively

II. *Functions*

1. Proposal of capital expenditures
2. Recruitment and training of efficient plant force and supervisors
3. Proper conduct of employee relationships and community relationships
4. Production and shipment in accordance with product specifications and schedules
5. Recommendation of studies and actions to promote company objectives

Inspection is to be performed by the quality control manager of the division, accounting and disbursement by the finance office.

III. *Relationships*

The plant manager reports to the Production Manager of the operating division.

FUNCTIONS OF THE PLANT MANAGER IN THE MEDIUM-SIZE COMPANY

1. Direct responsibility over the following functions:
    a. Production control
    b. Manufacturing engineering (industrial and plant engineering)
    c. Quality control
    d. Local purchasing
    e. Office administration
    f. Production
    g. Employee relations
2. Production of quality products in accordance with specifications and according to production schedules
3. Approval and initiation of capital expenditures
4. Training of personnel
5. Utilization of staff services
6. Maximum utilization of equipment
7. Maintenance of effective inventory control

MANUFACTURING: COORDINATION REQUIREMENTS IN A MEDIUM-SIZE COMPANY

Responsibility for Coordination:

1. With Sales—
    a. Establishment of master schedules and planning of opera-

tions for each plant on the basis of forecasts from the
marketing department
b. Receipt of orders to manufacture from the Sales Department and scheduling of plant work accordingly
c. Release of finished orders to the Sales Department
d. Adjustment of customer complaints

2. With Research and Engineering—
a. Planning new products
b. Conforming to research and engineering standards
c. Getting Research and Engineering consent and conforming to its standards in making practical changes in specifications, dimensions, and tolerances
d. Cooperation in engineering activities and research studies

3. With the Treasurer and Controller's Division—
a. Immediate jurisdiction over Works Accountants, but responsibility to Treasurer and Controller for adherence to
accounting policies and procedures

4. With the Purchasing Division—
a. Adherence to purchasing policies and procedures regarding the requisition of productive materials, supplies,
equipment, tools and service; policies of centralization
and decentralization
b. Aiding in the reduction of material costs
c. Immediate jurisdiction over purchasing agents, who will,
however, be responsible to the Director of Purchasing for
adherence to purchasing policies and procedures as well
as in the disposition of scrap

5. With the Legal Counsel and Employee Relations Divisions
for—
a. Working within the framework of employee relations
policies
b. Requesting assistance in planning, promotion, and transfers
c. Planning manpower requirements for each plant in line
with the master production schedule at least 60 days
ahead of changes
d. Administration of the suggestion system

e. Participation in labor negotiations and representing the company in union negotiations

f. Direct jurisdiction over personnel representatives at the plants, but with adherence to general personnel policies

COORDINATION REQUIREMENTS OF THE SALES DEPARTMENT IN THE MEDIUM-SIZE COMPANY

1. Functional responsibility to the Treasurer and Controller for:

   a. Prices and terms

   b. Obtaining records, data, sales history for proper sales administration and inventory control

   c. Retaining customer goodwill in credit and collection policies

   d. Furnishing invoices of completed orders for collection purposes

   e. Collaboration on payrolls and expense vouchers

2. Functional responsibilities to Research and Engineering for:

   a. Cooperation in arranging customer contacts

   b. Suggestions for re-design and new products

   c. Information about new competitive products

   d. Investigation of new products

   e. Assistance in developing acceptable quality

3. Functional responsibilities to Manufacturing for:

   a. Advice on sales forecasts and master production schedules

   b. Advice on inventory

   c. Liaison between customers and factory but without exercise of authority in the plants

   d. Transmitting customer complaints to the plant

4. Functional responsibilities to Law and Employee Relations:

   a. Obtaining legal interpretations regarding sales and compliance with governmental regulations

   b. Referring contractual agreements and leases for review

   c. Conforming to company's legal and employee relations policies

   d. Assistance in formulating patent policies as they affect customers

APPENDIX E

SUMMARY OF CONTENTS

THE MANAGEMENT GUIDE
(Standard Oil Company of California)

Introduction

The Nature and Purpose of the Management Guide
The Management Guide in Organization Planning
The Management Guide as a Tool of Management
Scope of the Booklet

The Background of the Management Guide

The Need for Job Descriptions
The Use of Job Descriptions
The Shortcomings of Job Descriptions
The Need for Job Descriptions for Management
The Earliest Form of the *Management Guide*
Subsequent Forms
The Standardized Conception and Form
The Present Conception and Form

The Elements of a Management Guide

Functions
Responsibilities and Authority
Relationships

Responsibility, Authority, and Accountability
The Application of a Management Guide

The Type of Position Covered
The Use of Management Guides

Some Considerations in the Construction of a Management Guide

Universal Responsibilities
Delegation of Authority
Observance of the Line of Control
Staff Positions
Some Practical Points on the Construction of a Guide

An Illustrative Management Guide

President
Manager, Personnel Department
Manager, Organization Department
Manager, Research and Development Department

ORGANIZATION NOMENCLATURE IN A LARGE COMPANY (FORD)

Component Designation*	Use of Component Designation	Corresponding Position Title*
Staff (Finance Staff)	A principal component of the Central Office—reports to the President and the Executive Vice President.	Vice President- (Vice President- Finance)
Office of— (Office of Public Relations)	A principal component of the Central Office—not otherwise designated as a Staff—reports to the President and the Executive Vice President.	Director, or Title Indicating Specialty (Tax Counsel)

* Examples of component designations and position titles are indicated in parenthesis. Specialty titles are limited to authorized exceptions. Deviations from standard usage are to be cleared with the Organization Department, Central Office.

APPENDIX F (Cont'd.)

Component Designation*	Use of Component Designation	Corresponding Position Title*
Group (Basic Products Group)	A number of Divisions under the executive direction of a Vice President—reports to the Vice President—Manufacturing.	Vice President- (Vice President- Basic Products Group)
Division (Ford Division)	A principal manufacturing or operating component of the Company—reports to the President and the Executive Vice President or a Vice President in charge of a Manufacturing Group.	Vice President and General Manager, or General Manager
Office (Plant Engineering Office) (General Sales Office)	A principal component of a Central Office Staff—reports to a Vice President, or A principal non-manufacturing component of a Vehicle Division General Office—reports to the Division Head.	Director, or Title Indicating Specialty (General Sales Manager)
Operations (Manufacturing Operations)	A principal manufacturing component of a Vehicle or Defense Product Division General Office—reports to the Division Head.	Manager, or Title Indicating Specialty (General Manufacturing Manager)
Plant (Dearborn Engine Plant)	A manufacturing facility of a Division—reports to Manufacturing Operations of a Vehicle Division or Defense Product Division, or to a Division Head of a Manufacturing Division.	Plant Manager, or Plant Superintendent

* Examples of component designations and position titles are indicated in parenthesis. Specialty titles are limited to authorized exceptions. Deviations from standard usage are to be cleared with the Organization Department, Central Office.

APPENDIX F (Cont'd.)

*Component Designation**	*Use of Component Designation*	*Corresponding Position Title**
Regional Sales Office (Central Regional Sales Office)	A regional sales activity of a Vehicle Division—reports to the General Sales Office of the Division.	Regional Sales Manager
District Sales Office (Detroit District Sales Office)	A district sales activity of a Vehicle Division—reports to a Regional Sales Office.	District Sales Manager
Parts Depot	A parts warehousing and distributing facility of a Vehicle Division—reports to the Parts and Accessories activity of the Division.	Depot Manager
Department	Normally the first organizational breakdown of each of the following: an Office; Operations (staff activities); a Manufacturing Division General Office; a Plant (both staff and manufacturing activities); a principal manufacturing or production area of a Division or Plant; and a Regional or District Sales Office.	Manager, Superintendent, or General Foreman
Section	The first organizational breakdown of a Department. Also indicates an activity of less than Department status which reports to a component above Department level.	Supervisor, General Foreman, or Foreman

* Examples of component designations and position titles are indicated in parenthesis. Specialty titles are limited to authorized exceptions. Deviations from standard usage are to be cleared with the Organization Department, Central Office.

APPENDIX F (Cont'd.)

Component Designation*	Use of Component Designation	Corresponding Position Title*
Unit	The first organizational breakdown of a Section. Also indicates an activity of less than Section status which reports to a component above Section level.	Supervisor, or Foreman
Sub-Unit	The first organizational breakdown of a Unit.	Supervisor, or Foreman

* Examples of component designations and position titles are indicated in parenthesis. Specialty titles are limited to authorized exceptions. Deviations from standard usage are to be cleared with the Organization Department, Central Office.

Bibliography

The following titles indicate either sources from which material was drawn for the subject headings indicated or references for further reading in specific areas of organization not discussed in this study.

GENERAL BIBLIOGRAPHY ON ORGANIZATION

LAWRENCE A. APPLEY, "Basic Factors in Modern Organization Development," PERSONNEL, November, 1938, pp. 49-56.

CHESTER I. BARNARD, *Organization and Management*, Harvard University Press, Cambridge, Massachusetts, 1948, pp. 111-133, 207-244.

.................., *The Functions of the Executive*, Harvard University Press, Cambridge, Massachusetts, 1938.

ALVIN BROWN, *Organization of Industry*, Prentice-Hall, Inc. New York, 1947.

R. C. DAVIS, *The Fundamentals of Top Management*, Harper & Brothers, New York, 1951.

HENRY S. DENNISON, *Organization Engineering*, McGraw-Hill Book Company, Inc., New York, 1931.

HENRI FAYOL, *General and Industrial Management*, Pitman Publishing Corporation, New York, 1949.

P. SARGANT FLORENCE, *The Logic of Industrial Organization*, Kegan, Paul, Trubner & Co., Ltd., London, 1933, pp. 114-154. New and revised edition, University of North Carolina Press, Chapel Hill, N. C., 1952.

PAUL E. HOLDEN, LOUNSBURY S. FISH and HUBERT L. SMITH, *Top-Management Organization and Control*, McGraw-Hill Book Company, Inc., New York, 1951, pp. 13-74.

HARRY ARTHUR HOPF, *Management and the Optimum*, an address before the Sixth International Congress for Scientific Management, London, July 15-18, 1935; reprinted Hopf Institute of Management, Ossining, N. Y., 1935.

ALBERT LEPAWSKY, *Administration,* The Art and Science of Organization and Management, Alfred A. Knopf, New York, 1949, pp. 219-416.

JAMES D. MOONEY and ALAN C. REILEY, *Onward Industry,* Harper & Brothers, New York, 1931.

HERBERT A. SIMON, *Administrative Behavior,* The Macmillan Company, New York, 1947, pp. 20-44.

LEWIS C. SORRELL, Discussion, in "Theories and Types of Organization," *Production Executives' Series No. 83,* American Management Association, 1929, pp. 40-51.

L. URWICK, *The Frontiers of Administration: The Need Is Urgent to Make Leadership a Reality,* Six lectures presented at the University of Toronto, published by *Manufacturing and Industrial Engineering.* Toronto, Canada, 1952.

PART I: THE DYNAMICS OF ORGANIZATION

Stage I: Division of Work

HENRY S. DENNISON, *Organization Engineering,* McGraw-Hill Book Company, Inc., New York, 1931, pp. 133-142.

HARRY S. FREEDMAN, "Scientific Management in Small Business," *Harvard Business Review,* May, 1950, pp. 33-41.

WILLIAM M. HOAD, "Organizational Problems of Small Business," *Michigan Business Review,* January, 1950, pp. 10-14.

PAUL E. HOLDEN, LOUNSBURY S. FISH and HUBERT L. SMITH, *Top-Management Organization and Control,* McGraw-Hill Book Company, Inc., New York, 1951, pp. 13-35.

JAMES D. MOONEY, "Organizing the Small Plant," in Edward H. Hempel (Editor), *Small Plant Management,* McGraw-Hill Book Company, Inc., New York, 1950, pp. 146-167.

ELMORE PETERSEN and E. GROSVENOR PLOWMAN, *Business Organization and Management,* Richard D. Irwin, Inc., Chicago, Ill., 1948, "Primary Departmentation," "The Criteria of Departmentation." pp. 200-255.

ROBERT W. PORTER, *Design for Industrial Co-Ordination,* Harper & Brothers, New York, 1941.

SCHUYLER WALLACE, *Federal Departmentalization,* A Critique of Theories of Organization, Columbia University Press, New York, 1941.

Stage II: Personality

ALEX BAVELAS and DERMOT BARRETT, "An Experimental Approach to Organizational Communication," PERSONNEL, March, 1951, pp. 366-371.

ERNEST DALE, "How Business Decisions are Made," MANAGEMENT NEWS, April 30, 1951, pp. 3-4.

SIGMUND FREUD, Group Psychology and the Analysis of the Ego, The Hogarth Press Ltd., London, 1922.

ERICH FROMM, Man for Himself, Rinehart and Company, Inc., New York, 1947, pp. 50-117.

THOMAS ROY JONES, "Dog Fights and Organization Charts," Dun's Review, December, 1938, pp. 5-8.

CARROLL L. SHARTLE, "Leadership and Executive Performance," PERSONNEL, March, 1949, pp. 370-380.

S. STANFELD SARGENT, Social Psychology, The Ronald Press Company, New York, 1950, pp. 154-174.

EDUARD SPRANGER, Types of Men, The Psychology and Ethics of Personality, translated by Paul J. W. Pigors, M. Niemeyer, Halle a.d. Saale, Germany, 1928, pp. 109-248.

Stage III: The Span of Control

ALVIN BROWN, Organization of Industry, Prentice-Hall, Inc., New York, 1947, pp. 81-86, 182, 202-203, 221-223, 237-238, 264-268, 313-315, 359.

R. C. DAVIS, The Influence of the Unit of Supervision and the Span of Executive Control on the Economy of Line Organization Structure, Bureau of Business Research, Research Monograph No. 26, The Ohio State University, Columbus, Ohio, 1941.

B. B. GARDNER, "Conserving and Developing Our Human Resources," Personnel Series No. 127, American Management Association, New York, 1949, p. 11.

V. A. GRAICUNAS, "Relationship in Organization," in Luther Gulick and L. Urwick (Editors), Papers on the Science of Administration, Institute of Public Administration, New York, 1937, pp. 183-187.

SIR IAN HAMILTON, The Soul and Body of an Army, Edward Arnold & Co., London, 1921, p. 229.

ELMORE PETERSEN and E. GROSVENOR PLOWMAN, "The Levels Theory of Organization," Business Organization and Management, Richard D. Irwin, Inc., Chicago, Ill., 1948, pp. 84-106.

L. URWICK, "Organization as a Technical Problem," in Luther Gulick and L. Urwick (Editors), *Papers on the Science of Administration*, Institute of Public Administration, New York, 1937, pp. 52-57.

CHARLES R. WALKER and F. L. W. RICHARDSON, JR., *Human Relations in An Expanding Company*, Yale Labor and Management Center, New Haven, Connecticut, 1948, pp. 14-18.

JAMES C. WORTHY, "Organizational Structure and Employe Morale," *American Sociological Review*, April, 1950, pp. 169-178.

Stage IV: The Staff Assistant

ALVIN BROWN, "The Assistant," in *Organization*, Hibbert Printing Company, New York, 1945, pp. 179-188.

A. G. HAYEK, "Use of Personal Assistants," *British Management Review*, December, 1950, pp. 53-61.

"Functions of an Assistant to the President," Policyholders Service Bureau, Metropolitan Life Insurance Company, New York, N. Y.

HENRY E. NILES and M. C. H. NILES, "Assistance in Coordination," PERSONNEL, August, 1938, pp. 26-38.

E. W. REILLEY, "Why Short-Change the Chief Executive on Staff Assistance?" PERSONNEL, September, 1947, pp. 85-92 (much valuable material has been obtained from this clear and informative article).

Stage V: Functionalization

MARVIN BOWER, "Untangling the Corporate Harness," *Mechanical Engineering*, December, 1938, pp. 904-908.

ERNEST R. BREECH, Executive Vice President, Ford Motor Company, Policy Letter to Staff Vice Presidents and Division Heads, on "Relationships Between Divisions and Staffs," No. 8, July 13, 1950, mimeographed.

ALVIN BROWN, *Organization of Industry*, Prentice-Hall, Inc., New York, 1947, pp. 228, 243-244, 325, 338-339, 356, 359-360.

HENRY H. FARQUHAR, "The Modern Business Staff," *The Society for the Advancement of Management Journal*, May, 1939, pp. 60-67.

J. FISHER, *Discussion of the Line and Staff Principle in Organization*, United States Steel Corporation of Delaware, Pittsburgh, Pa., February, 1950.

E. P. LEARNED, D. N. ULRICH, and D. R. BOOZ, *Executive Action*, Harvard University Press, Boston, 1951, Chapters 10 and 11.

J. K. LOUDEN, "Line and Staff—Their Roles in the Organization Structure," *Advanced Management,* June, 1949, pp. 76-82.

ARTHUR W. MACMAHON, JOHN D. MILLETT, and GLADYS OGDEN, *The Administration of Federal Work Relief,* Public Administration Service, Chicago, 1941, "The Rival Claims of Hierarchy and Specialty," Chapter 11, pp. 244-68.

WILLIAM R. SPRIEGEL and JOSEPH K. BAILEY, "The Staff Function in Organization," *Advanced Management,* March, 1952, pp. 2-6.

F. W. TAYLOR, *Shop Management,* Harper & Brothers, New York, 1911, pp. 92-127.

Stage VI: Group Decision-Making

E. M. ANDERSEN and G. T. SCHWENNING, *The Science of Production Organization,* J. Wiley & Sons, Inc., New York, 1938. "Committee Types," pp. 145-155, "Advantages and Disadvantages of Committees," pp. 181-192.

WILLIAM B. GIVEN, JR., *Bottom-Up Management,* Harper & Brothers, New York, 1949, pp. 3-50.

JOHN J. HADER, "Committee Process and Committee Chairmanship," *Handbook of Business Administration* (W. J. Donald, Editor), McGraw-Hill Book Company, Inc., New York, 1931, pp. 1676-1684.

PAUL E. HOLDEN, LOUNSBURY S. FISH and HUBERT L. SMITH, *Top-Management Organization and Control,* McGraw-Hill Book Company, Inc., New York 1951, pp. 59-73.

GEORGE B. DE HUSZAR, *Practical Applications of Democracy,* Harper & Brothers, New York, 1945, pp. 1-33, 83-102.

E. C. LINDEMANN, "The Authorities, Functions and Limitations of Committees," *Handbook of Business Administration,* McGraw-Hill Book Company, New York, 1931, pp. 1676-1688.

"Management," in *Better Living,* Employee Magazine of E. I. du Pont de Nemours & Company, March-April, 1949, pp. 1-8.

CHARLES P. McCORMICK *Multiple Management,* Harper & Brothers, New York, 1938, pp. 1-155.

FRANK W. PIERCE, *Developing Tomorrow's Business Leaders,* an address before the Society for the Advancement of Management, December 6, 1945. Standard Oil Company of N. J., New York, N. Y., pp. 4-7.

JOHN B. THURSTON, *Coordinating and Controlling Operations,* Funk & Wagnalls Company, New York, 1948.

Board of Directors

ROBERT A. GORDON, "The Board of Directors" in *Business Leadership and the Large Corporation,* The Brookings Institution, Washington, D. C., 1945, pp. 116-146.

MELVIN T. COPELAND and ANDREW R. TOWL, *The Board of Directors and Business Management,* Division of Research, Graduate School of Business Administration, Harvard University, Boston, 1947.

JOHN C. BAKER, *Directors and Their Functions,* Division of Research, Graduate School of Business Administration, Harvard University, Boston, 1945.

RICHARD C. PATTERSON, JR., "The Responsibilities of Directors," an address before the Harvard Graduate School of Business Administration, Cambridge, Mass., March, 1940.

GEORGE A. SLOAN, "The Corporate Board of Directors," *The Conference Board Economic Record,* July 24, 1941.

PAUL E. HOLDEN, LOUNSBURY S. FISH and HUBERT L. SMITH, "The Board of Directors," in *Top-Management Organization and Control,* McGraw-Hill Book Company, New York, 1951, pp. 16-20; 213-238.

J. O. McKINSEY, in W. J. Donald, "Functions of Boards of Directors, Board Committees, and Officers," *Handbook of Business Administration,* American Management Association, New York, 1931, pp. 391-401.

G. E. BATES, "The Board of Directors," *Harvard Business Review,* Vol. 19, 1940, pp. 74-76.

Stage VII: Decentralization

GEORGE C. S. BENSON, "A Plea for Administrative Decentralization," *Public Administration Review,* Summer, 1947, pp. 170-178.

NEIL W. CHAMBERLAIN, *Management in Motion,* Yale Labor and Management Center, New Haven, Conn., 1950.

RALPH J. CORDINER, "The Implications of Industrial Decentralization," *General Management Series No. 134,* American Management Association, 1945, pp. 24-32.

PETER F. DRUCKER, *The New Society,* Harper & Brothers, New York, 1949, pp. 263-280.

HYACINTHE DUBREUIL, *A Chance for Everybody: A Liberal Basis for the Organization of Work,* Chatto and Windus, London, 1939.

BORIS EMMET and JOHN E. JEUCK, *Catalogues and Counters*, A History of Sears, Roebuck and Company, The University of Chicago Press, Chicago, Illinois, 1950, pp. 358-373, 675-676.

WILLIAM B. GIVEN, *Bottom-Up Management, op. cit.*, pp. 50-62.

R. A. GORDON, *Business Leadership in the Large Corporation*, The Brookings Institution, Washington, D. C., 1945, pp. 46-105.

Metropolitan Life Insurance Company, *Centralization or Decentralization of Management*, Policyholders Service Bureau, The Company, New York.

G. E. MILWARD (Editor), *Large-Scale Organization*, A First-Hand Account of the Day-to-Day Organization and Management of Large Industrial Undertakings and Public Services, MacDonald & Evans, London, 1950.

DON G. MITCHELL, "Big Business in Small Plants," *Advanced Management*, December, 1950, pp. 2-5.

JOHN ALLEN MURPHY, "What's Behind Today's Trend Toward Decentralization?" *Sales Management*, October 1 and 15, November 1 and 10, 1946.

CLAUDE V. SWANK, "Some Principles of Decentralized Operation," *Production Series No. 176*, American Management Association, 1948, pp. 3-9.

D. B. TRUMAN, *Administrative Decentralization*, The University of of Chicago Press, Chicago, 1940.

L. URWICK, "Executive Decentralization with Functional Coordination," THE MANAGEMENT REVIEW, December, 1935, pp. 355-68.

JAMES C. WORTHY, "Democratic Principles in Business Management," *Advanced Management*, March, 1949, pp. 16-21.

The General Motors Case

The General Motors illustrative case has been based to some extent on first-hand studies, to some extent on the following materials:

ALBERT BRADLEY, "Setting Up a Forecasting Program," *Annual Convention Series No. 41*, American Management Association, 1926.

DONALDSON BROWN, "Centralized Control with Decentralized Responsibilities," *Annual Convention Series No. 57*, American Management Association, 1927, (see also *Handbook of Business Administration, op. cit.*, pp. 1465-1474).

........................, "Industrial Management as a National Resource," *The Conference Board Management Record*, April, 1943, pp. 142-148.

PETER F. DRUCKER, "The Corporation as Human Effort," in *Concept of the Corporation*, The John Day Company, New York, 1946, pp. 20-129.

GM and Its People: An American Industrial Team, Public Relations Department, General Motors Corporation, Detroit, Michigan, February, 1949.

F. H. HARBISON and ROBERT DUBIN, *Patterns of Union-Management Relations*, Science Research Associates, Chicago, Ill., pp. 54-62.

ALFRED P. SLOAN, JR., *The Principles and Policies Behind General Motors*, an address before Automobile Editors of American Newspapers at General Motors Proving Ground, Milford, Mich., September 28, 1927.

........................, *Adventures of a White-Collar Man*, Doubleday, Doran & Company, Inc., New York, 1941.

EDGAR W. SMITH, (then) Assistant to the President, General Motors Export Company, "Organization and Operating Principles," *Handbook of Business Administration, op. cit.*, pp. 1474-1488.

PART II: THE MECHANICS OF ORGANIZATION

HENRI FAYOL, *General and Industrial Management, op. cit.*

LOUNSBURY FISH, "Organization as the Mechanism of Management, *General Management Series No. 142*, American Management Association, 1948, pp. 14-26.

............, "Organization—Foundation of Management," in Catheryn Seckler-Hudson, *Processes of Organization and Management*, Public Affairs Press, Washington, D. C., 1948, pp. 89-98.

R. E. GILLMOR, *A Practical Manual of Organization*, Funk & Wagnalls Company, New York, 1948.

GEORGE L. HALL, *The Management Guide*, Standard Oil Company of California, San Francisco, California, 1948.

JOSEPH B. HALL, "Leadership in an Evolving Organization," in Marvin Bower (Editor), *The Development of Executive Leadership*, Harvard University Press, Cambridge, Mass., 1949, pp. 97-114.

CHARLES R. HOOK, JR., "Organization Planning—Its Challenges and Limitations, *Personnel Series No. 141*, American Management Association, 1951, pp. 15-22.

HARRY ARTHUR HOPF, "The Evolution of Organization," *National Association of Cost Accountants Yearbook 1932*, The Association, New York, 1932, pp. 68-102.

. . . ., *Organization, Executive Capacity and Progress,* An address delivered before the Annual Conference of the Life Office Management Association, September, 1944; reprinted as Publication No. 4, of the Hopf Institute of Management, Ossining, New York, 1945.

JOHN B. JOYNT, "Gaining Acceptance of New Ideas," Address to the Systems and Procedures Association of America, October 20, 1950, mimeographed.

. . . ., "Organization Planning for Improved Output," *Office Management Series No. 130,* American Management Association, 1952, pp. 3-14.

ROBERT T. LIVINGSTON, *The Engineering of Organization and Management,* McGraw-Hill Book Company, Inc., New York, 1949.

J. O. McKINSEY, *Organization and Methods of the Walworth Manufacturing Company,* Cases and Problems No. 3, The University of Chicago Press, Chicago, Ill., 1922.

Metropolitan Life Insurance Company, *Business Organization,* Policyholders Service Bureau, The Company, New York, June, 1947.

National Industrial Conference Board, *Organization Standards and Practices,* Studies in Business Policy No. 18, The Board, New York, 1946.

WILLIAM H. NEWMAN, *Administrative Action,* The Techniques of Organization and Management, Prentice-Hall, Inc., New York, 1951, pp. 237-313.

WELLS NORRIS, "How Ampco Reorganized," *American Business,* June, 1949, pp. 10-11; 34.

E. W. REILLEY, "The Control Staff as an Aid to Management," *Office Management Series No. 107,* American Management Association, 1944, pp. 3-13.

RUSSELL ROBB, "The Organization of Administration," in C. Seckler-Hudson (Editor), *Processes of Organization and Management,* Public Affairs Press, Washington, D. C., 1948, pp. 99-111.

BREHON SOMERVELL, "Organization Controls in Industry," *General Management Series No. 142,* American Management Association, 1948, pp. 3-13.

JOSEPH M. TRICKETT, "Organization Planning," *Advanced Management,* March, 1948, pp. 16-21.

L. URWICK, "Principles of Management," *British Management Review,* Vol. VII, No. 3, 1948, pp. 15-48.

. . . ., "Scientific Principles and Organization," *Institute of Management Series No. 19*, American Management Association, 1938.

. . . ., *The Elements of Administration*, Pitman, London, 1943, Harper & Brothers, New York, 1943, New and Revised Edition to be published in 1953.

. . . ., "The Function of Administration with Special Reference to the Work of Henri Fayol," in *Papers in the Science of Administration, op. cit.*, pp. 115-130.

ALVIN ZANDER, "Resistance to Change—Its Analysis and Prevention," *Advanced Management*, January, 1950, pp. 9-11.

Measures of Organization Effectiveness and Their Shortcomings

CONRAD ARENSBERG and DOUGLAS McGREGOR, "Determination of Morale in an Industrial Company," *Applied Anthropology*, September, 1942.

E. WIGHT BAKKE, *Bonds of Organization*, Harper & Brothers, New York, 1950.

A. L. COMREY, J. M. PFIFFNER and H. P. BEEM, *Studies in Organizational Effectiveness, I. The U. S. Forest Survey*, University of Southern California, Los Angeles, Calif., 1951 (mimeographed).

ERNEST DALE, "Payroll Costs in Industrial Relations," MANAGEMENT NEWS, October, 1949, p. 3.

SEYMOUR MELMAN, "Rise of Administrative Overhead in the Manufacturing Industries of the United States, 1899-1947," *Oxford Economic Papers* (new series) Vol. III, No. 1, January, 1951, pp. 62-112.

CLARENCE E. RIDLEY and HERBERT A. SIMON, *Measuring Municipal Activities*, International City Managers' Association, Second Edition, Chicago, Ill., 1943.

HERBERT A. SIMON, DONALD W. SMITHBURG and VICTOR A. THOMPSON, *Public Administration*, Alfred A. Knopf, New York, 1950, pp. 488-512.

U. S. Budget Bureau, *Production Planning and Control in Office Operation*, The Bureau, Washington, D. C., 1949.

Organization Manuals

GEORGE L. HALL, *The Management Guide*, Standard Oil Company of California, San Francisco, California, 1948.

EILEEN AHERN, *How to Prepare and Maintain a Supervisor's Policy Manual,* Research Report No. 11, American Management Association, New York, 1947.

ALVIN BROWN, "The Record of Organization," *Organization, op. cit.,* pp. 289-293.

F. R. HARRISON, "The Place of Organization and Procedure Manuals in Business Administration," mimeographed, 1951. (The author is Associate Professor of Industry, Western Reserve University.)

Organization Charts

C. S. ASCHER, "Organization—Mercator's Projection," *Public Administration Review,* Autumn, 1943, pp. 360-364.

ALVIN BROWN, "Charts" in *Organization, op. cit.,* pp. 295-302.

C. G. BROWNE, "The Concentric Organization Chart," *Journal of Applied Psychology,* December, 1950, pp. 375-377.

Company Organization Charts, Studies in Personnel Policy No. 64, National Industrial Conference Board, Inc., New York, 1944.

JOHN J. FURIA, *How to Make and Interpret Functional Organization Charts,* Graduate Division for Training in Public Service, New York University, 1943, Public Business Management Series No. 2.

............, "Making and Interpreting Functional Organization Charts," PERSONNEL, January, 1944, pp. 221-230.

P. H. LITTLEFIELD, "What's Wrong with Organization Charts?" THE MANAGEMENT REVIEW, June, 1947, pp. 315-317.

"Organization Charts," in L. P. Alford and John R. Bangs, Editors, *Production Handbook,* The Ronald Press Company, New York, 1944, pp. 40-54.

W. C. PUCKEY, "Some Principles of Organization," *British Management Review,* Vol. VII, No. 3, 1948, pp. 77-86.

THE CONTENT OF MAJOR MANAGEMENT FUNCTIONS

General

CHESTER I. BARNARD, *The Functions of the Executive,* Harvard University Press, Cambridge, Mass., 1938, pp. 215-234.

W. L. BATT, "Duties of a Chief Executive in a Business of Moderate Size," Paper presented at the International Management Congress, Paris, June, 1929.

Sune Carlson, *Executive Behavior; A Study of the Work Load and Working Methods of Managing Directors*, C. A. Stromberg Aktiebolag, Publisher, Stockholm, Sweden, 1951.

James B. Du Prau, "The Chief Executive—His Job and His Staff," *General Management Series No. 155*, American Management Association, 1952.

George L. Hall, *The Management Guide, op. cit.*

"The President's Round Table," *General Management Series No. 150*, American Management Association, 1950, pp. 3-14.

"The Presidents' Round Table," *General Management Series No. 152*, American Management Association, 1951, pp. 17-35.

Accounting and Control

Thornton F. Bradshaw and Charles C. Hull, Editors, *Controllership in Modern Management*, Richard D. Irwin, Inc., Chicago, Illinois, 1949, pp. 113-144.

William V. Deane, "How Westinghouse Organizes Accounting Functions," *The Journal of Accountancy*, March, 1951, pp. 402-407.

Evaluating Managerial and Supervisory Jobs in the Controller's Department, The Controllership Foundation, Inc., New York, 1949.

S. D. Flinn, "Administration of a Large Accounting Department," *National Association of Cost Accountants Bulletin*, November, 1950.

J. G. Glover and C. L. Maze, *Managerial Control*, The Ronald Press Company, New York, 1937.

B. E. Goetz, *Management Planning and Control*, McGraw-Hill Book Company, Inc., New York, 1949, pp. 28-29.

J. Hugh Jackson, *The Comptroller: His Functions and Organization*, Harvard University Press, Cambridge, Mass., 1948, pp. 27-47.

J. P. Jordan, "Setting Up An Organization," *1929 Year Book of the National Association of Cost Accountants*, pp. 7-35.

Edmound Landauer, "Management from a Distance," *Handbook of Business Administration, op. cit.*, pp. 1488-1496.

A. G. L. Matthias, "Type of Organization and Plan of Control Leading to Profits," *1935 Year Book of the National Association of Cost Accountants*, pp. 86-106.

Metropolitan Life Insurance Company, *Functions of the Controller*, Policyholders Service Bureau, The Company, New York, 1947.

T. H. Patterson, "A Program of Limited Decentralization of Accounting Functions," *National Association of Cost Accountants Bulletin*, June 1, 1948, pp. 1191-1200.

JOHN S. REYNOLDS, "Is Your Head Office Necessary?" *National Association of Cost Accountants Bulletin,* September, 1950.

E. B. RICKARD, "A Study in Decentralization: Controllership in a Divisional Organization," (Ford Motor Company), *National Association of Cost Accountants Bulletin,* January, 1950, pp. 567-599.

FLOYD H. ROWLAND, "Simplification in Accounting Through Simplification in Organization," *1928 Year Book of the National Association of Cost Accountants,* pp. 99-110.

D. H. VOORHIES, *The Functions of Corporate Secretaries, Treasurers and Comptrollers,* Standard Oil Company of California, San Francisco, Calif., 1944, "The Comptroller," pp. 21-30.

Advertising

Metropolitan Life Insurance Company, *Functions of the Advertising Manager,* Policyholders Service Bureau, The Company, New York, no date.

Organization of the Advertising Function, A Study prepared by McKinsey & Company, Management Consultants, for the Association of National Advertisers, New York, 1946.

VERGIL D. REED, "Advertising Organization," in *Marketing Handbook,* Paul H. Nystrom, (Editor) The Ronald Press Company, New York, 1948, pp. 307-336.

Engineering

RALPH M. BARNES, *Industrial Engineering and Management,* Problems and Policies, McGraw-Hill Book Company, Inc., New York, 1931.

R. CONRAD COOPER, *Organization of Industrial Engineering Activities,* United States Steel Corporation, New York, 1952.

DEXTER S. KIMBALL and DEXTER S. KIMBALL, JR., *Principles of Industrial Organization,* McGraw-Hill Book Company, Inc., New York, 1947, pp. 150-171.

J. K. LOUDEN, "Staff Organization for Control," *Advanced Management,* January-March, 1943, pp. 17-23.

WILLIAM H. SCHUTT, *Process Engineering,* McGraw-Hill Book Company, Inc., New York, 1948.

WILLIAM STANIAR, *Plant Engineering Handbook,* McGraw-Hill Book Company, Inc., New York, 1950, pp. 29-34.

J. E. THOMPSON, *Engineering Organization and Methods,* McGraw-Hill Book Company, Inc., New York, 1947.

Industrial Research

D. B. HERTZ, *The Theory and Practice of Industrial Research,* Mc-Graw-Hill Book Company, Inc., New York, 1950.

D. H. VOORHIES, *The Co-ordination of Motive, Men and Money in Industrial Research,* Standard Oil Company of California, San Francisco, Calif., 1946.

Internal Auditing

FRANK A. LAMPERTI, "Organization Planning—Its Purpose, Scope, and Relationship to Internal Auditing," *Internal Auditor,* December, 1949, p. 57.

Metropolitan Life Insurance Company, "Organization of the Internal Auditing Function Between Parent and Subsidiary Operations," *Internal Auditor,* December, 1944, p. 23.

Marketing

MARVIN BOWER, "Sales Organization," in Paul H. Nystrom (Editor), *Marketing Handbook, op. cit.,* pp. 605-640.

Metropolitan Life Insurance Company, *Functions of the Sales Executive,* Policyholders Service Bureau, The Company, New York, no date.

J. A. MURPHY, "Why Decentralization Takes Root in Sales Management," *Sales Management,* November 10, 1946.

L. URWICK, E. ASTON and F. H. CORDUKES, *Organizing a Sales Office,* Pitman Publishing Corporation, New York, 1937.

Office Management

HARRY ARTHUR HOPF, "Office Management and Its Future," Address before the 23rd Annual Conference, National Office Management Association, 1942.

COLEMAN MAZE, *Office Management: A Handbook,* The Ronald Press Company, New York, 1947, pp. 18-38.

Metropolitan Life Insurance Company, *Functions of the Office Manager,* Policyholders Service Bureau, The Comapny, New York, no date.

Personnel

LAWRENCE A. APPLEY, "Essentials of a Management Personnel Policy," PERSONNEL, May, 1947, pp. 430-436.

............, *Functions of the Personnel Executive,* Bulletin No. 1, Industrial Relations Section, California Institute of Technology, Pasadena, Calif., 1940.

DAVID W. BELCHER, "Personnel Management in the Small Organization," *Business Management Aids,* University of Illinois, Urbana, Ill., no date.

HAROLD B. BERGEN, "A Personnel Program for a Small Plant," *Mechanical Engineering,* May, 1940, pp. 1-4.

H. H. CAREY, "An Outline of Personnel Activities," PERSONNEL, May, 1947, pp. 384-387.

K. R. DAILEY, "The Organization and Administration of Industrial Relations Departments in Large Firms," Proceedings of the Seventh Annual Industrial Relations Conference, University of Minnesota, Minneapolis, Minn., March 24 and 25, 1949, pp. 19-28 (mimeographed).

GLENN GARDINER, "The Operating Executive and the Personnel Department," *Personnel Series No. 121,* American Management Association, 1948, pp. 3-12.

I. DENT JENKINS, "The Personnel Function in Profile," paper presented at Personnel Administration in Hospitals, An Institute Sponsored by the New York State School of Industrial and Labor Relations, Cornell University, in Cooperation with The American Hospital Association, October 25, 1950 (mimeographed).

CLIFFORD E. JURGENSEN, "Personnel Administration in Small Firms: A Practical View," PERSONNEL, July, 1949, pp. 24-34.

Metropolitan Life Insurance Company, *Functions of the Personnel Director,* Policyholders Service Bureau, The Company, New York, no date.

G. R. MOXON, *Functions of a Personnel Department,* Institute of Personnel Management, London, England, 1951.

MARY CUSHING NILES, "Decentralizing Personnel Management," *Advanced Management,* September, 1949, pp. 125-132.

PAUL PIGORS and CHARLES A. MYERS, *Personnel Administration,* A Point of View and A Method, McGraw-Hill Book Company, Inc., New York, 1951, pp. 17-23.

GENEVA SEYBOLD, *Organization of Personnel Administration, Studies in Personnel Policy No. 73,* National Industrial Conference Board, New York, 1945.

............, "Personnel Administration in the Small Company," *Studies in Personnel Policy No. 117,* National Industrial Conference Board, New York, 1951.

FRANCIS SPODICK, *How to Establish and Maintain a Personnel Department,* Research Report No. 4, American Management Association, 1944.

L.Urwick, *Personnel Management in Relation to Factory Organization,* Institute of Labor Management, Aldwych, England, 1943.

Dale Yoder, *Personnel Management and Industrial Relations,* Prentice-Hall, Inc., New York, 1951, pp. 16-21.

Production

L. P. Alford and John R. Bangs, Editors, "Plant Organization," in *Production Handbook, op. cit.,* pp. 1-39.

W. N. Mitchell, *Organization and Management of Production,* McGraw-Hill Book Company, New York, 1939, pp. 70-114.

Public Relations

Philip Lesly, Editor, *Public Relations Handbook,* Prentice-Hall, Inc., New York, 1950.

Purchasing

Stuart F. Heinritz, *Purchasing,* Prentice-Hall, Inc., New York, 1947.

Howard T. Lewis, *Procurement: Principles and Cases,* Richard D. Irwin, Chicago, 1948, Chapter 3, pp. 49-50 (First Edition).

Metropolitan Life Insurance Company, *Functions of the Purchasing Agent,* Policyholders Service Bureau, The Company, New York, no date.

National Association of Purchasing Agents Manual, 1938.

The Secretary

D. H. Voorhies, *The Functions of Corporate Secretaries, Treasurers and Comptrollers, op. cit.,* "The Secretary," pp. 5-12.

The Treasurer

Metropolitan Life Insurance Company, *The Functions of the Treasurer,* Policyholders Service Bureau, The Company, New York, no date.

D. H. Voorhies, *The Functions of Corporate Secretaries, Treasurers and Comptrollers, op. cit.,* "The Treasurer," pp. 13-20.

THE ORGANIZATION OF SELECTED INDUSTRIES AND SERVICES

Banking

HARRY ARTHUR HOPF, *Problems of Bank Organization,* An address delivered before the joint meeting of the American Society of Mechanical Engineers and the Taylor Society, New York, 1927 (reprinted from the *Bulletin of the Taylor Society,* Vol. XII, No. 2).

Canning

CLARKE KNOX, *Office and Factory Manual for Fruit and Vegetable Canners,* San Francisco, Calif., 1924.

Dairies

MARTIN MORTENSEN, *Management of Dairy Plants,* The Macmillan Company, New York, 1938.

Flour Milling

E. L. PEARSON, *Organization and Management in the Flour Milling Industry,* Sir I. Pitman's & Sons, Ltd., London, 1925.

Foundries

J. J. GILLESPIE, *Foundry Organization and Management,* Sir I. Pitman's & Sons, Ltd., London, 1937.

Government

Administrative Management in the Government of the United States, Government Printing Office, Washington, D. C., 1937.

Commission on Organization of the Executive Branch of the Government, HERBERT HOOVER, Chairman, McGraw-Hill Book Company, Inc., New York, 1949.

ARTHUR W. MACMAHON, JOHN D. MILLETT and GLADYS OGDEN, *op. cit.*

HERBERT A. SIMON, DONALD W. SMITHBURG, and VICTOR A. THOMPSON, *op. cit.*

DWIGHT WALDO, *The Administrative State,* The Ronald Press Company, New York, 1948.

Insurance

HARRY ARTHUR HOPF, "Significant Aspects of Organization," Article No. V, in "New Perspectives in Management," in *The Spectator*, January, 1944; "Organization of Administration," Article No. VI, in "New Perspectives in Management," in *The Spectator*, February, 1944, pp. 20-25, 33, 35-37; "Instruments Essential to Control," Article No. VII, in "New Perspectives in Management," in *The Spectator*, March, 1944, pp. 8-12, 45-49; "Historical Development of Organizational Structure," Article No. XIII, in "New Perspectives in Management," in *The Spectator*, November, 1944, pp. 36-41, 58-64, 72-73.

JOSEPH B. MacLEAN, *Life Insurance*, 7th Edition, McGraw-Hill Book Company, Inc., New York, 1951, "Internal Organization of the Home Office," Chapter 18.

G. F. MICHELBACHER, *Casualty Insurance Principles*, 2nd Edition, McGraw-Hill Book Company, Inc., New York 1942, "Organization of the Insurance Carrier," Chapter 3; "Organization of the Claim Department,"; Chapter 15; "Organization of the Agency Systems," Chapter 16.

Mail-Order Business

BORIS EMMET and JOHN E. JEUCK, *Catalogues and Counters*, A History of Sears, Roebuck and Co., The University of Chicago Press, Chicago, Ill., 1950, pp. 124, 358-373, 675-676.

Mining

D. C. DAVIES, *Organization and Scientific Management as Applied to the Coal Industry*, Port Talbot, 1925.

S. H. TRUSCOTT, *Mine Economics, Sampling-Valuation-Organization*, Mining Publications Ltd., London, 1937.

Municipal Activities

CLARENCE E. RIDLEY and HERBERT A. SIMON, *Measuring Municipal Activities*, International City Managers' Association, Chicago, Ill., 1943.

D. C. STONE, *The Management of Municipal Public Works*, Public Administration Service, Chicago, Ill., 1939.

Petroleum

"Standard Is Strong in Disunion," *Business Week,* June 22, 1946.
"The Jersey Company—I. Its Principles of Management; II. Its Affiliates in Practice," *Fortune,* October, 1951, pp. 98-103, 174-184; 105-
107, 186-200.
Your Job, Standard Oil Company of New Jersey, New York, 1946.

Power Plants

W. N. POLAKOV, *Power Plant Management,* Job Analyses and Functions, McGraw-Hill Book Company, Inc., New York, 1932.

Public Utilities

KEITH S. McHUGH, "The Organization of the Bell System," Statement before a Subcommittee of the Committee on Post Office
and Civil Service, U. S. House of Representatives, Washington,
D. C., May 7, 1948.
Metropolitan Life Insurance Company, *Business Organization, op.
cit.,* pp. 26-36.

Retailing

H. R. BARNETT, *Man Management in Chain Stores,* Harper &
Brothers, New York, 1931.
E. H. GAULT, *Control of the Retail Units of Chain Stores,* Bureau
of Business Research, University of Michigan, Ann Arbor, Mich.,
1935.
MICHAEL J. JUCIUS, H. H. MAYNARD, and CARROLL L. SHARTLE, *Job
Analysis for Retail Stores,* Research Monograph No. 37, Bureau
of Business Research, The Ohio State University, Columbus, O.,
1945.
PAUL M. MAZUR, *Principles of Organization Applied to Modern Retailing,* Harper & Brothers, New York, 1927.
HERMAN C. NOLAN and HAROLD H. MAYNARD, *Drug Store Management,* McGraw-Hill Book Company, Inc., New York, 1941.

Steel

JAMES B. DU PRAU, *The Chief Executive—His Job and His Staff, op.
cit.*
Metropolitan Life Insurance Company, *Business Organization, op.
cit.,* pp. 30-32.

Textiles

Anglo-American Council on Productivity, Productivity Team Reports: Cotton Spinning, Cotton Doubling, Cotton Weaving, New York, 1950 and 1951.

C. CANBY BALDERSTON, *Management of a Textile Business,* A Study of the Operation of an Individual Enterprise, The Textile Foundation, Washington, D. C., 1938.

A. E. CLIFFORD, *Textile Organization and Production,* H. R. Carter, Belfast, 1951.

HIRAM S. DAVIS, *Vertical Integration in the Textile Industries,* Industrial Research Department, Wharton School of Finance and Commerce, University of Pennsylvania, Philadelphia, Penna., 1938.

G. T. SCHWENNING, (Editor), *Management Problems with Special Reference to the Textile Industry,* University of North Carolina Press, Chapel Hill, N. C., 1930.

Transportation

MARVIN L. FAIR and ERNEST W. WILLIAMS, *Economics of Transportation,* Harper and Brothers, New York, 1950, pp. 201-214.

KENT T. HEALY, *The Economics of Transportation in America,* The Ronald Press Company, New York, 1940, pp. 76-78, 315-319.

Metropolitan Life Insurance Company, *Functions of the Traffic Manager,* Policyholders Service Bureau, The Company, New York, 1937.

"Operating Methods and Procedures—The Railroad Organization," in "Railways" *Encyclopaedia Britannica,* 1951.

Organization and Traffic of the Illinois Central System, Illinois Central Railroad Company, Chicago, Ill., 1938.

T. W. VAN METRE, *Traffic Management in Domestic Commerce,* McGraw-Hill Book Company, Inc., New York, to be published in 1953, Chapter 1.

THOMAS WOLFE, *Air Transportation,* McGraw-Hill Book Company, Inc., New York, 1950, Chapter 15, pp. 361-381.

NEW DEVELOPMENTS IN ORGANIZATION

HARRY ARTHUR HOPF, "Evolution in Organization During the Past Decade," paper presented to the Eighth International Management Congress, Stockholm, Sweden, July, 1947; Hopf Institute of Management Publication No. 10.

HERBERT A. SIMON, "Modern Organization Theories," *Advanced Management,* October, 1950, pp. 2-4.

Operational Research

A. S. CAHN, "The Warehouse Problem," Abstract 505, *Bulletin of American Mathematical Society,* Vol. 54, November, 1948.

GEORGE B. DANTZIG, *Linear Programming,* Paper presented before the Symposium on Numerical Methods, July, 1948, Los Angeles, California (mimeographed).

GEORGE B. DANTZIG, *Suggestions on the Classification Problem in Linear Programming,* Program Standards and Cost Control, Comptroller Headquarters, USAF, October 11, 1948 (mimeographed).

PHILIP M. MORSE and GEORGE E. KIMBALL, *Methods of Operations Research,* The Technology Press of Massachusetts Institute of Technology, and John Wiley & Sons, Inc., New York, 1951 (especially the Introduction, pp. 1-10b and the last chapter on Organizational and Procedural Problems, pp. 137-145).

LIEUTENANT COLONEL DAVID B. PARKER, "Our Greatest Secret Weapon," *This Week Magazine,* New York Herald Tribune, August 5, 1951, pp. 7, 30-32.

HERBERT SOLOW, "Operations Research," *Fortune,* April, 1951, pp. 105-107; 146-148.

MARSHALL K. WOOD and GEORGE B. DANTZIG, (United States Army Air Force Comptroller) "Programming of Interdependent Activities," *Econometrics,* July-October, 1949, pp. 193-211.

Index

331

D

E

F